Praise for *Your Personal Renaissance*

Diane Dreher speaks to a deep longing for meaningful life work that is unrequited for so many. She does so with grace, power, and fascinating stories. Her deep knowledge and clear, strong voice make Dreher the perfect guide. I urge you to join her for a life-changing journey.
 —Frances Moore Lappé,
 author of *Diet for a Small Planet* and *Getting a Grip*

We're all searching for more passion and meaning in life. In this brilliant book, Diane provides a spiritual compass for the journey to create a life that fits skin tight over your true self.
 —Jerry Lynch, author of *The Way of the Champion*

In *Your Personal Renaissance,* Diane Dreher acts as a wise, compassionate, buoyant life coach, directing our energies away from what dulls and diminishes us and toward those desires that have always given us zest and a sense of accomplishment. And it's also such a delight to read that I can't imagine anyone finishing it without feeling the joy she promises. It's a book, and outlook, much needed in these times.
 —Ron Hansen, author of *A Stay Against Confusion* and *Atticus*

Your Personal Renaissance is unique—a self-help book grounded in real lessons from history, not glib parables awkwardly situated in a hypothetical here-and-now. The book is lively and interesting, and its advice is sound. *Your Personal Renaissance* is well worth reading and—even more importantly— well worth using as a guide to a better life.
 —Christopher Peterson, Professor of Psychology,
 University of Michigan

Diane Dreher invites us to wisely use the wisdom of the Renaissance to transform our lives and embrace our deepest purpose, gracing us with practical inspiration and motivating insight on every page.
 —Gloria De Gaetano, founder, the Parent Coaching Institute

Diane Dreher's *Your Personal Renaissance* amounts to a wonderful fusion of theory and practice that is both inspirational and pragmatic. It provides each of us a clear, provocative, and compelling pathway for creating—and toward realizing—our own personal Renaissance.

—John Vasconcellos, California State Senator emeritus

This is a special book, a spiritual book, a practical book, a responsible book. . . . The author takes to heart (and writes with a great deal of heart) two of my favorite truths: *Nothing endures but change* and *what you perceive to be real is real in its consequences*. Diane Dreher warmly encourages the reader to make needed changes creatively and challenges the perceptions that so many of us harbor about the inevitability of how we now live our lives.

—Carl E. Thoresen, PhD, Professor Emeritus of Education, Psychology and Psychiatry/Behavioral Sciences, Stanford University

Diane Dreher directs our attention toward extraordinary individuals like Leonardo da Vinci and Queen Elizabeth I of England, identifies the qualities that allowed them to step out into greatness, and then offers practices designed to let us awaken those qualities in ourselves. The cumulative effect is irresistible: as we align ourselves imaginatively with women and men who embody Renaissance ideals, something of their courage, resilience and creativity begin to flow into our own lives. A splendid guide to personal transformation.

—Carol Lee Flinders, PhD, author of *Enduring Grace* and *Enduring Lives*

Dreher has beautifully integrated the wisdom from the Renaissance, spiritual and religious principles, and contemporary positive psychology, offering a wonderfully engaging, remarkable, and practical program to help the reader discover more meaning, purpose, calling, and vocation in life. It is truly a must read.

—Thomas G. Plante, PhD, Professor of Psychology and Director of the Spirituality and Health Institute, Santa Clara University

Your Personal
RENAISSANCE

ALSO BY DIANE DREHER

The Tao of Inner Peace
The Tao of Personal Leadership
The Tao of Womanhood
Inner Gardening

Your Personal
RENAISSANCE

12 Steps to Finding
Your Life's True Calling

Diane Dreher, PhD

Da Capo
LIFE
LONG

A Member of the Perseus Books Group

Designed by Jeff Williams
Set in 11.75-point Berkeley Book by the Perseus Books Group

Library of Congress Cataloging-in-Publication Data
Dreher, Diane, 1946-
    Your personal Renaissance : 12 powerful practices for finding your life's true
calling / by Diane Dreher. — 1st Da Capo Press ed.
        p. cm.
    Includes bibliographical references and index.
    ISBN-13: 978-1-60094-001-9 (alk. paper)
    ISBN-10: 1-60094-001-3 (alk. paper)
    1. Self-actualization (Psychology) I. Title.

BF637.S4D75 2008
158—dc22

                                                                    2007049456

Published by Da Capo Press
A Member of the Perseus Books Group
www.dacapopress.com

Da Capo Press books are available at special discounts for bulk purchases in the
United States by corporations, institutions, and other organizations. For more information, please contact the Special Markets Department at the Perseus Books Group,
2300 Chestnut Street, Suite 200, Philadelphia, PA 19103, or call (800) 255–1514, or
e-mail special.markets@perseusbooks.com.

10 9 8 7 6 5 4 3 2 1

For those with the courage
to follow their hearts
and create a new Renaissance
within and around them.

Contents

PHASE II

MAKING THE RENAISSANCE PRACTICES WORK FOR YOU

Acknowledgments

Writing this book has been an ongoing discernment journey as many people have shared their gifts with me. I would like to thank my colleagues in Santa Clara's Spirituality and Health Institute; and Jane Ferguson, Carol Lee Flinders, Tim Flinders, William J. Rewak, S. J., Theodore J. Rynes, S. J., Shauna Shapiro, Juan Velasco, and Ann Wittman, S.C.S.C., for their insights on meditation and spiritual growth; and Hans Boepple, Chris Boscia, Michelle Chappel, Tina Clare, Michael Collopy, Carl Djerassi, Frank Dreher, Josepha Edman, Christina Fialho, Jane Goodall, Ron Hansen, I. King Jordan, Paula Leen, Jerry Lynch, Robert Mason, Anne Quaranta, David Reed, Karel Sloane, Elizabeth Thompson, Gertrude Welch, and Erna Wenus for their stories and insights. I am grateful to the many researchers in positive psychology and neuroscience whose work has influenced my own, especially Teresa Amabile, Mihaly Csikszentmihalyi, David Feldman, Kristin Neff, Robert Numan, Jaak Panksepp, Christopher Peterson, Tom Plante, Martin Seligman, Shauna Shapiro, Patti Simone, C. R. Snyder, and Shelley Taylor.

I would like to thank my agents, Jill Marsal and Sandra Dijkstra, and my editor, Kathryn McHugh; my production editor, Meredith Smith; and my copy editor, Linda Barker; as well as my colleagues at Santa Clara University in the English department, the Ignatian Center, DISCOVER, and the Osher Lifelong Learning Institute. I am grateful for the assistance of Carole Wentz in English; university librarians Cindy Bradley, Gail Gradowski, Leanna Goodwater, and Alice Whistler; my research assistants Cece Garrison, Erin Schoenfelder, and Kate Holloway; my students; and the participants in my surveys, retreats, and workshops.

For personal support, I acknowledge these people and many others, including Gloria DeGaetano, Tom Judd, Janette Lewis, Christiaan T. Lievestro, Sunny Lockwood, Elizabeth Moran, Pat Patrick, William J. Sullivan, John Vasconcellos, Col. Frank H. Dreher and Mary Ann Dreher, Michael and Marilyn Numan, Frank Dreher, and Heidi Dreher-Numan. Above all, I am grateful to my husband, Robert Numan, for sharing his gifts, his love, and life's journey with me.

Applying the creative principles in this book, a portion of the proceeds will be used to bring a new Renaissance to the great city of New Orleans, helping our neighbors there rebuild their lives and restore a national treasure to our country and the world.

The Sense of Calling

Creating Your Personal Renaissance

Nature, that framed us of four elements
Warring within our breasts for regiment,
Doth teach us all to have aspiring minds.
—CHRISTOPHER MARLOWE, TAMBURLAINE[1]

Are you ready for a Renaissance in your life? Longing for greater joy and meaning? Do you feel stuck in a dead-end job, debilitating routine, confining relationship, or money problems? Perhaps you're facing a major change—anything from graduation, downsizing, retirement, or divorce, to recovery from a natural disaster—or you're searching for a long-deferred dream.

A personal Renaissance can come in different ways. For a downsized engineer, it may mean writing a book and beginning a new life as a leadership consultant. For someone else, it's going back to school for an MBA in order to leave a lackluster job behind. One woman's personal Renaissance means leaving an abusive relationship to begin living her own life. Another may find her Renaissance homeschooling her daughter or starting her own company, while a retired couple may find theirs volunteering at a local food bank and becoming more active in their community.

Wherever it leads, your personal Renaissance will bring you a creative new beginning, freeing you to become more joyously and authentically *yourself*. This process usually begins with a growing restlessness, a feeling that there must be something more in life. It happens as a stockbroker watches his income rise but feels progressively empty inside, when a successful career woman recognizes she never has time for herself because she's too busy pleasing others, or when a frustrated manager finally realizes he's been living somebody else's life.

Do you feel an underlying sense that something's missing from your life? Do any of the following statements sound familiar?

Lately, I've been feeling restless and unhappy.
I can't express an important part of who I am.
With all the changes around me, I feel like I just don't fit any more.
I've outgrown my current situation but don't know what to do.
My life is just an endless round of responsibilities; it's not fun any more.
Something's missing from my life but I don't know what it is.
My life is changing and I need to set new goals.
I feel a growing need to do something more with my life.

If you resonate with any of these statements, you are experiencing creative discontent and are ready for your own new Renaissance.

What Is a Calling?

Seeking your calling is a process of discovery that continues throughout your life, informed by your questions, your conflicts, and your deepest dreams. It is the journey known by many names, from Homer's *Odyssey* to the pilgrimage in Dante's *Divine Comedy* and the quests of the knights of the round table, to the vision quests of Native Americans, and the path of the Chinese sage, Lao Tzu. Abraham Maslow called it self-actualization. Joseph Campbell knew it as "the hero's journey." It is the dynamic voyage of self-discovery central to the Renaissance, and it is our journey, yours and mine, as we seek to live with greater joy and purpose, becoming more deeply, more authentically ourselves.

As you become more aware of your calling, it weaves like a bright thread through the daily fabric of your life, and as you move through life's seasons, into new roles in your work, family, and community, every stage in life invites you to discover your calling on another level. In the Renaissance, Shakespeare and his contemporaries realized that each of us goes through many seasons, "plays many parts." Ideally, we all begin developing our callings in childhood by exploring our world and discovering what we love to do. During your teens to early twenties, you move forward in your calling as you enter college or take your first job. You may discover new callings in love, marriage, and family life or be called to community service, caregiving, or mentoring others. Your quest will begin again with each promotion, downsizing, or desire to reach out in a new direction, and as you mature, you will hear a new call to creative retirement.

Psychologists see the sense of calling as essential for fulfillment in life, finding it the "most important life value" in the United States, Italy, Canada, Belgium, Portugal, South Africa, Poland, Croatia, Israel, Australia, and Japan. Pursuing your calling can make you happier, healthier, and more energetic, filling you with the joyous engagement known as "flow," and bringing greater meaning to your life.[2]

Creative Discontent: The Source of Calling

In whatever season of life you find yourself now, your inner restlessness is a sign that your life is changing. You are poised on the edge of possibility, ready to begin the journey to become more fully yourself.

Hundreds of years ago, men and women knew a powerful secret: that creative discontent is the first stage in the archetypal journey of renewal that leads to your calling in life. To understand more about your sense of calling, let's go back over five hundred years to a time when the quest for calling inspired the Renaissance, an era of dynamic change much like our own.

The invention of the printing press unleashed a flood of information equaled only by the advent of the computer and the Internet. Explorers sailed boldly across uncharted seas to discover new worlds, just as modern astronauts have walked on the moon and ventured through vast oceans of space. With his telescope, Galileo discovered the moons of Jupiter and a new vision of the solar system, while our astronomers have discovered new planets and sent space probes to Mars. Exploring new worlds within, William Harvey discovered the circulation of the blood and Antony van Leeuwenhoek invented the microscope, discovering red blood cells and bacteria, while our scientists today have developed nanotechnology and mapped the human genome.

In an age of unprecedented exploration and creativity, Renaissance men and women were empowered by the sense of calling or vocation (from the Latin *vocare,* to call). Martin Luther, John Calvin, and generations after them believed that *everyone* had a calling, from kings to commoners—artists, artisans, bakers, carpenters, diplomats, doctors, farmers, lawyers, merchants, ministers, teachers, parents, husbands, wives, and people like you and me. Believing that their lives held divine significance, that they were each given special talents, Renaissance men and women became artists, poets, humanists, saints, scientists, political leaders, devoted parents, and committed citizens. Their identities were informed by a sense of personal destiny, faith in a meaningful universe and their place within it.[3]

By contrast, our own new millennium is filled with what psychologist Martin Seligman has called an "unprecedented epidemic of depression." Suffering from chronic anxiety, isolation, and lack of meaning, too many people today feel powerless, experiencing what Seligman has called "learned helplessness," the feeling that nothing they do in life will make any difference.[4]

We could be on the edge of another Renaissance, but there is one vital difference: unlike today's victims of learned helplessness, Renaissance men and women believed in their own inner resources, seeing themselves as creative agents, not passive victims of fate. Their philosophers proclaimed the human power to discover, choose, and create; Shakespeare's plays linked characters' fates with their choices; and Francis Bacon affirmed that knowledge is power.[5]

Today, while we have worlds of information at our fingertips, we too often lose touch with ourselves, ignoring our own inner resources. Because many people don't take time to look within, to ask where they're going, too often they race down the road of life, full speed ahead—in the wrong direction.

Have You Been Pursuing What You Want— or What You *Think* You *Should* Want?

As a college professor, I've seen too many people rush into decisions about their futures without doing the essential inner work. When LSAT results were announced last year, our college pre-law advisor spent hours counseling despondent students who'd learned that they had no aptitude for law. They had grown up watching lawyers on television; their fathers, mothers, or uncles were lawyers; and during their four years of college they had taken pre-law courses, done legal internships, and applied to law schools, looking everywhere but within themselves. Another colleague was asked to write letters of recommendation for PhD programs, MBA programs, counseling programs, and teacher education programs—all by the same student, who had graduated with honors last spring but never looked within herself to consider her calling.

These students are not alone. The *New York Times* reports that 58 percent of American workers have gone through at least one major career change and over a third of students enrolled in colleges today are reentry students over age twenty-five seeking new directions in life.[6] Some of this has been caused by our rapidly changing economy, but much of it occurs because people today don't take the time to look within. I've seen many people graduate, take the first entry-level job they could find, then years later ask me for letters of recommendation to do something completely different. I've known lawyers, corporate vice presidents, and computer engineers, outwardly successful but inwardly haunted by the nagging realization that somewhere they'd lost a vital part of themselves.

Millions of Americans languish in learned helplessness because they look outside themselves to find themselves in consumerism and conformity. Our culture has forgotten the vital wisdom of the Renaissance, a time when people realized that each of us is unique, blessed with personal strengths we can use to find a sense of calling and live with greater creativity, joy, and meaning.

I realized how much we have lost with the fading of this Renaissance wisdom a few years ago in a literature class at Santa Clara University. While discussing one of Milton's sonnets, I told my students that Milton was anxious to use his talents to pursue his vocation. The confusion on their faces told me they didn't know what I was talking about. "'Vocation' comes from the Latin *vocare*—it means 'calling,'" I said. "A vocation is your calling, your life's work. How would you describe your calling today?"

Silence. The students shifted uneasily in their chairs. I rephrased my question: "What do *you* want to do with your lives?" More silence. Struggling to make a connection, I asked why they had come to college. They said they wanted to buy new cars, to make a good income, to live as well as their parents. I couldn't believe what I was hearing. "Beyond making money," I asked, "don't you have a deeper reason for your work?"

Silence again. The students looked at each other anxiously. Finally, one young man said, "So I can support a wife and family." I shook my head. "More than money, more than paying the bills, there has to be something *more* to our efforts to give our lives meaning. People in the Renaissance believed they were given special talents, or gifts, as part of the divine plan, that it was their responsibility to use these gifts wisely and well. A calling means using our talents, our lives, to make a significant contribution to the world."

My students looked at me blankly. "Surely people still feel that way today?" I added hesitantly, "When I was in college, my friends and I worried about 'finding ourselves,' about doing something meaningful with our lives." My students smiled, obviously amused. My college days must have seemed as far away as Milton and the seventeenth-century Puritans.

After class, I walked back to my office, concerned that my students, bright, endearing young people on the edge of adulthood, were out of touch with deeper questions of purpose and meaning. I knew I had to write this book.

Making Vocation Visible

My students were confused because our culture doesn't reinforce us for finding our callings. Neuroscientists tell us that naming a feeling helps us understand and deal with it more effectively. Unlike today, life in the Renaissance was informed by the vocabulary of vocation. That inner restlessness, the longing you feel for something more, for the chance to follow your heart, to develop your deepest potential—in the Renaissance this feeling was known as a call to vocation. Because our culture lacks such a vocabulary, when you feel restless and discontent, you may worry that something's wrong with you, while your Renaissance counterparts saw these feelings as the first step on the journey to greater fulfillment in life.[7]

In a process known as the "self-fulfilling prophecy," psychologists have found that our expectations shape our experience. On many levels, from personal performance to relationships, you and I apparently get what we expect. Because generations of Renaissance men and women expected to discover their callings, they found them in remarkable ways. Their vocations illuminated their lives as they combined ideals and action into unprecedented contributions to science, religion, culture, politics, and the arts. A poor Dutch boy grew up to become the great humanist Desiderius Erasmus. Artemisia Gentileschi transcended an abusive early life to become the most important woman painter of the Renaissance. Caterina Adorno transformed her unhappy marriage, managed a large hospital, and became St. Catherine of Genoa. And a poor boy from the English countryside whose parents could sign their names only with an X found his calling on the London stage as William Shakespeare.[8]

In seventeenth-century England, George Fox grew increasingly restless, searching for meaning, walking alone with his Bible through the countryside, sitting "in hollow trees and lonesome places till night came on; and frequently in the night walked mournfully about." He discovered his calling in 1643, founding the Society of Friends, or Quakers. A similar bout of restlessness and depression afflicted young Isaac Newton during his first year of college at Cambridge in 1662. Within two years, he had found his calling as a scientist and mathematician, discovering the law of gravity and beginning his pioneering work in physics. Some people find their callings in crisis. In sixteenth-century Naples, Vittoria Colonna fainted and fell from her horse when she learned of her husband's death. Taken to a nearby convent, she recovered, beginning a new life writing poetry, living simply, and working with the poor. She performed acts of charity, wrote sonnets praised by the poet Ariosto, and became close friends with Michelangelo.[9]

As you may know, Renaissance means "rebirth," a rebirth of faith in our potential, a belief that what we do matters. For cultures, as for individuals, when we reach out courageously to express our ideals, our lives blossom into new possibilities. In the mid-nineteenth century, a group of New England writers created an American Renaissance. In the early twentieth century, African American writers and artists created the Harlem Renaissance.

From the fourteenth through the seventeenth centuries, during the Renaissance in Western Europe, generations of men and women found their callings and changed the world, questioning preconceived notions in philosophy, religion, science, politics, and the arts. Botticelli, Leonardo, and Michelangelo celebrated the glories of the natural world and the power of the human form. Recognizing the uniqueness of every individual, Renaissance artists painted the first portraits, and ordinary men and women began recording their lives in spiritual autobiographies. Unlike contemporary mass media that often isolates and overwhelms us, the guiding principles of Renaissance culture affirm that we are intimately connected to the world around us, and that you and I have the power to make a difference.

We make this difference by finding our callings. To understand how men and women can find their callings today, for the past five years I've done empirical research with hundreds of people from ages 18 to 80—college students, working adults, and retired people. My findings show that it is never too late to discover your own life pattern, never too late to become more creatively and authentically yourself. A sense of calling can occur at any age and in any occupation, from paid employment to your own education, art work, caring for your family, or community service. People who find their callings feel a sense of joy and personal satisfaction. Intrinsically motivated by what they do, not by the external rewards it may bring, they get so involved in their work that time passes quickly. Inspired and energized, they see their lives as part of a larger pattern of meaning, love their work, and feel it makes a positive contribution to the world.[10]

From my research and over two decades of workshops, retreats, and personal counseling, I have uncovered a simple process that you can use to find your calling today, a process that has been used in clinical practice and presented at national conferences through Santa Clara's Spirituality and Health Institute. As I've worked with thousands of people, from the late teens through retirement age, I have seen the creative awakenings that occur when they discover their gifts, detach from impediments, discern their deepest values, and chart their new directions in life, taking the same vital path to fulfillment that inspired the Renaissance. Uncovering this hidden Renaissance wisdom and revealing this path to you was my purpose in writing this book.[11]

Living More Creatively

Our Renaissance counterparts aspired to live creatively. Becoming aware of their personal gifts and values, they developed what contemporary psychologists call intrinsic motivation, an attitude that can make you happier, healthier, and more successful. By contrast, studies have shown that living reactively, being driven by external rewards and pressures, can undermine your sense of self. Reacting to the push and pull of good and bad events, rewards and disappointments, other people's demands and expectations, can produce anxiety and depression. When you live creatively, you follow your own inner compass, unshaken by life's highs and lows because you see beyond what Shakespeare called "the slings and arrows of outrageous fortune."[12]

This book will help you live more creatively, strengthening your intrinsic motivation as you cast away unproductive habits to discover a calling uniquely your own. In a series of simple exercises designed to bring more energy, vitality, and fun into your life, you will reconnect with the part of yourself that is forever young, as playful and curious as a child. You'll find powerful lessons from other people who have lived creatively. Over the years, I have done research on the lives of over one hundred artists, scientists, scholars, writers, citizens, saints, and political leaders from the early Renaissance through the Enlightenment, a period of over four hundred years. I have also studied contemporary men and women who are living their own new Renaissance lives. Woven through this book are their stories, examples of courage and creativity to light your path today.

What to Expect

As you move through the steps in this book, you will find yourself:

- Happier, more energetic, more deeply yourself
- More inner directed, focused, and confident
- More relaxed, playful, and open to new possibilities
- Able to recognize and reject what drains you
- Able to embrace what energizes and inspires you
- More aware of creative opportunities
- Surrounded by supportive friends and mentors
- Experiencing greater joy and meaning in life.

Offering a practical, twelve-step guide to personal renewal, *Your Personal Renaissance* is literally the message of this book. During Phase One, the first four chapters will take you through the stages of Discovery, Detachment, Discernment, and Direction. Your progress in each stage will be supported by stories, assessments, personal exercises, and checklists.

In chapter one, you will discover your gifts, asking: "What brings me joy? What am I good at?"

In chapter two, you will begin eliminating all the things that drain your creative energy, asking, "What's blocking me from becoming my true self? What do I need to release?"

In chapter three, you will discern your deepest values, asking, "What do I really care about? Which choices leave me empty and frustrated? Which ones make me feel more alive?"

In chapter four, you will combine your gifts and values to chart your new direction, asking, "Where am I headed in life? What is the next step? How can I stay on course?"

Once you have chosen your direction, the next eight chapters will take you into Phase Two, introducing you to eight powerful Renaissance practices: (1) Faith (2) Examen (3) Community (4) Contemplation (5) Creativity (6) Reading and Reflection (7) Exercise and (8) Discipline and Dedication. Together, these practices will create a supportive counterculture to help you move forward in your calling.

Written in short sections that can be read in a single sitting, this book combines the best of the old and new—powerful principles from Renaissance lives supported by the latest psychological research. You will also find examples from my life and the lives of other contemporary men and women. Some of these people you will recognize; others are my students, clients, and colleagues, whose names have been changed to protect their privacy.

One powerful secret you will discover in this book is that *small actions over time produce monumental results*. Anyone who has ever planted a garden, played a musical instrument, run a marathon, or acquired any new skill knows the amazing power of consistent effort over time. When you begin any new endeavor, your efforts actually transform the world within you, the inner workings of your brain. Neuroscientists have found that as you learn a new skill, your brain begins growing new neural connections. Each time you practice that skill, you stimulate your brain to continue their growth. The transition from awkward beginnings to graceful proficiency occurs when these new connections become established.

As you follow the program in this book—embracing your gifts, shedding unproductive habits, living your values, and developing a stronger sense of yourself—the small steps in this course will create a Renaissance within and around you, dramatically transforming your life.

How to Get the Most from This Book

To benefit from this book, you'll need to:

- Get yourself a journal to record your journey.
- Focus on one chapter at a time, doing the exercises, and checking in with the reminders at the end.

- Be kind to yourself. You will find your calling through joy and love, not stress or obligation.
- Use this book, don't just read it. Whenever you see the words "Personal Exercise," take positive action by doing the exercise. Remember, each small step builds your neural connections, increasing your creative momentum.
- Listen to yourself, recognizing what energizes you and what drains you.
- Make a copy of the Renaissance principles below and review them daily.
- Trust the process, trust yourself, and trust the creative power of the universe.

Now I invite you to join me in a journey back through time and into your own creative future. As my friend Dr. Carol Flinders found in her research on mystics, within each of us "there is a map to higher consciousness," an inner pattern that can bring greater meaning to our lives.[13] As you follow this journey, you will join Leonardo da Vinci, William Shakespeare, St. Teresa of Avila, Galileo Galilei, John Donne, Queen Elizabeth I, and countless others, and you will discover for yourself the deep and sustaining joy of finding your calling: your personal Renaissance.

RENAISSANCE PRINCIPLES

~ Your calling is your vocation of destiny, bringing greater joy and meaning to your life.

~ Your daily choices shape your life and inform the world.

~ There is a part of you that is forever young, playful, curious, and true that leads you to your calling.

~ Detach from the noisy world around you to follow the deepest values of your heart.

~ You are here to discover your gifts and use them to fulfill your destiny.

~ Discernment means following what inspires you and releasing what diminishes you.

~ You excel by focusing on your strengths, not dwelling on your weaknesses.

~ New Renaissance men and women affirm creative growth for themselves and one another.

~ Small actions over time produce monumental results.

~ When you reach out to follow your calling, the universe supports you with a world of possibilities.

The Discernment Journey:
Renaissance Wisdom for Your Life Today

CHAPTER 1

Discovery

Realizing Your Joys and Talents

Now there are diversities of gifts, but the same Spirit.

—1 Corinthians 12:4

What brings you joy? What do you love to do? Many people today are so caught up in their daily routine that they've lost touch with their dreams.

That was Linda's experience. It was a hectic Monday morning as she put down the phone and printed out the next round of sales figures. Reaching for her coffee cup, she glanced at the family photos on her desk. Her husband, Joe, was a manager for a top computer firm, Scott was in high school now, and Molly had just left for college. Her eyes grew misty. She was proud of Molly—so young, so eager, and so filled with aspirations. Once, Linda had dreamed of becoming a journalist. But she'd dropped out of school when she got married, taking a secretarial job so Joe could get his MBA. And there were always responsibilities—the children, the new house, and all the bills, so she'd kept on working. She had a wonderful family and was office manager for a busy Ford dealership, but as she looked out her glass cubicle past the gleaming cars on the showroom floor, she wondered if she'd ever find time for her dreams.

If you, too, are caught up in an endless round of responsibilities, if your life's journey has been feeling like an uphill battle, it's time to take a different path. You will find your calling not by a forced march through the mire of obligations but by following the gentle path of joy and love. Italian Renaissance artists and philosophers saw love as the creative power of the universe. In your life as well, reconnecting with what you love will fill you with the powerful joy of discovery.

Do you know anyone with this kind of joy? I saw it years ago in Linus Pauling, the Nobel prize-winning chemist, when I was in college. He spoke to a group of students gathered on the University of California Riverside commons lawn, and his blue eyes sparkled as he told us about his life as a scientist, about following his curiosity and exploring new ideas. I could see that he loved his work, that science was his calling. It was late afternoon. The sun's parting rays were at his back, but he had his own light and was positively radiating energy, enthusiasm, and the joy of discovery. His bright spirit has been an inspiration for me ever since.

In the Renaissance, people believed that each of us is given a unique set of gifts as part of the divine plan. Although there are over six billion people on the planet, current research confirms that each of us is unique. In the history of the world, there has never been anyone exactly like you. Even identical twins have different fingerprints and different personalities. My husband, Bob, is an identical twin, sharing many interests with his brother, Michael. Both are psychology professors specializing in brain research but, unlike Michael, Bob has a deep love of animals. When Bob and I walk through town, strange cats and dogs come up to him as if he were St. Francis of Assisi. Three stray cats have followed him home and now live in our yard. Bob's special bond with animals is one of his gifts.

In this chapter you will take the first step toward finding your calling by discovering your gifts, the talents and strengths that make you who you are, the treasure of your uniqueness.

Looking Back and Looking Within

When you were a child, you began discovering your gifts by exploring your world and learning what you loved to do. How does this work? Follow me back through the long tunnel of time to thirteenth-century Tuscany.

Centuries ago, a young boy stood on a sunny hilltop outside Florence watching his father's sheep. He looked out at the rolling hills of green and gold, the small farms and olive groves. Then he led the sheep to where the grass grew sweet in the shade of cypress trees, picked up a rock, and began drawing. The boy loved to draw—on the ground, on stones, with whatever materials he could find. Studying a young ram, he sketched its image onto a large flat stone. He continued drawing as the afternoon wore on and the warm sun beat down on his back. Finally he stood up, wiped his hands on his worn brown tunic, and smiled as the image of a ram looked back at him from the stone. Then he turned abruptly, startled by the sound of horse's hooves.

"Buon giorno," said a man on horseback.

"Buon giorno, signore," said the boy, looking up at the man in a brown cape and red hooded cap.

The stranger dismounted, walked over to the drawing, and asked, "Who did this?"

"I did," said the boy.

"You?"

"Si, signore."

"What is your name?"

"Giotto di Bondone."

"How old are you?"

"Ten, signore—almost eleven."

"You have a gift, my son," said the stranger. "I am Giovanni Cimabue, painter of Florence." He paused, then asked, "Would you like to become my apprentice?"

Cimabue had revived the arts in Florence, even painted St. Francis of Assisi from life. Catching his breath, Giotto answered, "Si, signore . . . if my father is willing."

They walked to a small cottage, where Giotto's mother wrapped up his few belongings and his father gave his blessing. Bidding them farewell, Giotto set off to become an artist in early modern Florence.

Living and working with Cimabue, Giotto grew in stature, skill, and grace, filling the studio with his energy and wit. Legend has it that one day when Cimabue was out on an errand, Giotto painted a picture of a fly on one of his master's paintings. So real did it appear that when the artist returned, he swatted it repeatedly. Ultimately, Giotto's art surpassed even that of his master. He became the most important artist of the early fourteenth century, transcending the old medieval icons with a dramatic realism that heralded the dawn of Renaissance art.[1]

Your Gifts Are the Keys to Your Destiny

What was true for Giotto is true for you today. Discovering and using your gifts will bring you a powerful flow of creative energy, lighting the way to your calling.

Renaissance religious reformers taught that God gave everyone "diversities of gifts" and that once we discover our gifts, we have a personal responsibility to use them.[2] As generations of Renaissance men and women discovered their gifts, the old class system started breaking down. A poor shepherd boy like Giotto and an illegitimate son like Leonardo da Vinci could become two of the greatest artists of their times. Women, too, found their callings as artists. Madonna Properzia de Rossi became a noted sculptor and Artemisia Gentileschi a celebrated painter. Gentileschi received commissions in Rome, Venice, Naples, and London, where she painted portraits for King Charles I.

Not only artists, but scientists, saints, and scholars discovered their gifts, which led them to their callings. As you read their stories, look for a powerful secret: the underlying pattern.

In 1572, eight-year-old Galileo Galilei saw a new star appear in the supposedly unchangeable heavens. This star and the comet that blazed across the sky when he was thirteen aroused his lifelong curiosity about the cosmos. At seventeen, while attending mass in Pisa, he noticed a chandelier swinging in the cathedral and timed its motions against his pulse. This experience led him to study the laws of pendular motion, and he used his gifts to become a researcher in physics.[3]

St. Teresa of Avila was unusually devout as a child. While her friends played outside in the late afternoon, she would go to her room to read about saints' lives. Little Teresa loved saying the rosary, becoming especially attached to the Virgin Mary after her mother died. At seven, Teresa and her eleven-year-old brother, Roderigo, walked out of town on a self-appointed pilgrimage. When their uncle brought them home, they set up a hermitage in a nearby orchard, foreshadowing Teresa's future as a religious reformer.[4]

Young Isaac Newton was fascinated by time and motion, and was forever making kites, sun dials, and water clocks. He once made a working model of a mill, with the wheel turned by a mouse he put inside and called "the miller." Although most of his family were poor farmers, an uncle recognized his gifts and got him admitted to Trinity College, Cambridge, in 1661. Isaac spent his first year feeling alone and out of place, cleaning rooms and serving meals to support his education. But when he was awarded a scholarship, he became so absorbed in his studies that he often forgot to eat or sleep. His cat grew fat feasting on meals that turned cold while the young man sat at his desk, lost in his studies.[5]

At seven, Elena Lucretia Cornaro's intellectual gifts were discovered by the priest who taught her Latin and Greek. She began learning Hebrew, Arabic, French, and Spanish at age eleven; she later became the first woman in history to earn a doctorate, which was awarded at the University of Padua in 1678.[6]

Half a world away, in the Spanish colony that is now Mexico, Sor Juana Inés de la Cruz, as a child of age three, followed her sister to school, pleading to be taught to read. At seven, Juana begged to dress in boy's clothes, like one of Shakespeare's heroines, to attend the university in Mexico City, which admitted only young men. When her family refused, she studied Latin and read the books in her grandfather's library. At eight, she won a prize for her poetry in Mexico City, impressing the viceroy and vicereine, who became her patrons. By age fifteen, she had become the most learned woman in New Spain.[7]

Did you discover the secret, the common pattern in the lives of these Renaissance men and women? They all began discovering their gifts in childhood by doing what they loved, the same pattern that occurs in the lives of creative men and women today.

Born on a Navajo reservation in Arizona, twentieth-century artist R. C. Gorman began drawing at age three. Like Giotto, he herded sheep and drew pictures in the sand, in the mud, on rocks—with any materials he could find. Inspired by the beauty of the earth and the lives of his people, he grew up to paint archetypal images of Navajo women, developing an international reputation for his art. I saw him at his Navajo Gallery in Taos on my last trip to New Mexico. In his western shirt and colorful headband, R. C. Gorman was a creative original, radiating joy, charisma, and an intense love of life.[8]

As a child in Bournemouth, England, Jane Goodall displayed the love of animals, curiosity, and patience that made her a pioneering primatologist. When she was one year old, her father gave her a stuffed animal—a chimpanzee she named Jubilee—that became her favorite toy. At age four, Jane sat quietly in her grandmother's henhouse for four hours watching to find out how hens laid eggs.

After years of studying chimpanzees in Gombe, Tanzania, Dr. Jane Goodall now lectures around the world to protect wildlife and preserve the environment. The motto of the Jane Goodall Institute underscores her belief that *each* of us has a calling:

> *Every individual matters.*
> *Every individual has a role to play.*
> *Every individual makes a difference.*[9]

Your Child Self

There is a part of you that is forever young, forever in discovery. As children we naturally follow our curiosity, exploring and using our gifts. As we grow older, we collect layers of experience, demands, and responsibilities. Yet, beneath these layers, there remains an inner core of joy, playfulness, spontaneity, and inspiration. Your *child self* (CS) is your *core* self, your *creative* self, your *curious, clever,* and *compassionate* self, and, in the deepest sense, your *courageous* self, urging you to explore new possibilities. Our word "courage" comes from the French word *coeur,* which means "heart." Whatever you choose to call it, your inner self—CS—is your emotional center, the part of you that lives with heart, joy, and vitality. Studies have found that throughout their lives, artists, composers, scientists, writers, and other creative individuals draw upon the curiosity and core feelings of childhood.[10]

There is another part of you that shoulders all the responsibilities of adult life: your rational or responsible self (RS), called the "executive function" by neuroscientists, who have determined that planning and decision making are located in your brain's frontal lobes. In the Renaissance, our emotional and rational functions were known as *passion* and *reason*. Although Descartes saw these forces as polar opposites, today's neuroscientists have found that our feelings provide vital guidance, helping us make wiser decisions. Centuries ago, Renaissance Neoplatonists, too, believed that love, blended with reason, could refine our spirits and inspire us to fulfill our highest potential. This book will show you how to listen to your heart and balance these two vital parts of yourself.[11]

Keeping a Renaissance Notebook

Following his curiosity and passionate interest in the world, Leonardo da Vinci kept notebooks throughout his life. His notes in left-handed mirror writing, sketches of people and horses, and designs for catapults, snorkels, and flying machines give us a glimpse into the mind of this remarkable Renaissance man.

As a valuable tool for your inner journey, you, too, will need to keep a Renaissance Notebook, responding to each chapter's personal exercises and recording your own explorations, questions, goals, and insights. This week, treat yourself to a notebook you'll enjoy—a classic composition book if you value simplicity, a colorful silk or leather-bound journal if you prefer an esthetic touch.

Personal Exercise: Reflect on Your Childhood

Like Jane Goodall, R. C. Gorman, and our Renaissance counterparts, you, too, began discovering your gifts in childhood by doing what you loved. To get more in touch with your gifts, set aside twenty to thirty minutes to reflect on your childhood. Go off by yourself where you won't be interrupted, taking along your notebook and a pen or pencil. Take a deep breath, close your eyes, and relax. Let your mind wander back to a key childhood memory.

Even if you came from a dysfunctional family, think back on the times when you found relief, hope, and a joyous new sense of yourself. As a child, my friend Tina found solace by going off by herself in nature and by singing in the school choir. Today she lives in a house surrounded by venerable oaks and wildlife and works as a spiritual counselor with the healing power of sound.

When you've recalled your own memory of joy and empowerment, write down your answers to these questions about the memory:

- What were you doing?
- What did it look like and feel like?
- When you were a child, what were three things you loved to do?

Your key memory and favorite childhood activities will help you recall what psychologist Abraham Maslow called a "peak experience," an expansive feeling of joy and oneness filled with clues about your calling.[12]

Personal Exercise: Create an Exploration List

Since the Renaissance was an age of exploration, your next notebook entry will be an "Exploration List," a list of possibilities: activities you enjoyed as a child, things you've been wanting to do but keep putting off—anything from wandering through an art museum, to signing up for a dance class, or treating yourself to that box of crayons or bag of cleary marbles you loved as a child. Some of these ideas will seem simple, others scary, some even silly. Just write them down. Most of us are so locked into routines and responsibilities that we lose touch with our curiosity, intuitions, and deep personal interests. This list will connect you with your inner, curious self (CS) and help you develop the Renaissance habit of exploring. Research has shown that getting back in touch with your natural curiosity will enhance your creativity, vitality and overall well-being.[13]

Developing Your Gifts Throughout Life

Although you began discovering your gifts in childhood, you will continue developing them throughout life. Even if you wander off course, you can find your direction by getting back in touch with your gifts.

Renaissance poet John Donne was famous for his dazzling intellect and gift of words. He studied law at London's Inns of Court, where he was known for his metaphysical love poetry. We have a portrait of him from those early days, a dashing dark-eyed cavalier in a wide-brimmed hat, with a sensuous smile and studied pose.

Young "Jack" Donne dreamed of a political career. At twenty-four, he sailed to Cádiz to fight the Spanish, then to the Azores, Italy, and Spain. When he returned, his gifts were recognized by Sir Thomas Egerton, advisor to the queen, who made him his secretary, setting him up for a government career. But in 1601 Donne eloped with Egerton's teenaged niece, Ann More. Because marriages among the nobility were arranged by their families, Ann's relatives were outraged, had Donne imprisoned, and tried to get the marriage annulled. Donne sent his bride a short note from prison: "John Donne, Ann Donne, undone." And indeed he was. Although the couple was reunited, for years Donne and his family lived with relatives and patrons while he searched in vain for employment.

Aside from a few short-term jobs, Donne spent his thirties and early forties poor and unemployed, with time weighing heavily upon him. Living with a series of patrons, he read philosophy in their libraries, composed poetry about lovers "canonized for love," and wrote *Biathanatos,* a treatise on suicide. He worried about what he was doing with his life, his hopes, and his many gifts, and how in the world he would support his growing family. The answers came slowly.

In the prime of his life, the world seemed to have passed him by. Even when Elizabeth was succeeded by James I in 1603, Donne was still shunned at court. Restless and despondent, he searched for his calling, meditating on how best to use his gifts, making the Ignatian Spiritual Exercises, and writing his "Holy Sonnets." He entered the Anglican priesthood in 1615, becoming the king's chaplain, for the first time in his life assured a regular income. Two years later his wife died, leaving him a widower with seven children.

Donne became dean of St. Paul's Cathedral and was an exemplary preacher whose religious poetry and sermons inspired multitudes. In his *Devotions,* he wrote "No man is an island" and "Never send to know for whom the bell tolls; it tolls for thee."[14] He found his calling by embracing his gifts, which developed greater depth and scope, blossoming most fully in later life.

❧ *Personal Assessment: What's Changing for You?*

Are you entering a new season of life? Do you feel your priorities changing? If so, these questions can help you find your way:

- What choices no longer appeal to you?
- What choices attract you now?
- How can you use your gifts in this new season of life?

Record your answers in your Renaissance Notebook.

Sometimes a season of change brings a call to adventure. After twenty years as editor of a busy metropolitan newspaper, Art's decision took the newsroom by surprise. "Can it be true?" the reporters wondered. "Is he really resigning, selling his house, and joining the Peace Corps?" "Yes," Art assured them. He and his wife, Marge, had not taken leave of their senses. Years earlier, he had wanted to be a foreign correspondent and they'd both been inspired by a young president's call to service. But marriage had brought responsibilities, so he'd worked for the *San Jose Mercury News,* Marge had taught high school, and they'd raised their children in the suburban

Almaden Valley. But now their children were grown, the paper had been bought by a multimedia conglomerate, and it was time for a new adventure together. During the prior year, they had put their affairs in order, studied Spanish, and begun simplifying their lives. In a few months they sold their house, put their remaining possessions in storage, packed their bags, and took off to teach English, write, and work in a small Guatemalan village.

At an age when some people think of retirement, Al and Marge were beginning their new Renaissance of discovery.

Discovering New Gifts through Challenge

Perhaps you're facing a challenge that reveals gifts you didn't know you had. This happened in the Renaissance to Magdalen Herbert, who found herself widowed at age twenty-seven—with ten children!

Married in her teens to Sir Richard Herbert of Castle Montgomery in Wales, for years she lived a private life as a wife and mother. In 1596, when her husband died, she was left to care for seven sons and three daughters. She led her family in devotions, attended daily Mass, taught her children to read and write, and kept a well ordered household, expressing her gift of artistry in her exquisite embroidery, her penmanship, and her well-tended garden. When her eldest son, Edward, entered college, she moved the family to Oxford, entering a more public season of life. Her household became a center of lively discussions as the university community recognized her gifts of intelligence, wit, and hospitality. John Donne visited Oxford, becoming a lifelong friend of the family. After Edward's graduation, she moved to London, where she welcomed people of all classes and political opinions into her home. Performing acts of charity and becoming a patron of the arts, she was called upon as a mediator to resolve disputes in the community. Legend has it that when Magdalen Herbert was forty, Donne wrote his poem "The Autumnal" for her, claiming, "No spring or summer beauty hath such grace/ As I have seen in one autumnal face."[15]

Sometimes when you pursue a new calling, you become a creative catalyst for the people around you, challenging them to develop their own gifts as well. When Josie went back to school to get her degree in pastoral ministry, taking all-day Saturday seminars, her husband, Tom, became responsible for Saturday night dinners. The first week, Tom took her out to dinner. Then he began cooking grilled meats and baked potatoes. But he soon began exploring his curiosity, trying out new recipes, finding his culinary experiments a welcome change from his work as a realtor. Between appointments with clients, he explored gourmet food stores. He even began baking bread, specializing in a Swedish recipe from his native Minnesota. As they both enjoyed developing their gifts, Josie returned from her classes to gourmet meals, while Tom exercised his creativity in the kitchen.

Becoming Mindful of Your Energies

One secret for discovering your gifts is to pay attention to your energies. There's a joy and vitality that comes from using your gifts, from doing what you love. Psychologist Mihaly Csikszentmihalyi calls this "flow." If a task is too easy for you, you're bored; if it's too hard, you get frustrated. But when your gifts are equal to the task, you feel happy, exhilarated, one with the process. Studies have also found that when you use your gifts in a meaningful way, really *believing* in what you're doing, you will feel more alive.[16]

The opposite is also true. Negative atmospheres can drain you, and doing the wrong work can even make you ill. I've worked in toxic environments where morale was low and people were always quitting or getting sick. They obviously didn't want to be there.

I've also experienced the healing effects of following my calling. I've gone in to teach my class with an awful sinus headache only to become so caught up in the flow of ideas, the literature I love, and the enthusiasm of my students that at the end of class, I suddenly realized my headache was gone.

Have you ever experienced anything like this?

Personal Assessment: Track Your Energies

When Frank began tracking his energies, he finally discovered the work he loved. For years, after dropping out of college, he had drifted from one job to another, working in restaurants, tending bar, setting up equipment for rock concerts. He had kept busy and made lots of friends but he had no direction in life. When he finally took time to reflect, he realized that, aside from his friends, the two things that gave him the most energy were sports and television. He'd loved sports since childhood and learned to read with the *TV Guide,* but he'd never focused on these gifts before. Frank went back to school, earning a degree in broadcast communication. Now he works televising games for the San Francisco Giants and 49ers and for professional basketball, soccer, and ice hockey games and college athletics, providing essential technical support. Tracking his energies helped Frank finally find his direction and discover a job he loves.

You can track your energies by answering these questions in your Renaissance Notebook:

1. What activities energize you, make you feel stronger and more alive?
2. What activities or interactions drain you? Are you exhausted after being in a certain situation? With a particular person?
3. When you finish your current work, do you feel happy—or just relieved?
4. What activity can you count on to lift your spirits?

● ●

Your energies are a vital message from your core self (CS). They tell you whether you're using your gifts and following your heart or living by someone else's design.

Once you begin recognizing your gifts, you may notice that they come in two categories: *talents* and *strengths*. Talents—such as perfect pitch or the artistic gifts of a Mozart or a Michelangelo—are innate. Do you have a special talent for art, music, or sports? If so, this is one of your gifts.

Your other gifts are strengths, which you can develop with education and practice. Some strengths are skills—like cooking, computer programming, or public speaking—while others are character strengths. Psychologist Martin Seligman maintains that we each have five main character strengths or "signature strengths." Whether from skills or character, your strengths are an area of tremendous potential, for you can keep on developing them throughout your life.

The joy that comes from using your gifts is *not* the same as the pleasure from a good meal, money, or material goods, although our consumer culture would like us to think so. In fact, research has linked striving for material wealth with increased stress, isolation, anxiety, and depression. Products may bring you temporary pleasure, but using your gifts leads to the deep, sustaining joy of living your calling.[17]

RENAISSANCE QUESTION

To get beyond all the external programming in your life and back to your core self (CS), ask yourself:

"What do I really love to do?"

Write your answer in your Renaissance Notebook.

Shadows on the Path: Facing Your Fears

Research shows that you become healthier, happier, and more successful when you focus on what you love to do, but most people do just the opposite. According to a recent Gallup survey, most people in the United States, Britain, Canada, France, Japan, and China spend more time focusing on their weaknesses than on their strengths.[18]

When I ask people in my workshops why they don't focus on their gifts, they tell me:

- I'm afraid I'm not good enough.
- I'm afraid to change and leave my comfort zone.
- If I change, I might upset the people I care about.
- I'm afraid of embarrassing myself.
- I'm afraid of failure.
- I'm afraid of success.

Do these reasons sound familiar? Behind them all is the specter of fear—fear of change, fear of the unknown, fear of failure, fear of losing people's love, fear of success. Casting a dark shadow across the pathway to your dreams, fear can make you lose heart, freeze, or run away from what you want.

The only emotion stronger than fear is love. The steps in this book are designed to overcome your fears. Based on powerful principles from Renaissance lives supported by psychological research, these steps will connect you to a love of life so strong it will banish the shadows of fear.

One important step you can take right now is to perform a Renaissance in your thinking by *focusing on your strengths.* This is not only more enjoyable, but also more effective. In the business world, focusing on strengths is a guiding principle of Appreciative Inquiry (AI), a transformational approach to corporate change that asks people what is working well in their companies, then helps them build on these strengths to create new possibilities, solving old problems along the way.

For groups and for individuals, focusing on weaknesses produces, at best, only greater competence. At worst, it demoralizes us and drains our energy, producing learned helplessness.[19] Focusing on our strengths is the pathway to excellence. By following the steps in this chapter, you will create your own future of excellence, building a sustaining momentum as you become stronger, more courageous, more fully yourself.

❧ *Personal Exercise: Identify Your Gifts*

It's now time to identify your gifts. First, read through the five options below. Then choose *one,* set aside enough time to do it, and discover the treasure of your uniqueness.

1. Childhood Reflection.

Set aside an hour to reflect in stillness, bringing along your Renaissance Notebook. Take a walk, go to a favorite contemplative spot, or look through an old photo album. Let your mind relax and go back to your childhood, asking yourself:

- How did I spend my time?
- What did I love to do?
- What did teachers or other adults say I was good at?
- What was I curious about?
- What were my favorite accomplishments?
- What did I do well?

Write the answers in your Renaissance Notebook. Now put your notebook aside. Tomorrow review your notes. Look for the emerging Renaissance in yourself, just as Cimabue saw the young Giotto, answering these questions:

- What talents and strengths did your young self demonstrate?
- Were they artistic?
- Verbal?
- The gift of curiosity?
- Human relationships?
- Resourcefulness?
- Leadership?
- Teamwork?
- Perseverance?
- Love of nature?
- Courage?
- Humor?
- Something else?

Write the answers in your Renaissance Notebook.

2. Peak Experience.

Give yourself an hour when you won't be disturbed, taking along your Renaissance Notebook and a pen or pencil. If you're at home, close the door and turn off your phone. Or go to your favorite contemplative place, a park or a local library. Slow down, relax, and take two or three deep breaths. Now think of a time in your adult life when you felt fully and completely yourself, filled with expansive energy, joy, and vitality.

- What were you doing?
- What did it look like and feel like?

Write your answers in your notebook without stopping, as if you were taking dictation, then put your writing aside. Later, read over your description, circling any words that reveal your gifts, asking:

- Were your gifts artistic?
- Verbal?
- Curiosity?

- Human relationships?
- Resourcefulness?
- Leadership?
- Teamwork?
- Patience?
- Perseverance?
- Love of nature?
- Courage?
- Humor?
- Something else?

Write your answers in your Renaissance Notebook.

3. Mentoring Community.

In the Renaissance many people became mentors, helping each other discover their gifts. Tap into your own mentoring community by asking three people you know to list five of your strengths or talents. Then compare their lists, looking for patterns. Which gifts feel most like you, giving you energy, joy, and enthusiasm? Circle these, then record them in your Renaissance Notebook.

4. Signature Strengths Survey.

To draw upon the latest research in positive psychology, complete Martin Seligman's online survey, VIA-IS, on www.authentichappiness.org. You will need to sign in, answer some demographic questions, and fill out the survey, which will take about 45 minutes. Follow the instructions and print out your results. You can also find Seligman's survey in his book, *Authentic Happiness*. Review your survey results, asking: Which gifts feel most like me? Which ones give me a sense of energy, joy, and enthusiasm? Record these in your Renaissance Notebook.

5. Prayer.

Spend some time this week alone in prayer. Give thanks for your gifts and ask God to reveal them to you more fully in the next three days. Then simply notice what you find. At the end of each day reflect on what you learned. Ask yourself:

- What gave me joy today?

- When was I energized and inspired?
- What did I feel good about doing?
- What did I learn about myself?

Write the answers in your Renaissance Notebook.

After finding four or five gifts by one of these methods, check to see if your list includes both talents and strengths. If not, add any you are aware of. Then look back in your Renaissance Notebook at your answers to the other exercises in this chapter. Do these clues reinforce the gifts on your list? Do they offer additional insights? If so, add these to your list of gifts.

Moving Forward

At the end of each chapter you'll find questions and reminders to help you move forward in your personal Renaissance. Record your answers to these questions and the date in your Renaissance Notebook, scheduling any activities on your calendar. For this chapter:

1. Look over your list of gifts one more time. What do they tell you about yourself? Were there any surprises?
2. What was the most important thing you learned about yourself?
3. Pick one gift and ask yourself, "How can I use this gift next week?" Make this a small step, not a giant commitment. If one of your gifts is a love of nature, spend some time in your garden or a nearby park. If you enjoy learning, browse in a bookstore, visit a library, or get information on classes at the local community college or recreation center.
4. Pick one activity from your Exploration List to try out next week.

You should now have a clearer sense of your gifts and a grow-ing awareness of your inner (CS) self, the creative spark that brings you greater joy and power. Since this is quite an accomplishment, congratulate yourself and do something special to celebrate.

RENAISSANCE REMINDERS

~ There is a part of you that is forever young, playful, curious, and true that leads you to your calling.

~ You are a creative original with valuable gifts that will bring greater harmony to yourself and your world.

~ The more you use your gifts, the greater your joy in life will be.

~ You excel by focusing on your strengths, not by dwelling on your weaknesses.

CHAPTER 2

Detachment

Clearing the Path Within

You never enjoy the world aright,
till the sea itself floweth in your veins,
till you are clothed with the heavens, and crowned with the stars.
—THOMAS TRAHERNE, *CENTURIES OF MEDITATION*[1]

N ow that you've discovered your gifts, this chapter will
help you create more time to use them. You'll begin
clearing away whatever is draining your energy—everything from
daily distractions to your own doubts and fears, other people's expectations, consumerism, and overcommitment.

Like many people today, Jo Ann spends most of her time at
work. As the retreat director for Villa Maria by the Sea, she concentrates on helping others while continually denying herself. After working long days in the Villa office, she grabs a quick bite,
then sits at home at night with her computer, designing flyers and
catching up on e-mail from work. On weekends, she's back at the
Villa, welcoming visitors, helping set up day and weekend retreats.
Jo Ann took this job after a painful divorce, determined to fill the
emptiness inside. Starved for approval, she constantly volunteers
to do more, cramming her calendar with one responsibility after
another. But now the incessant activity is wearing her down and
she feels her life spinning out of control.

Overcommitted people like Jo Ann are driven by adrenaline, anxiety, and caffeine. Living at this frantic pace not only undermines our happiness and creativity, its continuous stress can weaken our memory and undermine our health. Racing around in constant anxiety puts our brains into an "alarm" mode, producing quick decisions and urgent action. While an alarm reaction serves us well in an emergency, when it becomes routine, it produces poor judgment, poor health, and a miserable quality of life.

Have you been living life like it's an emergency? If Jo Ann's story sounds familiar, you can overcome your own frantic cycle by cultivating your inner life. By clearing away mental clutter, you'll awaken your intuition, that reservoir of insight, information, and wisdom beneath your normal awareness that psychologists call "implicit memory." This inner wisdom not only inspired artists in the Renaissance, it's available to you, right now. Each of us has what Chicago psychologist John Neafsey calls "the potential to hear and follow the inner voice."[2] In this chapter, you'll begin listening to yourself on a deeper level, releasing what's blocking you from being your true self.

Revealing Your Renaissance Self

When Michelangelo began making his sculptures, he would first draw a rough outline on one side of a block of marble, then chip away the surrounding stone to release the magnificent form within. In his unfinished statues, we can see the dynamic figures emerging, apparently struggling to break free from their bondage of stone.

As you practice the detachment exercises in this chapter, you will undergo a similar liberation process. Remember to keep your eyes on your inner life, focusing on what brings you joy. Then it will be easier to chip away all the things that have kept *you* locked up, emerging to fulfill your shining potential.

Personal Exercise: Embrace Your Gifts

In the last chapter, you discovered your gifts. Research has shown that using these gifts regularly will cultivate your inner life, energizing and inspiring you. In 2005, psychologists found that people who used their strengths in a new way each day significantly reduced their depression and increased their happiness. Try this exercise for yourself. Take out your Renaissance Notebook, review your gifts, then:

- Use your gifts in a new way every day this week. This can be a small gesture. If one of your gifts is loving relationships, send someone a card or e-mail. Or try out some of the actions on your Exploration List. Be creative. Make this a game for yourself.
- Reflect on your gifts. Each day, remind yourself of what you do well. Don't undermine yourself with false humility by denying your gifts. Acknowledge them. Research has found that simply reminding yourself of your personal strengths will reduce stress and increase your vitality.[3]
- Affirm your strengths. Celebrate your uniqueness. Don't compare yourself to other people. Remember, you are a new Renaissance person with your own unique gifts and path in life. Tell yourself: "I am a creative original, creating a new Renaissance within and around me."

Smile as you move forward in your personal Renaissance.

Looking Back

Now that you're more in touch with your gifts, you're ready to move into the next step: detachment. Let's begin by going back in time to Renaissance England.

On a gray Sunday morning in sixteenth-century London, a young woman stood on a barge that was headed slowly down the

Thames, her red-gold hair the only brightness on this cold, dark day. The rain beat down relentlessly as the boatmen steered the barge toward the fatal Tower of London. Barely twenty-one, the young woman faced her fate alone. Her parents and brother were dead, her friends imprisoned, and her own sister had condemned her to this place. When the barge reached ground, she stepped ashore, raised her eyes to heaven, and said to the tower guards, "I pray you all, good friends and fellows, bear me witness that I come as no traitor." The guards fell silent. Many dropped to their knees, calling out, "God preserve your Grace! God save the Princess Elizabeth!" They led her to a prison chamber, bolting the heavy wooden door behind her.

It was March 17, 1554. Elizabeth's cousin, Lady Jane Grey, had just been executed, and in less than a month Sir Thomas Wyatt would lose his head on the block, along with seventy more suspected rebels. Elizabeth's life hung in the balance. She was accused, interrogated, and closely watched as the queen's men searched for evidence against her.

Elizabeth had always been a serious child. Seeking refuge from court politics and her father's moods, she had spent hours each day alone with her books. Throughout the many changes in her life, her favorite classical authors were an enduring source of comfort and strength.

After two months in prison, Elizabeth was taken to a house in Woodstock, to be kept under strict house arrest. Riding under guard through miles of English countryside, she was greeted by crowds with cheers and homemade cakes. Loved by the common people but seen as a criminal by her jealous half sister, Elizabeth's spirit remained unbroken. One day, she took her diamond ring and wrote on a window: "Much suspected by me. Nothing proved can be, Quod Elizabeth, prisoner." Surrounded by her sister's spies, she continued her studies, the long hours of enforced detachment strengthening her courage and determination.

In November 1558, her sister died. Suddenly, Elizabeth was queen of England. Embracing her vocation of destiny, she announced, "The burden that is fallen upon me maketh me amazed; and yet, considering I am God's creature, ordained to obey His appointment, I will thereto yield, desiring from the bottom of my heart that I may have assistance of His grace to be the minister of His heavenly will in this office now committed to me."

Elizabeth reigned for forty-five years over a Renaissance of exploration in learning, poetry, and dramatic art, a golden age of discovery known today as Elizabethan. Transcending narrow stereotypes, she became a great leader, practicing complex political strategies, answering ambassadors in French, Italian, Spanish, or Latin, the language of international diplomacy. She maintained her perspective by taking time to read and reflect, brightening her court with pageantry, music, and Shakespeare's plays. During the attack of the Spanish Armada in 1588, she rode her white horse among the English troops at Tilbury, inspiring them with her energy and eloquence. Flamboyant, strong-willed, charismatic, and much beloved, Elizabeth combined her gifts with the wisdom of detachment, living her vocation with the courage to be herself.[4]

Detachment and Courage Today

Although few of us have lives as dramatic as Queen Elizabeth's, following your calling always means living courageously, seeing beyond convention to acknowledge your gifts, affirm your uniqueness, and become who you are meant to be. Research has shown that people with *resilience*—the ability to overcome challenges and achieve excellence—have developed powerful inner lives.[5]

A period of enforced detachment concentrates your attention like the sun through a magnifying glass. Imprisoned in the Tower of London, Elizabeth was left alone to ponder the purpose of her life, transformed from an intelligent princess into a wise and virtuous queen. Throughout history, people have grown, through crisis, to embrace the deepest values of their hearts. Imprisoned for his faith in the 1660s, John Bunyan wrote his classic, *Pilgrim's Progress*.

In our own time, Nelson Mandela emerged from twenty-seven years in prison with a new vision of hope for South Africa.

Any major change in life can bring you new perspective—from a job layoff, a move, the end of a relationship, to a voluntary departure from everyday routine. Detachment always involves a journey from the world you know to a world of renewal, echoing the rites of passage—separation, initiation, and integration—described by anthropologist Arnold Van Gennep and the "hero's journey" studied by Joseph Campbell.[6] The wisdom of detachment enables you to see more clearly, act more authentically, and become more creatively, courageously yourself.

Personal Exercise: Take Time for Detachment

You can gain greater detachment by taking time away from your regular routine. Some ways to do this are to:

- **Take a Sabbatical or Retreat.** Universities and many progressive companies provide sabbaticals for their employees. If you don't have this option, arrange to spend a few vacation days in a quiet natural setting. Make a retreat with a church group or, if you prefer unstructured time, ask a retreat house for an "individually-directed retreat"—booking a quiet room for contemplation and meals in a garden or wood-side setting. SpiritSite.com provides an online directory of American retreat centers at http://www.spiritsite.com/centers/ and in Europe, many Catholic churches provide information about local retreat centers.
- **Find Yourself a Sanctuary.** Do you have a sanctuary, a refuge for peace and renewal? Like Renaissance poets Andrew Marvell and John Milton, many people today find sanctuary in their gardens. Others seek serenity in a quiet chapel or park. Some people set aside a place in their homes for meditation and reflection. Find a sanctuary for yourself and visit it regularly.
- **Take a Weekly Sabbath.** Give yourself a Sabbath—a day or part of a day—each week for rest, reflection, and renewal. Traditionally, the Sabbath was a day set aside for prayer and

renewal—from sundown Friday to sundown Saturday for Jews and Sundays for most Christians. Observing the Sabbath was an integral part of life in the Renaissance. For your personal Renaissance, set aside your own Sabbath, taking time each week to detach from routine, to relax and reflect.

• •

Dan, a dynamic entrepreneur in California's Silicon Valley, has a secret source of creativity: one afternoon a week of contemplative time. On Thursday afternoons, he goes off by himself, away from work and household responsibilities. Traveling light, with no baggage from work, only his Renaissance Notebook, he heads out to detach and decompress. Sometimes he goes to a favorite coffee shop, watching the world go by while reflecting on his life. Sometimes he takes a hike in a nearby nature preserve. Sometimes he walks by the bay, watching the shifting patterns of water, seabirds, sunlight and shadow. The time he invests in contemplative afternoons brings tremendous dividends: a larger perspective on life, new ideas, and creative solutions to current problems. At the end of the day, Dan goes home relaxed, returning to work the next day graced with the wisdom of detachment.

Identify Distractions

At first, people in my workshops cannot imagine taking such a Sabbath. Their schedules are too crammed with commitments, distractions that fill up their lives, taking them away from their core selves (CS). Do any of these distractions sound familiar?

Too much to do
Continual interruptions
A cluttered household
Other people's demands
Constant pressure, rushing, hurrying
Electronic interruptions: phones, e-mail

The Internet
Compulsive shopping
Television
A chronic complainer in your life
Mindless socializing
Gossip
Something else?

For now, just write your personal distractions in your Renaissance Notebook. You'll learn how to deal with them at the end of this chapter.

❧ *Personal Exercise: Take a Breather*

You can begin detaching from stress by taking a breather—literally. The next time you feel stressed out, take ten minutes to:

- Sit still, close your eyes, and feel your body relax as you take in a slow, deep breath and let it out.
- Breathe in peace and breathe out tension.
- Concentrate on your breathing, slowly breathing in, then breathing out anything you need to release.
- Relax, breathe in and out the thoughts that come to you, or simply concentrate on your breath.
- After about ten minutes, take a final slow, deep breath, release it, and open your eyes, returning to your activities relaxed and renewed.

Transcending Consumerism

Are you a shopaholic? Do you often find yourself buying something when you feel restless? A major distraction for many of us is consumerism. Materialistic values make us look outside ourselves to find ourselves, rather than inward. Even in the Renaissance, poet Thomas Traherne realized the perils of materialism. He described his blissful enjoyment of nature as a child before "the customs and manners of men" taught him to value money and possessions. He felt poor, miserable, and isolated until he learned once more to enjoy life's simple pleasures. Traherne became a minister, teaching others to avoid false values that he said "put grubs and worms in men's heads that are enemies to all pure and true apprehensions, and eat out all their happiness." Living simply, he spent his days writing, preaching, and contemplating nature, leaving a collection of poems and meditations that celebrate the radiant beauty of the natural world.

Today's culture takes materialism to a level Traherne never imagined—deluging us with mass-media advertising designed to reduce us from citizens to consumers, a market to be manipulated for profit.[7] According to psychologist Tim Kasser, advertising controls us by appealing to our four basic needs: safety, capability, relationship, and individuality. Reacting to advertising, many people buy SUVs to feel safe. They buy the newest computers and hand-held devices to feel more capable. Families buy cell phones, hoping to strengthen their relationships, and for decades teens have worn the latest trendy clothing to assert their individuality.

Preying upon our insecurities in a busy, impersonal culture, corporate brands offer seductive illusions of warmth, love, and acceptance, appealing to the needs of a time-starved, stressed-out population. Young people are especially vulnerable to corporate branding. Developmental psychologist Erik Erikson found that around age six, each of us begins learning the skills and values of our culture. Whether this means going to school, learning a trade, or working on the farm, we develop what he called "a sense of industry," the ability to use our culture's tools to make our own contribution to the world.

But if we are socialized as consumers, taught to acquire products instead of learning these vital skills, we cannot develop this sense of industry. Teenagers driven by consumer values are more prone to anxiety disorders, conduct disorders, attention deficit disorder, alcohol and drug abuse, and depression. Studies have also found that adults with consumer values have lower life satisfaction, both in America and internationally.[8] To build a better future for ourselves and our world, we must find healthier ways to meet our needs than just taking trips to the mall.

🌿 Personal Exercise: Review Your Exploration List

You can begin identifying your own unmet needs by examining your Exploration List, becoming better friends with your core self (CS). This list is a vital tool for understanding yourself. Like any tool, the more you use it, the better it serves you. As you review your list:

- Ask yourself, "What do I want to explore?"
- If you've done something on your list, ask, "How did that make me feel? What did I learn about myself?"
- Ask yourself, "What unmet needs do these explorations represent: Security? Capability? Relationship? Freedom? Beauty? Self expression? Something else?"
- Then ask, "What are some healthy ways I can meet these needs?"
- If you've been trying to meet your needs with an addiction, you'll need help to break this pattern. Meet with a therapist or counselor you trust; call your local priest, rabbi, or other religious leader; or attend a 12-step program (such as Alcoholics Anonymous, Codependents Anonymous, Narcotics Anonymous, Overeaters Anonymous). You can find them listed in your phone book or get referrals from a local church. Detaching from the shadow of addiction will bring greater light to your personal Renaissance.

Record your insights and actions in your Renaissance Notebook.

The Hidden Cost of Technology

Less is more. A hectic life drains you by pulling you in too many directions at once. Rushing around; multitasking; multiple demands; noise pollution from cars, radios, televisions, and stereos; advertisements; interruptions—all of this exhausts us by splitting our concentration. Doesn't it make you feel tired just reading about it?

Our technology has given us powerful new tools—but at a cost. Recently, the U.S. government began offering BlackBerries to employees at the National Institutes of Health, giving them instant Internet, e-mail, and phone access wherever they are. At first this seemed like another government extravagance, but it was a clever investment. For the cost of the device and wireless access, the agency is getting access to employees on nights and weekends, expanding their work days to 24/7.

Many families purchase cell phones for their children and a "family plan" to stay in touch. Again, this seems like a useful tool. But a recent study of over 1,300 adults in upstate New York found that regular cell phone use increased stress and lowered family satisfaction. Substituting phone calls for personal contact and blurring the boundaries between home and work ends up stressing people and undermining relationships.[9]

Personal Exercise: 7 Ways to Simplify Your Life

You can simplify your life and gain time for what you value by taking out your Renaissance Notebook and reviewing the list of distractions you made earlier. Then choose *one* of the seven exercises below to begin eliminating what drains you. (Don't try to do all seven at once—that would only drain your energy.) By making subtle but powerful changes, you will become progressively less hassled, more serene.

1. Avoid Temptation.

In the Renaissance, Magdalen Herbert used to say that "as our bodies take in nourishment" from the food we eat, so our souls are nourished by our daily activities.[10] Nurture your inner life by limiting exposure to consumerism:

- Cut down on aimless shopping. Don't wander through shopping malls for recreation.
- Make a list of what you need. Group errands together to spend less time shopping.
- Stop watching commercials.
- Stop reading mail-order catalogs.
- Stay off Internet shopping sites.

2. Stop Measuring Yourself by Others' Standards.

Honor your own needs and values. Don't let people's demands control you. Letting others tell you who you "should" be traps you in endless rounds of draining behavior. Take a cue from William Shakespeare. Enjoy your friends' company but don't waste time in mindless socializing. Living excessively, many Renaissance dramatists never reached their prime, dying in their late twenties or early thirties. Christopher Marlowe was reportedly killed in a tavern brawl and Robert Greene died from gluttony and alcoholism, while Shakespeare enjoyed his friends but also honored his gifts, balancing his life with time to write.[11] Like Shakespeare, you are a creative original with your own unique gifts, here to share your life with others, *not* surrender to them.

3. Don't Keep Doing Something if You've Outgrown It.

Throughout this book, you will read about Renaissance men and women who knew a valuable secret: throughout the changing seasons of our lives, the only way to make room for new growth is to "prune" away activities that no longer serve us.

Has something you once enjoyed become an obligation?

If this activity is only draining time and energy from your life, STOP doing it. Free up time for what you really care about.

4. Stop Hurrying.

Rushing is an epidemic in our culture. People dash off to work at "rush hour," react to one deadline and demand after another, and race through their days with what meditation teacher Eknath Easwaran has called the "hurry sickness." Rushing puts our bodies and minds into chronic stress, depleting our energy, undermining our health, and making us less effective. According to research in the *Harvard Business Review,* rushing undermines your creativity.[12]

As you release unnecessary activities, you will have less reason to rush from one thing to the next. But because your body has become accustomed to running in high gear, downshifting takes conscious effort. Whenever you catch yourself hurrying, tell yourself to SLOW DOWN. Take a deep breath, release it, and look around. Take another deep breath, release it, and return to your activities at a more natural pace.

5. Go On a Media Diet.

The average American watches at least four hours of television a day, nearly thirty hours a week. We turn on car radios or stereos automatically, and many people walk around "plugged in" to cell phones and iPods. When do we listen to our own thoughts?

Studies have shown that the more TV we watch, the lower our morale and self-worth, and that excessive use of screen technologies—TV, videos, and the Internet—can damage children's developing brains. Parent Coaching Institute founder and CEO Gloria DeGaetano advises parents to limit children's screen time and encourage more reading, play, exercise, and exploration.

Cutting down on distractions means exercising control over your environment, choosing whether to turn on your radio, TV, stereo, and other media or enjoy silence and communion with your own thoughts. Each household needs to set its own limits. Some of my friends have raised their children with no TV in the house. Others set limits on TV time and spend one night a week doing something together as a family. My husband and I keep our small TV in the closet and take it out only when we want to watch something.[13]

6. Deal with Unfinished Business.

Unfinished business (UB) nags at you, prevents clarity, blocks your creativity, and fills your mind with clutter that churns around incessantly. Getting UB down on paper will get it out of your mind while helping you take positive action.

- Make a UB list. List each item of UB and one action you can take to address it. For example:
  - ~Repair the garden gate: get parts at the hardware store.
  - ~Sign up for Pilates class: call the community center.
  - ~Get a birthday gift for a friend: visit an art supply store.
- Check your list daily, updating it by reviewing what needs to be done, recording actions and completions.
- Mark off each completed action with a check mark and date of completion.
- Recognize that you don't have to do everything. Cancel some UB you decide not to pursue with an X and your decision date.

This list will help clear your mind while keeping track of what needs to be done. It also creates forward momentum. I often find myself spontaneously taking action to complete a UB, then checking it off the next time I look at my list.

7. Eliminate Energy Drains, people or situations that exhaust you and pull you away from what you really care about.

- Draining Relationships. When you're around energy drains, you feel exhausted by their crises, chaos, and demands. These people invade your boundaries and lay their urgent problems at your feet, dragging you away from your own chosen path.
- Draining Activities. Energy-draining activities such as envy, excessive interest in other people's business, and gossip can be harmful to others while wasting your time, draining your energy, and blocking your creative growth. This week, begin noticing what drains your energy and take action.
- Set healthy boundaries. You are here to fulfill your destiny, not become a receptacle for chronic complaints. When someone launches into a litany of complaints, ask, "What are you going to do about it?" change the subject, or curtail the conversation.

- Don't get caught up in envy. It can poison your mind. If you find yourself envying someone else's accomplishments, tell yourself, "That's great that ____ did that. I can fulfill my dreams, too."
- Don't gossip. It's amazing how much time we spend talking about others, usually unfavorably. Make it a point *not* to talk about other people's business. When someone tries to engage you in gossip, change the subject; ask how that person is doing instead.

• •

Do you have an energy drain in your life? Perhaps this story sounds familiar.

After another long lunch with her friend, Nicole was exhausted. As usual, Lauren had talked nonstop, gossiping about people at work and complaining about her job, her health, her husband, her finances, and her difficult neighbors. Lauren was always in crisis. When they'd had adjacent cubicles at work, Lauren had struck Nicole as a talented designer, filled with energy but high on drama. Even after Lauren was transferred, they kept meeting for lunch. Nicole listened and tried to help, but Lauren didn't take her advice. She just continued to vent, and there was always something more.

Nicole went back to work with another headache, too worn out to deal with her latest design project, too exhausted for her evening workout with Dave. She'd have to call and cancel again. *But at least that lunch is over,* she thought, *and I won't be seeing Lauren for a while.* Then she saw the red light flashing on her phone. It was a voice mail from Lauren saying "I always feel better after talking to you. Let's have lunch again soon."

Nicole moaned. Tired of being Lauren's therapist, coach, and trash can for all of her complaints, she realized that her own life was out of balance. To reclaim some time for herself, she took one small detachment step: bringing a sandwich and taking walks at noon to decompress. When Lauren wanted to schedule another lunch, she told her, "I've decided to stop taking long lunches."

One small change can make a difference. Nicole's midday walks have relieved her stress, renewed her energy, and brought new perspective to her life and work. Without a constant energy drain, Nicole's headaches are gone, her work has improved, and she is enjoying a more balanced life.

To bring greater balance to your life, choose one of the previous detachment exercises. Take the first step and watch what happens. Remember the Renaissance principle: *Small actions over time produce monumental results*. You'll see.

Shadows on the Path: Dealing with Adrenaline Withdrawal

As you eliminate draining activities, you may begin feeling at loose ends. The incessant activity and noise in your life may not have fulfilled you, but it did fill you full—of adrenaline, excitement, and commotion. Simplifying can be unsettling until you adapt to your own natural rhythms. If you feel restless, pause and ask yourself, "What do I really *want* to do?"

Listen to your body. You might just want to relax.

You may find yourself with time on your hands—just by cutting down on TV or Internet, you could have up to thirty additional hours a week. Don't fall back into old patterns. Rest. Take care of yourself. Use this time creatively.

RENAISSANCE QUESTION

Use your newfound time to look around and explore new options. Have fun. Try some activities on your Exploration List. Ask yourself:

"How can I use my gifts today?"

And, most importantly, follow your heart.

Celebrate Creative Victories

As you move forward in your personal Renaissance, you will make many breakthroughs. With some you will see immediate results, but many breakthroughs are more subtle. These are the *creative victories,* important steps toward living more creatively that only you can know. A creative victory might mean beginning to detach from a major distraction, signing up for a new class to develop your skills, making an important phone call, completing a difficult task, submitting a grant proposal or article for publication. The results aren't clear yet, but you've done your part—made that call, written that article or proposal. Now it's up to the universe to do the rest.

With each creative victory, don't wait for external recognition. Your new Renaissance begins *not* at the end of the process, when you've finished a project or won some award, but at the magical beginning, when you reach out courageously to follow your heart. A powerful secret in pursuing your personal Renaissance is consciously celebrating these victories to mark your progress and build your positive momentum.

How will you celebrate? That's up to you. What do *you* consider a celebration? Take your CS out for tea or dinner with a friend. Or buy yourself a small gift, a colorful pen or pencil, a new CD, or a book you've wanted to read. Or treat yourself to a picnic, a walk in the woods, a movie you've wanted to see. Choose something that *you* enjoy.

When you're facing a long, difficult task, break it into manageable stages and plan a celebration after each stage. When I was writing my doctoral dissertation, I divided it into chapters, giving myself deadlines and planning celebrations. At the end of each chapter, I'd invite a friend to join me at a Chinese restaurant for dinner, my favorite treat at the time. These celebrations gave me energy, marked my progress, and strengthened my motivation, until, one celebration at a time, I finished my dissertation and received my degree.

Reclaiming Your Renaissance Spirit

In 1979, workers began removing the centuries of candle soot, dust, and grime from the paintings in the Sistine Chapel. In 1999, when the massive restoration was complete, the results were stunning. No longer hidden beneath the grimy surface, the bright blues, reds, oranges, and yellows shone forth with a brilliance art historians had never imagined. But some critics had become so accustomed to the sepia tones from the grimy surface that they found the original Renaissance colors shocking, complaining that the paintings were ruined.

We can become so accustomed to living inauthentically that at first our own originality stuns us—and the people around us. Some are bound to complain, "You've changed," and urge you to go back to the way you used to be. Yet, as you move forward on the path, you will delight in your own true colors, shining forth as the creative original you are.

Moving Forward

Now, let's review your progress in this chapter. Write your answers and today's date in your Renaissance Notebook.

1. How have you used your gifts lately? What brought you the most CS joy?
2. What have you learned from your Exploration List?
3. What detachment exercise have you been doing? How do you feel now?
4. What was your creative victory in this chapter? How are you celebrating it?

RENAISSANCE REMINDERS

Detach from the noisy world around you to follow the deepest values of your heart.

- ~ Remember to create positive momentum by doing what you love.
- ~ Take time for yourself. Honor your needs and your own creative growth.
- ~ Less is more. Detachment brings inner harmony. Don't confuse being filled full with being fulfilled.

CHAPTER 3

Discernment

Embracing Your Values, Living with Heart

Character is destiny.
—Heraclitus, *On the Universe*[1]

Our values develop our character and our character creates our destiny. When we're out of touch with our values, we are blown about like autumn leaves, caught up in mindless routines and subject to external events, impulse, and appetite. But when we affirm our guiding values, our lives are inspired by our deepest beliefs. Queen Elizabeth I's values helped her become a great leader, developing a calling uniquely her own. Like Elizabeth, you, too, have guiding values to inspire your life with meaning.[2]

Our Need for Meaning

We need meaning to give form and purpose to our lives.[3] History tells us that throughout world cultures, a breakdown in fundamental values leads to the breakdown of civilizations. What is true for nations is true for individuals. Clinical studies have shown that we cannot endure a life without meaning.[4]

Without meaning, we give up, failing in school, jobs, and relationships. As psychiatrist Viktor Frankl realized, without meaning, people die. They lose the will to live, their immune systems break down, they become depressed and physically deteriorate. Imprisoned in a Nazi concentration camp during World War II, Frankl saw some people's sense of purpose give them strength to endure, while others lost hope and died. He found his own purpose completing his book, *The Doctor and the Soul*. Although his manuscript was confiscated when he entered Auschwitz, reconstructing it on scraps of paper sustained him through years of hardship. Like Renaissance philosophers, Frankl believed in free will and personal responsibility, even in the direst of circumstances. Living with dignity, he believed, meant responding to challenge with a sense of purpose.

Confirming Frankl's observations, a recent UCLA study has shown that reflecting on your values can strengthen your health as well as your motivation. Study participants who discussed their personal values before undergoing a stress test had stronger immune systems—lower cortisol levels and healthier reactions to stress—than those who did not.[5]

To meet today's challenges with courage and resourcefulness, we must believe that what we do matters, that our actions are part of a larger pattern of meaning.

Shifting to Intrinsic Motivation

Following your values gives you the joy and wisdom of intrinsic motivation, while basing your self-worth on externals—results, rewards, and others' approval—produces chronic stress, anxiety, and compulsive behavior. When compulsive workaholics achieve their goals, they are temporarily relieved. But if they don't measure up—fail to get that promotion or get a B grade instead of an A—they collapse in inadequacy and depression. People often confuse workaholism with devotion to a calling. Yet these two are worlds apart, as distant as love and fear. While our callings inspire and energize us, workaholism drives and diminishes us. Workaholics are pushed by the compulsive need to prove themselves, afraid they are "not good enough," won't "have enough," dreading failure if they relax the hectic pace of their existence. In a culture that prizes external accomplishment and consumption, workaholism has become a widespread addiction, while living your calling requires the courage to do what you love, overcome external pressures, and follow your own guiding values.[6]

RENAISSANCE QUESTION

If you've been caught up in workaholism, you can break this destructive habit by shifting your focus. The next time you start judging yourself by external results, STOP. Instead, ask yourself:

"Why am I doing this?"

Instead of obsessing about outcomes, focus on your values, look for the wisdom each day brings. Be kind to yourself. Reassure your child self (CS). Trust the process. You are becoming a new Renaissance person, renewing your life one powerful step at a time.

Discerning between Love and Duty

Sometimes a sense of duty makes us ignore our values. Like Ben, we can wander off the path, following someone else's "shoulds." Grabbing a cup of coffee as he rushed out to the car, Ben drove off to another day of work at the superior court, where he witnessed an endless parade of troubled lives. Yesterday it was a felony assault case, today a juvenile drug offense. He gazed up at the green hills in the distance. He'd majored in forestry in college, dreamed of becoming a park ranger, but when he married Marlene, she'd urged him to get "a respectable job." For five years now he'd worked as a court reporter, recording all the courtroom dramas, mechanically going through the motions while feeling numb inside. He looked forward to Saturdays, when he could take an early morning hike in the hills before returning to a long list of chores.

Ben put on his favorite CD and zoned out. The light turned green as he approached the intersection, and he barely noticed the red blur on the right, a truck speeding wildly down the road. He felt a loud jolt, then his car spun wildly, crashing down on its side. Suddenly, everything was still except for the CD, stuck on the same few notes. He turned the key to shut the thing off, then slowly stood up, brushed off the shattered glass, and climbed out through the broken side door window.

The car was totaled and the truck nowhere in sight. "Felony hit and run," he muttered to himself. He heard the siren from an approaching ambulance. The medics insisted on putting him on a stretcher, taking him to the hospital to be examined. "You're lucky to be alive," they told him when they saw his car, adding that if he hadn't turned off the ignition, the car might have burst into flames.

Ben was treated for a few cuts and bruises and called Marlene, who took him home from the hospital. In the days after the accident, he realized that life had given him a second chance. He didn't know what he would do yet, but he *did* know that he and Marlene needed to talk, and that he was going to start living by his own values.

🌿 *Personal Exercise: Love or Duty?*

You don't need a major wake-up call like Ben's to find out if you're acting from love or duty. You can reflect on your daily routine and ask yourself:

- Why am I doing this? Because I want to? Because it *means* something to me—or because I should? Have to? Would feel guilty if I didn't?
- When I finish this task, how do I feel? Happy? Energetic? A sense of accomplishment? Or exhausted? Relieved? Glad it's over?[7]

Clearly, if you feel energized and value what you're doing, you are motivated by love. But if you're doing something out of obligation, feeling emotionally numb when you do it or drained when you finish, what is this telling you?

In this busy world of ours, many voices call to you from the outside—family, friends, employers, coworkers, and mass media advertising. But living your calling means turning within to listen to your heart, to follow your guiding values. This is the practice of discernment.

Looking Back

Discernment, from the Renaissance to today, involves a journey from *what is* to *what we are called to be*. In March 1522, a young man set out alone from his home in northern Spain. The decision was not easy. His own desire for glory, noble heritage, and family all argued against it. But he strapped on his armor and packed his mule for the 300-mile journey to the monastery of Montserrat that would change his life forever.

Iñigo Lopez was a young nobleman. He had lived in the courts of princes, cutting a dashing figure with his flashing smile, golden hair, and athletic grace. Known for his charm and courtly manners, he had read the books of chivalry and followed their example. He was enamored with beautiful women and was ambitious, charismatic, a natural leader. Yet in a dramatic departure from all he had been, he became what psychologist William James called "twice born," beginning a new life that would transform him into St. Ignatius Loyola.

Iñigo's discernment journey had begun the year before, when he was wounded defending the fortress of Pamplona from a French invasion. Struck in the leg by a cannonball, he was taken home to recover at the family castle of Loyola, where he suffered repeated settings of his shattered leg.

As he lay in bed for the long, painful months of recovery (a period of enforced detachment), he asked for books of chivalry, but there were none in the house, only a life of Christ and a book of saints' lives. So he read them, then drifted off in his imagination. He recalled his life at court—the duels, adventures, and deeds to impress the fair ladies. But these thoughts brought him only temporary pleasure, leaving him restless and discontent. When he imagined himself following the example of St. Francis or St. Dominic, he felt an enduring joy and peace. Discernment, he realized, meant stopping to examine his desires, asking which ones offered only fleeting pleasures, which a deeper and enduring joy.

And so, in his late twenties, he decided to leave behind all the pride and machismo of his former life. Arriving at Montserrat, Iñigo made his confession, gave his knights clothing to a poor vagrant, put on sandals and a sackcloth tunic. After a night's vigil in the chapel, he departed at dawn. Leaving his sword and armor at the altar of the Virgin Mary, he made his way to the town of Manresa, where he reflected on his life in meditations. This process of self-examination became the Ignatian Spiritual Exercises, still used by people today to discover their callings.

By practicing discernment, Iñigo discovered his calling one step at a time, making a pilgrimage to Jerusalem, then studying in Paris, where he took the name of Ignatius. He made friends with other devout young men, sharing his Spiritual Exercises, and together they entered the priesthood in 1534. They traveled to Rome, teaching and ministering to the poor until 1540, when the Pope confirmed them as the Society of Jesus. Ignatius opened a few schools to educate young Jesuits. Soon his schools were educating future leaders, the sons of princes and magistrates. Within ten years the Jesuits had discovered their mission of education, transforming higher education in Europe by establishing more than thirty colleges and founding high schools throughout Europe, Asia, and the New World.[8]

Ignatius's discernment journey was repeated on many levels throughout the Renaissance. Not only saints, but young men and women from all classes and occupations discovered their gifts and connected them with their guiding values, finding their callings by practicing discernment, one powerful step at a time.

Listening to Your Heart

Years ago, my friend Michelle Chappel was a psychology professor at Santa Clara University. With a PhD from Princeton, outstanding teaching evaluations, and an impressive research agenda, she was on her way to a successful academic career. Students would come to her office to ask what they should do with their lives. Should they go to graduate school? Get a job? Join the Peace Corps? Michelle would ask them what they really *wanted* to do, then tell them to follow their hearts, and they left her office with a new sense of purpose.

Then one day, Michelle realized she wasn't following *her* heart. Deep down inside, what she really wanted to do was make music. At first this seemed irrational, illogical, and risky. But a few months later, she took a leap of faith and resigned from the university to begin her new career writing songs, singing, and playing her guitar. Her first CD made the charts in South Africa, and she has continued to perform, record, and work as an international creativity consultant. Her workshops on creativity and discernment have helped thousands of people live their dreams.[9]

As St. Ignatius and philosophers of his time realized, our lives are motivated by desires. Some desires sustain us; others move us beyond ourselves. Our self-sustaining desires are to *consume*—food, water, material goods. Psychologist Abraham Maslow called these "deficiency needs." Our higher desires, or guiding values, are to *create*—to use our gifts to contribute to the world. We need the first desires in order to survive, the second in order to thrive, or as Maslow said, to "self-actualize." Over four hundred years ago, Shakespeare, too, realized this, writing:

> *. . . What is a man*
> *If his chief good and market of his time*
> *Be but to sleep and feed?—a beast, no more.*[10]

As physical beings, we have appetites, but if we only "sleep and feed," our souls are starved for meaning. We find meaning by practicing discernment.

Beneath all your cultural conditioning and external demands, you have a powerful source of inner guidance. As St. Ignatius realized, your feelings are your inner compass, for he found his calling by listening to his heart.[11]

The key to discernment is reflecting on your feelings, your energies, your responses to experience. You can do this by meditating, keeping a journal, talking with a spiritual director, counselor, or trusted friend, and by doing the personal exercises in this chapter.

You can begin practicing discernment right now by slowing down, taking a deep breath, and asking yourself: "What am I feeling now?"

Your inner world is like a deep mountain lake where winds and currents stir the surface. But deep beneath the shifting currents of popular culture, peer pressure, and external demands, are quiet depths of wisdom. As you dive beneath life's busy surface, the first feelings you may find are a tangled barrier of fears: fear of risk, fear of inadequacy, fear of rejection, fear of failure, fear of loss, fear of not meeting other people's expectations. These and other chronic fears can lock people into the rigid behavior pattern psychologist D. W. Winnicott has called the "false self" system, the ego defenses that block our core self (CS) and keep us trapped on the surface of life.

Personal Exercise: Face Your Fears

If you've come up against a barrier of fears, you can gain greater discernment by asking:

- "What am I *really* afraid of?"

- "What's the worst thing that can happen?"
- "Is this realistic?" and if so,
- "Can I deal with it?"

Legitimate fears are useful warning signals, helping you avoid danger. But many chronic fears are illusions, a mass of anxieties that blocks your personal growth. In the still, silent depths beneath these fears lie your deepest desires, your guiding values that connect with your calling at a point where love transcends fear. Recognizing these values will bring you deep feelings of peace and consolation, the transforming power of love. With consolation comes liberation, for the greatest obstacle between you and your calling, the greatest enemy of hope, is fear.[12]

. . . .

Setting Your Compass

Learning to recognize your inner polarities of love and fear, sunlight and shadow is the next step in discernment. These are the two settings on your inner compass that St. Ignatius called "consolation" and "desolation."

Consolation is a radiant communion that moves you beyond yourself into greater unity with life. It brings deep feelings of love, joy, insight, understanding, inspiration, clarity, altruism, authenticity, gratitude, oneness with others, peace, trust, appreciation, grace, generosity, openness, energy, growth, creativity, spirituality, and expansiveness.

Desolation cuts you off from others, closing you in on yourself. It brings dark feelings of fear, threat, misery, isolation, egocentrism, diminishment, frustration, confusion, anxiety, despair, hurt, hopelessness, defensiveness, hate, hostility, helplessness, self-pity, restlessness, turmoil, failure, guilt, self-hate, selfishness, animosity, agitation, compulsiveness, brooding, depression, and lack of meaning.[13]

Discernment means looking not only at your deeper feelings but also at the direction in which they lead. As St. Ignatius would say, "Do your feelings lead you toward or away from God," from grace, from fulfillment in life? Pleasant feelings can be shallow and fleeting, like the nostalgia Ignatius felt recalling his old life, while feelings of restlessness and emptiness can be important signals, warning you that you're going in the wrong direction. If you don't heed these signals, you may be like Ben, needing a serious wake-up call or the darkness of "hitting bottom" to break away from a dysfunctional job, situation, or relationship to find your true direction.

QUIZ: CONSOLATION OR DESOLATION?

To check your understanding of these concepts, take this short quiz, choosing "consolation" or "desolation" for each statement:

1. While walking along the creek trail, I was deeply moved by the beauty of nature.
   Consolation   Desolation

2. Yesterday I sprained my wrist and spent the rest of the day worrying about my health.
   Consolation   Desolation

3. Last week, a colleague at work criticized me. Today I was happy when I saw the same colleague make a stupid mistake.
   Consolation   Desolation

4. When we gathered at our professor's memorial service, my friends and I mourned his passing, but felt a deep appreciation for all he meant to us.
   Consolation   Desolation

5. I spent Saturday afternoon doing yard work.
   Consolation   Desolation

6. I spent last weekend visiting my relatives.
   Consolation   Desolation

Key (some of these are obvious):

1. consolation (appreciation of nature)
2. desolation (isolation, worry)

Others depend not just on the initial feelings but the *direction* in which they lead.

3. desolation (isolation—gloating at another's expense)
4. consolation (feelings of deep appreciation in the midst of loss)

5 and 6. The final two depend on your feelings about your yard (do you love gardening or consider it a chore?) and your family (loving or dysfunctional?).

Discernment Helps You Make Choices

In the Renaissance, discernment helped people make important choices. In 1643, George Fox realized that "there were two thirsts in me," one for material success, the other for a more spiritual life. He realized that "if I had a king's diet, palace, and attendance, all would have been as nothing," whereas his thoughts of the spiritual life brought him feelings of love and "admiration at the infiniteness of it." Following these feelings of consolation, Fox founded the Society of Friends, or Quakers, and traveled throughout England, Holland, the West Indies, and Colonial America to spread his message of peace and social justice.

When John Locke earned his master's degree at Oxford in 1658, he could have remained there as a tutor or listened to his friends who urged him to become a minister. He studied medicine and even tried diplomacy, going on a political mission to France in 1665. But these choices left him restless and dissatisfied. He finally returned to Oxford, convinced that his calling was to help people gain greater understanding. Finding consolation in philosophy, Locke became a great leader of the Enlightenment, and his political vision became the cornerstone of a new American democracy.[14]

In a recent study of discernment, psychologist Martin Seligman asked his students at the University of Pennsylvania to participate in one pleasurable activity (watching a movie or eating a favorite dessert) and one altruistic activity (doing volunteer work or helping someone), then write about how they felt. The students discovered that the pleasant activities gave them only fleeting pleasures, while their altruistic actions brought them greater joy and fulfillment. From the Renaissance through today, living our deepest values brings us powerful feelings of joy and vitality, making us happier, more energetic, more authentically ourselves.[15]

Discerning Your Life Direction

Years ago, when she lived in North Carolina, Julie would tell her friends about her dream of owning a bed and breakfast, welcoming guests with Southern cooking and hospitality. But her days were spent in scientific research. With a PhD in pharmacology, she worked as a toxicologist for a major tobacco company. Her job was to find evidence that their product was "perfectly safe" so they could present their findings to the courts.

Julie ran the experiments, examined the data, then ran the experiments again. The results were undeniable: the product contained potentially dangerous substances. When she presented her evidence to her supervisors, they said her findings were unacceptable and told her to "reframe" the data. In essence they wanted her to lie. None of her scientific training had prepared her for this. She couldn't lie, and so she quit.

Following her values brought major changes and led to a new Renaissance in Julie's life. She took a job with a feed supply company in Minnesota, where she ran tests on a variety of products. The Minnesota winters were a shock, but she found the research atmosphere congenial and began making new friends. One of her colleagues, Don, took her hiking and canoeing in the Minnesota lake country. They realized they were kindred spirits, sharing a love of the outdoors, drama, and music, enjoying symphony concerts and plays at the Guthrie Theater. The next summer they were married at Don's lakeside home. Don supported Julie when she changed careers and began studying at the local culinary academy, becoming a chef at a downtown restaurant. He's planning to take early retirement so they can realize another dream, opening a bed and breakfast where they can welcome guests with Julie's cooking and Southern hospitality.

As Julie's story shows, when you have the courage to live your values, you invite a new beginning into your life. Perhaps your choices are not as dramatic as being asked to lie, but discernment can also help with more subtle choices. On the surface, two professions, two jobs, two directions in life may appear equally desirable. You could decide by calculating the assets and liabilities on a balance sheet. But reason alone overlooks the wisdom of the heart.

I've had a job that paid well and had many advantages but the office politics conflicted with my values, leaving me feeling drained and diminished. Discernment, for me, meant listening to my heart and leaving that job.

Reflecting on your feelings can help you turn from superficial advantages, a false sense of obligation, or outright desolation to discover your true direction in life.

🌿 *Personal Exercise: Discernment Questions*

Where could you benefit from greater discernment in your life? Are you at a point of choice in a job, career, or relationship? Looking for a new direction in life?

Think of one area in your life where you could benefit from greater discernment. Then begin noting your feelings of consolation and desolation.

- Where do you find consolation?
- Where do you find desolation?
- What are your feelings telling you?
- What directions do they point to?

Record your answers in your Renaissance Notebook.

🌿 *Personal Exercise: Discern Your Values*

Knowing your guiding values will help you find greater meaning in life. These values may be *altruism, beauty, compassion, cooperation, courage, creativity, empathy, fairness, family, fortitude, freedom, friendship, honesty, independence, ingenuity, integrity, justice, kindness, love, loyalty, nature, patriotism, peace, perseverance, religion, resourcefulness, service, spirituality, vision,* or something else. To discern your own guiding values, read through the following exercises, choose one, and set aside time to complete it.

1. Think of Three People You Admire (from history or people you know). Write each person's name in your Renaissance Notebook. Beneath each name list the qualities you most admire. When you've finished, put your writing away. On another day, read over your lists, circling three or more values you most admire. These are your guiding values.
2. Reflect on What Brings You Consolation. Go off by yourself with your Renaissance Notebook and a pen or pencil. Think of a time when you were doing something that brought you consolation, inspired you with joy and purpose, connected you to the deeper meaning of life. What were you doing? Write down as many details as you can. Then put your writing away. On another day, read what you've written, looking for three or more values that stand out. These are your guiding values.
3. Personal Reflection and Inventory. In your Renaissance Notebook, list three accomplishments that you're most proud of. Then ask yourself what values each one represents. Write them down. Then circle the three values that stand out most for you. These are your guiding values.

. . . .

Shadows on the Path: Dealing with Desolation

As you practice discernment, you'll find consolation a joy. But don't disparage desolation. It can be a valuable guide as you navigate through life's challenges and changes. When you experience desolation, remember:

Don't Give in to the Darkness

When you encounter the stormy weather of desolation, acknowledge what you're feeling but don't go off by yourself and brood. As Renaissance scholar Robert Burton advised:

- Tell a trusted friend or counselor how you feel.
- Write in your journal.
- Pray. Meditate. Ask God or your Higher Power for help.
- Take care of yourself. Rest. Get enough sleep. Drink pure water and eat fresh, healthy food in moderation.
- Get moving. Get moderate exercise and fresh air. Take a walk, go for a run, work in your garden.
- Think of what brings you joy. Look for the sunlight beyond the shadows.
- Listen to your favorite music.
- Reach out. Call a friend. Send a card or e-mail. Do someone a favor. Volunteer for a favorite cause.
- Don't rush into major decisions. Desolation can cloud your vision.
- Get back in touch with nature. Breathe in the abundant beauty of life.

Look for the Larger Patterns

Ask yourself where you were headed when you ran into desolation. Were you caught up in surface currents—chasing sensation, ambition, or power and moving away from what you value? Is desolation telling you to look in your heart and choose another direction?[16]

Using both settings on your inner compass will bring greater joy and meaning to your life.

Moving Forward

Now let's review your progress in this chapter. Write your answers and today's date in your Renaissance Notebook.

1. What are your guiding values?
2. In your life now, what brings you the most CS joy and consolation?
3. What brings you desolation? And what are you doing about it?
4. Do you feel called in a new direction? If so, what is it?
5. What was your creative victory in this chapter and how are you celebrating it?

Congratulations! You have now discovered two valuable treasures on your discernment journey: your personal gifts and your guiding values. Research has shown that recognizing these values will bring you greater happiness and fulfillment.[17] In the next chapter you will combine your gifts and values to chart your true direction in life.

RENAISSANCE REMINDERS

Discernment means following what inspires you and releasing what diminishes you.

As you consult the inner compass of your heart:

~ Use consolation to move toward what brings you joy and meaning.

~ Use desolation to move from darkness to greater light.

~ Be kind to yourself as you practice the wisdom of discernment.

CHAPTER 4

Direction

Turning Your Ideals into Action

[I]t is an ever-fixèd mark
That looks on tempests and is never shaken;
It is the star to every wand'ring bark,
Whose worth's unknown although his height be taken.
—WILLIAM SHAKESPEARE, SONNET 116[1]

Now that you've discovered your gifts and values, you're ready to find what Shakespeare called "the star to every wand'ring bark": your own north star to guide you toward your dreams.

For centuries, explorers navigated by the sun and stars. Renaissance mariners had magnetic compasses but still steered their course by the wind, the rising and setting sun, and Polaris, the north star. Setting off to discover new worlds in their small wooden ships, or "barks," they ventured into unknown seas and uncharted territories, marked on maps as *terra incognita*.

You, too, venture into unknown territory when you follow your heart to seek your calling. There is no map because each journey is unique. Yet your path will reveal itself, one step at a time, offering surprises and revelations along the way. Studies have shown that as you keep your eyes on your guiding star, living by your deepest values will transform your life.[2] This chapter will help you discover your star and chart your new direction.

Your Job Is Not Your Calling

We are so far from the Renaissance today that people often think a "vocation" means making a living. During my retreats and workshops, people often say, "I don't have a calling. I'm only a _____" (insert housewife, student, retired person, or working at a job that only pays the bills). I tell them: "Your job is not your calling. You are always more than what you do—what matters most is the *spirit* in which you do it."

Although companies urge employees to identify with their corporate mission, we are much more than what we do for a living. Years ago, I met Mike Narciso, a photographer who knew this lesson well. Living in a hillside cottage with his friendly St. Bernard, Mike took a job in a cannery to pay the bills. But his calling was photography, which he always referred to as "my work." "Never confuse your job with your work," he told me.

Many new Renaissance men and women take a "day job" to pay the bills while pursuing their life's work. For years, Gertrude Welch worked as a secretary at Santa Clara University, but her real calling was working for social justice. Through the years, she has marched with Cesar Chavez, volunteered at migrant camps and homeless shelters, gone on peace delegations to Nicaragua, the Middle East, and the former Soviet Union, met with political leaders and written them countless letters. In the 1980s, she retired from the university to work full time for peace and justice. In 2001 she was proclaimed "Woman of the Year" by the State of California in recognition of her life's work.

During the seventeenth century, there were also people like Mike and Gertrude, who recognized the vital difference between their jobs and their work. One of these was Antony Van Leeuwenhoek, whose life's work continues to revolutionize our world today.

Born to a tradesman's family in the Netherlands in 1632, he was apprenticed at sixteen to a linen draper in Amsterdam, where he grew fascinated with the lenses used to inspect cloth. At twenty-two, he married and opened a draper's shop in Delft, where he sold cloth, needles, and ribbons to support himself and his family. But while he made his living selling cloth, his real passion was science.

He made magnifying glasses and over 247 microscopes, using them to examine his drinking water, rainwater, and water from a nearby lake. Finding strange microorganisms, protozoa and bacteria, he called them little "animalcules." Studying his saliva, his blood, and muscle tissue from meat, he made detailed sketches, writing the Royal Society in London in 1673 to describe his findings. The society's members were amazed that without any formal education Leeuwenhoek had made this important contribution to science. His letters and reports continued. In 1680, the Royal Society made him a member, and, in later years, he became world famous. Distinguished visitors came to his shop, including Tsar Peter the Great in 1698. When Leeuwenhoek died at age ninety, a black lacquer cabinet, carefully wrapped by his daughter Maria, was sent to the Royal Society. Inside were his microscopes and magnifying glasses, bequeathed to them for future research.

By looking more deeply, Leeuwenhoek found a new world beneath the surface of daily life. On another level, you, too, will find your calling by looking more deeply at the world within and around you. Finding your calling is not attaining some distant dream. You do not have to walk on the moon, win the lottery, climb Mount Everest, or make it on *American Idol*. As Martin Luther told people in 1535, any task that you perform with love can be your calling. The key is to follow your heart.[3]

Personal Exercise: Chart Your Direction

By following your heart, you will discern your true direction—not that of your boss, your friends, or your parents, but your own.

In the last chapter you learned how St. Ignatius found his direction by reflecting on his deepest desires. Your reflections on consolation and desolation may have helped you recognize your own direction as well. To discover more about your direction, take out your Renaissance Notebook, review your Exploration List, and ask yourself:

- Do any childhood hobbies or interests call me to pursue them further?
- Do any entries point to an early dream deferred?

If so, write them down. Now take a deep breath, give yourself time to reflect, and answer these questions with the first thought that comes to mind:

- What do I really *want* to do? Not what I "should" do, what someone else wants me to do, but what my heart calls me to do.
- Is there something I've been wanting to do but keep putting off?
- Does a challenge or problem call out to me for an answer?
- Do I feel an inner longing to move in a certain direction?

We are all here to grow, expand, create. As psychologist Abraham Maslow once said, "A musician must make music, an artist must paint, a poet must write, if he is to be ultimately at peace with himself."[4] Until you connect with your heart's desire, you can spend your time doing a reasonable job at anything, but without heart, it remains only that—a job, not a calling.

Don't rush as you chart your direction. Make sure you follow your own star, not someone else's expectations. Gain greater clarity by writing down the names of three or four significant people in your life: your parents, your boss, a close friend, your spouse or significant other. Next to each name, write what you think this person wants you to do.

Now close your eyes, take a deep breath, and connect with your CS, that authentic, inner part of you that leads to greater joy and meaning. What does your CS tell you? What do you *really* want to do? Say the answer to yourself and write it down. This is your direction, your own guiding star.[5]

YOU CAN CHART A NEW COURSE AT ANY AGE

In the Renaissance, most people began seeking their callings in their mid-teens to mid-twenties, years of dramatic change when traditional cultures have always performed their rites of passage. During these formative years the brain's frontal lobes mature, enabling us to engage in impulse control, long-range planning, complex decision making, and purposeful action.

This momentous transition from adolescence to adulthood begins our first discernment journey. Yet we now know that our brains continue developing throughout our lives. Each season of life calls us to another journey as we meet new challenges and discover new possibilities. By continuing to learn throughout life, we develop our brains, increase our vitality, and deepen our sense of purpose.[6]

Imagining Your Future Self

Psychologists say that we make many decisions based on visions of our future selves. We each have a *best possible self*—how you would be if you followed your star—and a *worst possible self*— what your life would be like if your deepest fears were realized. Whether you're aware of them or not, these possible selves shape your life.

We base our possible selves on people we know. You can see this in the example of Sir Thomas More. At twelve, More became a page in the household of John Morton, archbishop of Canterbury and lord chancellor of England. Accompanying his mentor to Canterbury Cathedral, young Thomas was inspired by the statues of saints, flickering candles, songs, and prayers. Recognizing Thomas's intellectual and spiritual gifts, Morton sent him to Oxford, but after two years More's father withdrew him, sending him to London to study law. A distinguished lawyer and judge, John More wanted his son to follow in his own footsteps.

John More and John Morton were two defining polarities in Thomas More's life. To his mentor, he owed his religious devotion and the education that made him a leading scholar in his time. To his father, he owed his feelings of a son's obedience and love of family. The tension between his sacred and secular duties remained with More throughout his life.

Searching for direction, More spent years in a pattern familiar to many of us—multitasking, trying to do it all. Between ages twenty-two and twenty-six, he practiced law, served in Parliament, studied Greek, and lectured on St. Augustine at a local church. Rising early and working late, he began and ended his days in prayer at a London monastery, trying to decide between religious vows and a secular life.

At twenty-seven, he made up his mind, marrying and committing to his legal practice. He became an ambassador and advisor to Henry VIII, who knighted him in 1521. More shared his wit and learning with his large household, especially his daughter Margaret, who became one of the most learned women of her time. In 1529, the king made More lord chancellor, the highest position in the realm next to the king himself.

Famous throughout Europe for his book *Utopia*, publicly More had followed his father's path with his legal career, family, and worldly honors, yet in private he maintained a monastic life. He taught his family theology and the classics, practiced daily devotions, spent each Friday in prayer at the chapel of his home in Chelsea, and, beneath his golden chain of office and robes of state, wore a hair shirt to keep him ever mindful of his faith.[7]

Personal Exercise: Define Your Best Possible Self

Now it's time to discover your own best possible self. Research in positive psychology has shown that writing about your possible self can bring you greater clarity, health, and well-being.[8] For the next four days, spend fifteen minutes with your Renaissance Notebook.

1. Begin each session by going off where you won't be disturbed.

2. Close your eyes, take two or three slow, deep breaths, and then see yourself as you would be if your deepest dreams came true. What do you and your world look like? Feel like?
3. Then open your eyes and list in your Renaissance Notebook what you visualized.
4. When you finish, put your writing away.
5. On the next two days, repeat the process.
6. On the fourth day, read over your three lists and combine them, writing a final description of your best possible self.
7. Check your results by asking how you feel about this self. Happy? Excited?
8. If you do *not* feel positive, ask if this is *your* best possible self or someone else's. If it's not really you, do the exercise again, this time writing about your *own* deepest dream.

Realizing Your Vision with Hope

Now that you know your best possible self, the next step is to bring it to life. There is always a creative tension between what you are and what you'd like to be. Many people become discouraged by this gap between their ideals and reality, retreating into mindless distractions. This section will help you bridge the gap with three powerful strategies from hope psychology: Goals, Agency, and Pathways—G-A-P.

University of Kansas psychologist Rick Snyder spent years studying successful leaders in religion, business, academic, and civic life. He found they all used similar strategies to set goals, maintain their motivation, and develop pathways or steps toward their goals. He called this set of skills "Hope Theory."[9] You can build your own hope skills with these strategies.

Setting Goals

To move forward in life, you need goals. Healthy people are always growing, pursuing their goals, reaching outward and upward, like plants in gardens. The most effective goals are meaningful, measurable, and manageable.

Meaningful

By using your inner compass and the exercises in this book, you've found a direction that brings your life meaning. Now you can set a strategic goal to get you there.

Measurable

- Make your goal specific so you know what to do. Instead of saying "I want to be more active in my community," ask what that would look like. If you mean "I want to build houses for Habitat for Humanity," call a Habitat chapter to volunteer.
- Make your goal positive, not "I *don't* want to be lonely" but "I want to meet new friends." Then set specific subgoals— join a community group, take a class, invite a colleague for coffee or lunch. Studies have shown that positive goals are not only more effective, they increase your psychological well-being.

Manageable

- Set a stretch goal—not too easy, not too hard, something you could accomplish in the next six months. If what you want seems too far away, don't lose heart. Focus on what you *can* do. Break the distance to your dream into smaller subgoals, then take one step at a time, celebrating your creative victories along the way.
- Make your goal performance based. Focusing on results (like "winning a game") only produces stress and undermines your performance. You can't control everything, but what you *can* do is give your best effort. Tell yourself, "I'm

going to play my best game" or "do my best." Then focus on the process.

Finally, commit to your goal. Write it down on an index card.[10]

Building Your Motivation

Now that you've set your goal, build your motivation or "agency."

- Look at your index card every day and visualize yourself achieving your goal. Feel the excitement. Smile as you accept this new reality into your life.
- Remember a past success, a challenge you overcame and the skills you used. See yourself using those skills now.
- Overcome false humility—feeling inadequate and putting yourself down. Think of someone you admire, someone too caught up in the adventure of living to waste time with personal put-downs. *True humility is being present:* accepting yourself as you are and embracing the adventure of life. If you catch yourself putting yourself down, STOP, take a deep breath, and focus on being present.
- Be kind to your CS. Maintain your energy and positive momentum by getting enough sleep, healthy food, and exercise.
- Meet with positive friends who encourage each other and celebrate each other's progress.
- Draw upon the boundless energy of joy. As my friend psychologist Jerry Lynch says, "If it's not fun, you're done."[11] Have fun with the process.

Overcoming Roadblocks

Some people begin new projects with enthusiasm, but then give up when they meet difficulties. Pathways map out the route to your goal and can help you overcome resistance. When driving cross-country, you don't just get in your car and go. First you plan, navigate with a map, or check your route on the Internet. On your new Renaissance journey, use pathways to help you reach your goal.

- When you look at your index card and see yourself achieving your goal, ask yourself, "What do I need to get there?" Then write down the specific steps.
- If there's something you need, a tool, skill, or information you don't have, get the tool, learn the skill, or ask someone for help.
- Anticipate roadblocks. Plan backups and alternate routes, so if one path is blocked, you'll have a good alternative.
- If something doesn't work out, learn from the experience, follow an alternate pathway, or modify your goal if necessary, but keep moving forward.
- Multiply your effectiveness with a positive network. You'll find that asking for help when you need it is not a sign of weakness but a source of strength. Cultivate win-win friendships with people who nurture and support each other's journeys.[12]

Jeff used these skills to move from disappointment to achievement. He began college as an accounting major, planning to become a CPA like his father. But he found his business classes dry as sawdust and got mediocre grades until he discovered his passion for science. He switched majors to biology, earned top science grades, and applied to medical school, but received only rejection letters. With advice from his biology professor, he developed an alternate pathway, working in a medical lab after graduation, then applying to graduate school in pharmacology. Two years later, with a master's degree in pharmacology, Jeff applied to medical school again. He was rejected again—another blocked pathway. But he didn't give up. He applied to medical schools outside the country and spent two years studying medicine in Mexico. When he sent out his applications again, he was admitted to medical school at the University of Rochester, completed his residency, and became a successful internist. Today he's president of his medical group. Jeff's hope skills helped him become an outstanding doctor.

QUIZ: HOW HOPEFUL ARE YOU?

How hopeful are you? To find out, take this short hope test developed by psychologist Rick Snyder and his colleagues at the University of Kansas:[13]

Read each item carefully, selecting the number that best describes you, and put that number in the blank provided. 1=definitely false; 2=mostly false; 3=mostly true; 4=definitely true.

1. ___ I energetically pursue my goals.
2. ___ I can think of many ways to get out of a jam.
3. ___ My past experiences have prepared me well for the future.
4. ___ There are lots of ways around any problem.
5. ___ I've been pretty successful in life.
6. ___ I can think of many ways to get the things in life that are most important to me.
7. ___ I meet the goals that I set for myself.
8. ___ Even when others get discouraged, I know I can find a way to solve the problem.

Scoring: Add the scores for all 8 items. A total score of 24 means that you are very hopeful. The odd-numbered items (1, 3, 5, 7) measure your strength in *agency;* the even numbers (2, 4, 6, 8) your strength in *pathways.*

Total Score: Agency____ Pathways____

(Source: © 1991 by the American Psychological Association. Adapted with permission.)

How did you do? No one fails the hope test. It's just an indicator, showing where you are now and where you can build greater effectiveness. If your agency score was low, strengthen it by following the advice on agency. If your pathways score was low, follow the advice to strengthen your pathways. If your total score was lower than you'd like, focus on action items in both sections. Hope is a strength, a skill you can keep on building throughout life. The stronger your hope skills, the more power you'll have to create your personal Renaissance.

Check Your Inner Compass

As you move forward in your journey, don't let success or the demands of daily life make you wander off course. Remember to check your inner compass.

The English statesman Sir Francis Bacon had many gifts. His father, Sir Nicolas Bacon, was England's highest judge; his uncle Lord Burghley was Queen Elizabeth's chief advisor. At sixteen, Francis studied philosophy at Cambridge, determined to develop a new scientific philosophy to benefit humanity. But two years later his father died, leaving him emotionally and financially adrift.

To establish himself, Bacon studied law at Gray's Inn, becoming a successful attorney. Elected to the House of Commons at age twenty, he built a powerful political career, eventually rising to become lord chancellor of England. But in 1621 he was convicted of taking bribes, forced out of office, banished, and dishonored. At the end of his life, Bacon wrote with regret that he had been born to be a philosopher but had betrayed his values by chasing after worldly power. His gifts, he confessed, had been "misspent . . . in things for which I was least fit; so as I may truly say, my soul hath been a stranger in the course of my pilgrimage."[14]

In your life's journey, success will bring its own challenges. Remember to check your inner compass and stay on course with your values.

Dealing with Challenges

"For every action, there is an equal and opposite reaction," according to Sir Isaac Newton's Third Law of Motion. Be prepared for opposition in your discernment journey.

Michelangelo

Michelangelo's father, Lodovico di Leonardo Buonarroti Simoni, wanted to apprentice his sons in the silk and wool guilds to bring more money into the family. But young Michelangelo frustrated his father's wishes by neglecting his schoolwork and drawing in secret. Believing art to be a trade unworthy of his family, Lodovico scolded and beat his son. Still the boy persisted. Finally, when Michelangelo was fourteen, his father gave in, apprenticing him to the artist Domenico Ghirlandajo, and Michelangelo became one of the greatest artists of the Renaissance.[15]

Sor Juana Inés de la Cruz

Limiting gender stereotypes told Renaissance women to remain in men's shadows—submissive, chaste, silent, and obedient. Their opportunities for scholarship were severely limited. Sir Thomas More's daughter, Margaret More Roper, continued her classical studies as a wife and mother, supported by her father, who championed education for women. But other women were not so fortunate. Sor Juana Inés de la Cruz grew up in the seventeenth-century colony of New Spain, her active mind and love of learning a vital part of her nature. With her intelligence and beauty, she had become the protégée of the viceroy and vicereine in Mexico City. But the university did not admit women, so at sixteen she entered the convent, which offered silence, solitude, and the only honorable way she could live as a scholar. Sor Juana's convent became her university. Studying science while working in the kitchen, she noted the interactions of eggs, sugar, and water. She watched two girls spinning a top and, by sprinkling flour around it, found that it spun not in circles but in spirals. She wrote poetry and plays and her fame spread throughout New Spain. But the bishop of Puebla reprimanded her, saying her studies were unfit for a nun. In 1691, she responded, defending a woman's right to learn and calling her love of learning a gift from God.[16]

Aphra Behn

In the Renaissance, there were no women actors in Shakespeare's plays. All women's roles were acted by boys. It is Shakespeare's poetic genius that brought Juliet, Rosalind, and Cleopatra to life on the London stage. There were no women writing for the London stage until Aphra Behn's first play, *The Forced Marriage,* in 1670. Behn's life was a drama in itself as she overcame personal challenges with resourcefulness and determination.

The details of her early life are hazy. According to some accounts, she was born near Canterbury around 1640. Then her family sailed to the colony of Suriname where her father was to serve as lieutenant general, but he died at sea. The family sailed on to Suriname, a tropical paradise, where Aphra grew up amid characters who later appeared in her literary work, including the slave who inspired *Oroonoko.* Later Aphra returned to England, a stunning young woman in her twenties, and married a Mr. Behn, a Dutch merchant who shortly died of the plague. In search of new pathways, the witty and resourceful Aphra caught the eye of King Charles II and in July 1666 sailed to Antwerp as a spy in his majesty's secret service. She sent back regular reports, but communications broke down. With each report, she asked her employers for her salary to pay her expenses. But there was no answer. Her requests became pleas, she sold her jewels, wrote court officials, but the money never came. Disgusted after five months of government service, she took out a loan to return to England, finding London in ruins after the Great Fire of 1666. Amid the confusion, unable to obtain her salary to repay the loan, she was sent to debtors prison.

As London emerged from the ashes, Aphra Behn, too, began again, finally obtaining her salary and release from prison. Instead of surrendering to misfortune, she wrote about it, turning problems into pathways. Conflict, lost love, life's daily dramas she wove into plots for plays and novels. For two decades, she filled the London stage with racy romantic dramas, and her many friends included poet laureate John Dryden. The first woman in England to make her living as a writer, Aphra Behn created new pathways, transforming adversity into art.[17]

Shadows on the Path: Don't Lose Hope

When you face challenges, don't lose hope. Confronting large, complex problems, some people become immobilized, unable to act, succumbing to the slow poison of cynicism.

Kevin was a gifted nature writer. Years ago, he wrote articles on water politics, the shrinking of the Ogallala Aquifer, the underground water source essential to the American Midwest. He spent months in the Alaskan wilderness tracking early signs of global warming. But as time went by, he became so depressed by the magnitude of the problems that he felt helpless. When he tried to write, he would sit with a glass of scotch, staring for hours at his notes and the blank computer screen. Finally, he just gave up. The problems were too vast. There was nothing he could do. So he did nothing. Surrendering to cynicism, he neglected his gifts, lost in the shadows of learned helplessness.

Today's global challenges are enormous, too complex for one person to solve. But each of us has vital gifts, and together we *can* make a difference. Years ago, ten people in Menlo Park, California, became concerned about urban sprawl and environmental degradation. Together they established the Peninsula Open Space Trust (POST), raising money to buy local land to preserve it from development.

Today, with over 17,000 donors, POST has saved 60,000 acres of open space—windswept beaches, rugged canyons, redwood forests, and valleys filled with wildflowers—refuges for wildlife and retreats for communion with nature, a gift to the future and to us all.

In 2004, a young couple in their twenties established a micro-lending Web site, facilitating positive partnerships between citizen investors and small business entrepreneurs in developing countries. While traveling in East Africa, Matt and Jessica Flannery decided they wanted to do something personal to help the people they met. At the time, Jessica was working for a nonprofit and Matt was a computer programmer. After researching possibilities and talking with experts in economics, law, technology, and microfinance, they set up their Web site, KIVA, which enables anyone to make a loan for as little as twenty-five dollars. Helping a shopkeeper in Ecuador, a baker in Afghanistan, a gift shop owner in Ukraine, or a seamstress in Kenya with funds to buy a sewing machine, refrigerator, or goods to stock their shelves, KIVA brings positive momentum and new hope to their lives. In its first eighteen months, the company made loans of over four million dollars, helping our neighbors around the planet realize their dreams of a better life.

If you're facing a major challenge—whether global or personal—don't let the magnitude of the problem overwhelm you. Don't be like Kevin, dwelling on what you can't do. Ask, "What *can* I do?" Use your hope skills to take positive action.

1. Think of something you *can* do with your gifts. Set a manageable goal you can achieve in the next six months. If your goal is larger than that, break it into smaller subgoals.

2. Chart realistic pathways, small steps to take you toward your goal.

3. When you face roadblocks, be resourceful like Aphra Behn.

If your roadblock is external, choose an alternate pathway. If that doesn't work, ask yourself, "What else can I do?" Be creative. Get help, change your approach, or modify your goal.

If your roadblock is internal, don't sabotage yourself with fear, worry, or self-doubt. Think of one *small* step to move toward your goal. How can you build your sense of agency, break an unproductive habit, get more knowledge or experience? Find consolation with prayer, positive self-talk, or a supportive friend. Remember a time you overcame adversity. Take a class, talk to friends, ask for help, find a mentor, read up on the subject. The important thing is to keep moving forward.

4. Finally, be kind to yourself. Don't lose heart. Scholar Christopher Booker has found that beneath all the major plots in world literature lies the same archetypal pattern—the hero's conflicts and challenges while pursuing a goal. Psychologists tell us that how we respond to challenge shapes the evolving story of our lives.[18]

RENAISSANCE AFFIRMATION

Some people see opportunities where others see only problems. The same situation can make a coward out of one person and a hero out of another. As John Milton wrote in 1644, "the matter of them both is the same."[19] To a great extent, what happens around you depends upon what happens within you. By responding creatively to your challenges you will build strength of character and transform your world. Remind yourself that you can overcome challenges by saying: "I now accept a new Renaissance in my life."

Moving Forward

Now it's time to record your own new goal and direction. Write your answers and today's date in your Renaissance Notebook.

1. My direction in life is

   _____

2. Which connects my gifts

   _____

3. With my guiding values

_____

4. My new goal is to

_____

(Remember to make your goal meaningful, manageable, and measurable.)

The first three steps to my goal are:

1. _____

2. _____

3. _____

Once you've found your direction and identified the first three steps, start moving forward. Don't feel you need to plan every detail in advance. You cannot anticipate everything. One step will lead to another. As you follow your star, you will be surprised by jewels on the path—remarkable coincidences, unexpected opportunities, new possibilities along the way.

Congratulations! You have now completed Phase One of your journey. The next chapter will take you into Phase Two, introducing you to eight powerful Renaissance practices to help you move forward with greater momentum.

You are well on your way to creating your own personal Renaissance. Since this is a creative victory, congratulate yourself and do something special to celebrate.

RENAISSANCE REMINDERS

Your daily choices shape your life and inform the world.
As you move forward, remember to:

- ~ Keep your eyes on your true direction, your own guiding star.
- ~ Keep building your strength in agency and pathways.
- ~ See roadblocks as challenges and respond creatively.
- ~ Keep checking your inner compass, watching for patterns of consolation and desolation.

Making the Renaissance Practices Work for You

CHAPTER 5

Faith

Trusting Your Life and Your World

Faith is the substance of things hoped for,
the evidence of things not seen.
—HEBREWS 11: 1–21

In Phase One of this book, you began discovering your gifts, discerning your values, and setting a new goal to move forward with a sense of calling. Because contemporary culture offers little support for living your calling, the next eight chapters will take you into Phase Two, offering eight powerful practices to support your new Renaissance life.

The Life-Changing Power of Practices

The ideals and aspirations of Renaissance men and women were reinforced by the regular practice of faith, introspection, community, meditation, involvement in the arts, reading, exercise, and sustaining discipline. At first, these practices might seem irrelevant to your life today. You may wonder, "How could meditating, meeting a friend for lunch, or painting a picture possibly help me in my calling?"

Because the power of these practices defies logic, it often eludes us, locked away in the hidden wisdom of the Renaissance. These valuable tools are not techniques. As my friend theologian Bill Spohn once told me, "A technique does something *for* you while a practice does something *to* you." While a technique like learning a new software program may improve your work, these Renaissance practices will progressively transform your life.

Like seeds slowly germinating beneath the surface, these practices will surprise you with new growth—insights, inspirations, and forward momentum. How does this happen? Small actions over time produce monumental results. Neuroscientists tell us that making such small changes in our behavior creates new connections in our brains, transforming us from within.

Individually, these Renaissance practices have been validated in research with thousands of people ranging in age from their late teens through retirement. Together these practices comprise what the Search Institute in Minneapolis calls "developmental assets," habits correlated with greater success, health, and well-being in over one million Americans.[1]

The Practice of Faith

The first of these practices is faith. In today's pluralistic society, faith means different things to different people. Yet ultimately it is a belief in the order of the universe and our place within it, the ability to find courage in our struggles, meaning in our daily lives. Despite the chronic anxiety and challenges of our times, our faith affirms that our actions have meaning and that somehow life makes sense.

However you define your personal faith, having a sense of calling means believing that your talents, your efforts, can make a difference. As you found in chapter three, psychologists and theologians agree that human beings have an essential *need* for meaning, and studies have found strong connections between faith and health.

Throughout human history, the great spiritual traditions have affirmed that we are part of the infinite pattern of life. Fifteen centuries before the Renaissance, Rabbi Hillel posed three questions still central to our lives today:

If I am not for myself, who will be for me?
If I am for myself alone, what am I?
If not now, when?[2]

Despite doctrinal differences, most people in the Renaissance attended regular religious services and practiced daily prayer. Their faith sustained them through wars, plagues, and political upheaval, assuring them that their lives had a purpose. As a young poet, John Milton dreamed of writing a great English epic. His faith sustained him when his dream was deferred by political turmoil, personal tragedy, and the English Civil War. Finally, in his late fifties, he began his masterpiece, *Paradise Lost,* with the invocation:

> *What in me is dark,*
> *Illumine, what is low raise and support;*
> *That to the height of this great Argument*
> *I may assert Eternal Providence,*
> *And justify the ways of God to men.*[3]

Invoking the muse is an epic convention, a petition to the classical muse of poetry. But Milton's invocation opened his poem with a prayer, affirming his faith as he embraced his calling in life.

RENAISSANCE QUESTIONS

Today many people live in confusion because they have no invisible means of support. Do you have the faith to sustain you in your calling? Take a moment now to ask:

~ Do I feel my life has a purpose?

~ Do I feel at home in my world?

(box continues)

(Renaissance Questions continued)

- Do I have a source of inspiration and support?
- Do I believe in the goodness and potential of my life—or am I haunted by inadequacy?

This chapter will help you answer these questions.

Strengthening Your Faith

I have many friends with a deep sense of faith. Some are vowed religious—Jesuit priests at my university and a Holy Cross sister in Wisconsin. Another friend is a Quaker, who lives her faith by working for peace and justice. Still others are Buddhists, sustained by their contemplative practice. Some friends are active in their churches or synagogues, while another friend lives in a mountain cabin, finding her inspiration in quiet walks through the green forest cathedral.

Whatever your personal faith, it is strengthened by regular practice. Whether this involves formal worship services, silent reflection, or meditation, regularly participating in the rituals of your faith brings you spiritual reference points to help you navigate through life.

This chapter offers examples of faith in Renaissance and contemporary lives along with practices in gratitude, spiritual modeling, and compassion. Some practices will appeal to you more than others. I ask that you try all three then choose one for your ongoing spiritual practice.

Practice 1: Gratitude

Our word "gratitude" is derived from the Latin word for "grace." For centuries, people have paused to give thanks for their daily blessings, not only in the Renaissance but throughout the Christian, Jewish, Muslim, Buddhist, and Hindu traditions. Today, research has shown that "counting our blessings" not only decreases stress but increases our energy, enthusiasm, alertness, sense of meaning, and well-being. When people ranging in age from their late teens through their seventies kept daily gratitude journals, they had higher optimism, fewer health problems, and better overall well-being than their peers.[4]

Personal Exercise: Your Daily Gratitude List

Try this gratitude practice for yourself. For the next week, at the end of the day, list five things you're thankful for in your Renaissance Notebook, like this:

Date: _____

1. _____
2. _____
3. _____
4. _____
5. _____

Some days you may think of more than five things, but aim for at least five a day.

By the end of the week, ask yourself if this exercise has made a difference in your life. Some people feel better in general. Others find themselves noticing blessings and new possibilities throughout the day.

Before she adopted this practice, Ellen was exhausted and discouraged. As a new social worker, she was overwhelmed by the problems of poverty, hunger, and homelessness she witnessed every day. She saw few results for her efforts and when she addressed one problem she found many more to take its place. Yet there were results—small ones—the young mother she had reached, the troubled boy who'd found a foster father, and the homeless family slowly rebuilding their lives. Ellen shared her concerns with a mentor at work, a woman she'd long admired. Her friend told her, "Don't expect immediate results. We are not so much called to be successful as we are called to be *faithful*." Then she told her about the gratitude practice. Following her friend's advice, as Ellen completed work each day she began writing down five things she was grateful for—from small joys like the willow tree outside her window to the chance to do something she believed in, the people she met, her colleagues, and her own friends and family. She began feeling less stressed, more aware of small blessings throughout the day. She also adopted another practice of her friend's, keeping a button from her daughter's coat in her pocket as a reminder to be grateful for the present moment.

Looking Back

Faith gives us the strength to persevere through challenging times, the courage to overcome obstacles, the light of hope to guide our way.

As the eldest son of a noble family in sixteenth-century France, Francis de Sales was expected to pursue a career at court. His father sent him to college to learn fencing, dancing, and riding. He studied these out of obedience, but felt called to the priesthood, attending theology lectures as well. After graduation, his father sent him to study law at the University of Padua, which had an international reputation in theology. For the next few years Francis studied both subjects, trying to balance family duty with the call of his heart. But when he received his law degree, his father announced that it was time for him to support the family by practicing law, marrying, and producing an heir. His younger brother, Louis, was expected to become a priest.

Francis prayed for guidance. As he rode through the woods, his sword and scabbard fell to the ground, landing in the shape of a cross. Taking heart from this symbol, he confided in his brother, who had no desire to be a priest, then approached his father, finally obtaining his consent to enter the priesthood. Francis was ordained in 1593, becoming a saint and one of the key figures of the Counter-Reformation.[5]

St. Francis's contemporary, Jeanne de Chantal, was sustained by faith through many seasons of her life. Born into the French nobility, she was married at twenty to Christophe, the young Baron de Chantal, who became her soul mate. By all appearances, Jeanne was a model Renaissance lady, with her long dark hair, sparkling eyes, and radiant smile. When her husband was home, she dressed in the shimmering silks he loved and became a gracious hostess to family and friends.

When her husband was away serving as a soldier and courtier, Jeanne oversaw the castle of Bourbilly. Dressed plainly in wool, she began each day in prayer, attended daily mass, kept the books, visited farmers on the estate, distributed bread and clothing to the poor, and ministered to the sick with healing herbs. She raised her son and three daughters with devotion, teaching them their prayers and lessons while also teaching the local children to read.

When Christophe returned home, seriously wounded in battle, Jeanne carefully nursed him back to health. But, shortly thereafter, he was fatally injured in a hunting accident. Widowed at twenty-eight, the grief-stricken baroness received several marriage proposals but knew this season of her life was over. Giving her husband's clothes and her own finery to the poor, she lived simply, focusing on her children and her prayers and tending those in need.

In 1604, she met Francis de Sales, who became her spiritual director, offering her books and lessons in discernment. As her children grew up, she increased her ministry to the poor, feeling called to a more devotional life. Her eldest daughter, Marie-Aimée, married the Baron de Thorens, the younger brother of St. Francis de Sales. In 1610, after arranging for her son's education, she obtained her father's blessing and took her younger daughters to Annecy, where she founded the Convent of the Visitation, a religious order dedicated to serving the poor. She was canonized as a saint in 1767.[6]

SCIENCE AND SPIRITUALITY

Some people in the Renaissance believed that science and spirituality were incompatible. Yet others, like English doctor Sir Thomas Browne, found inspiration all around them. Although Browne was educated in science at the universities of Padua and Leiden, he wrote of his expansive compassion for the natural world along with people of other nations and beliefs. "I love to lose myself in a mystery, to pursue my reason to an *O altitudo*," he wrote in his spiritual autobiography, inspired by a vision of faith that transcended all he knew.

Centuries later Albert Einstein wrote that "The most beautiful thing we can experience is the mysterious. It is the source of all true art and science." This reverence for the intricate pattern of life is equally apparent in Galileo's descriptions of the moons of Jupiter or twentieth-century astronomer Carl Sagan's rhapsodic references to the "billions and billions" of stars in the cosmos and the fact that you and I are composed of the very elements of the stars. Like these scientists from the Renaissance to modern times, we, too, proclaim our faith when we embrace the radiant mystery of life.[7]

Faith and Calling Today

The power of faith inspires many creative people today. Fiction writer Ron Hansen discovered his calling in church. He and his twin brother, Rob, grew up in an Irish Catholic parish in Omaha, Nebraska, their childhood discoveries framed by daily mass and the rituals of the liturgical year. One Sunday when Ron was about five, he heard the priest read the Gospel and suddenly realized that he *knew* the story, that here was a familiar pattern echoing through time to touch his life as well. This fascination with the power of story is woven into his novels, including my favorite, *Atticus,* a finalist for the National Book Award.

Ron is my friend and colleague in the English department at Santa Clara University. He still attends daily mass, now in the Santa Clara Mission, and sees his writing as informed by his faith. The process of writing is always a revelation. Ron considers it a form of prayer, likening it to Ignatian meditation. "You go into a meditation with the intention of solving a problem or calming a particular want, and other things that are unrecognized irritants or blessings begin to percolate up. Writing does that, too," he explains, "but in the guise of a fictional character or a choice of topic." In writing about others, he learns more about himself. "I find I'm often anticipating dilemmas or conquering old issues through my protagonists, antagonists, and plots," he admits, "but the underlying themes are not always apparent to me at the time of composition." Following his calling brings moments of grace. Ron says, "I often recognize a feeling of serenity when I find myself at the end of a work period, and that serenity comes not just from pride in a job well done but from freedom and relaxation and the other gifts we associate with prayer."

In living his faith, Ron acknowledges the importance of regular practice. "Daily mass," he says, "is my greatest source of sustenance. If nothing else goes well but I have that, it feels like a pretty good day. Also, an annual week-long retreat in silence and prayer seems increasingly important to me. And nature, particularly the oceans and the wide, scary, sun-baked desert, often put God right in front of me." Ron realizes that "because of the world we're in, faith and prayer do not come as naturally as they apparently did" for people in the past. But, as with any important relationship, exercise, or endeavor, consistent practice is essential.

"Seekers should realize they're exercising muscles most people don't even know they have," he says. "And it takes a great deal of practice and learning to feel fully comfortable in one's faith. It often looks bizarre from the outside but can be a wonderful source of life and nurture from the inside. Even Sunday worship isn't enough though. You have to make it as regular as any other form of exercise to really get the benefits."[8]

Practice 2: Find a Spiritual Model

For centuries, people have benefited from "spiritual modeling," the influence of inspirational men and women on our lives. Psychologists have found that we experience "elevation," a feeling of warmth, joy, and inspiration, when we witness acts of kindness or even read about them.

Yet, these days, inspiring role models can be hard to find. Because of this, many young people suffer developmental deficits. When I began my research on vocation, I found that nearly 80 percent of the California college students I surveyed lacked positive role models. Those who had them mentioned mainly sports figures and rock stars. Other studies of today's youth have revealed similar results.[9]

By contrast, spiritual models and mentors were promoted by Renaissance culture, which also offered a wealth of spiritual models in books. St. Ignatius was inspired by reading about St. Francis and St. Dominic. St. Teresa of Avila found special comfort reading the lives of St. Jerome, St. Augustine, and St. Clare. Elena Cornaro spent each day reading about the saints, striving to imitate them as a scholar and friend of the poor. Other sources of spiritual models were history and the classics, important influences for Queen Elizabeth and sources for Shakespeare's plays.

Finding spiritual models today is more difficult but well worth the effort. My friend Carol Flinders wrote her book *Enduring Lives* about four contemporary women of faith: Etty Hillesum, Jane Goodall, Sr. Helen Prejean, and Tenzin Palmo, all of whom possess what she calls a "very powerful interior life," making them compelling spiritual models for our time.[10]

Have you been inspired by someone you know, someone from the past you've discovered in a book or movie? I've found many of my own spiritual models—Elizabeth I, Mohandas Gandhi,

Franklin and Eleanor Roosevelt—in books and films. Studies have shown that focusing on spiritual models can help you deepen your faith and develop greater strength of character. Spiritual directors have used this practice for years, advising people to reflect on the lives of people they admire.[11]

🌺 *Personal Exercise: Find a Spiritual Role Model*

To experience spiritual modeling for yourself, take out your Renaissance Notebook and give yourself time to reflect:

- Think of someone you admire—from history or the present day.
- What quality do you admire most about the person?
- Now ask yourself, "How can I develop more of this quality in myself?"
- Think of one action you can take to develop the quality.
- Close your eyes and visualize yourself expressing it.
- Take one step this week to actively express this quality in your life.

To become better acquainted with your spiritual model, do an Internet search, read a biography or autobiography, get a picture for your home or office. As I write this chapter, I have a picture of Eleanor Roosevelt smiling down at me from above my desk.

Shadows on the Path:
Moving from Approval to Acceptance

Many conscientious people live in the shadows of self-doubt. Feeling unworthy and insecure, they block their own path to happiness. They constantly seek approval, afraid of doing something wrong. Whenever they do make a mistake, they tell themselves "You never do anything right," "You're not good enough."

Megan's friends couldn't understand why she got involved in one abusive relationship after another. She was a successful realtor, friendly and outgoing. But she was anything but friendly to herself, her inner dialogue a constant stream of self-criticism. After another romantic breakup, she went into therapy, where she realized that these relationships had mirrored her deep feelings of insecurity. Megan decided to take a "sabbatical" from dating in order to develop a better relationship with herself. She joined a mindfulness meditation group, where she practiced accepting her feelings. To affirm her commitment to a healthier life, she bought herself a ring, a gold band studded with tiny emeralds to wear on her left hand. After a few weeks meditating, exercising, and spending time with friends, Megan began accepting herself more. She felt less driven, had more fun in her life, and was even more successful at work. Over dinner one night she told an old friend about the meaning of her ring, which opened up their relationship to greater trust and understanding. They began spending more time together. Today, she is married to her best friend, who loves and appreciates her for who she is.

Does Megan's story sound familiar? Whether in our relationships, our work, or our finances, the outer world of our experience mirrors our inner dialogue. If you feel you're not good enough, if you're haunted by shadows of self-doubt, you crave *approval*. Struggling to meet some standard of perfection—your own or someone else's—just to feel okay, you can become caught up in a drama of compulsive "doing" that dominates your life and distorts your relationships. You may feel good after an accomplishment or word of praise, but a few minutes later, if you make a mistake, disappoint someone, or fail to meet your own expectations, you feel terrible. Defeated. Worthless.

Acceptance is something else entirely. If someone accepts you, you can make a mistake, be late, fail a test, burn the dinner, forget to do something, and that person will still love you. Some people are blessed with acceptance from their parents, partners, or close friends. Others find it only with a faithful dog or cat. But ultimately each of us must find it within ourselves.

Transcending reason and logic, unconditional acceptance is healing and life-affirming, a gift of grace. Indeed, the highest form of acceptance is divine love that embraces us in spite of our imperfections, healing our fractured lives to make us whole.

RENAISSANCE QUESTION

Do I relate to myself with approval or acceptance?

Practice 3: Self-Compassion

In the Renaissance, some people experienced an extreme lack of self-acceptance, becoming so obsessed with their faults that they believed not even the infinite grace of God could save them. Robert Burton's *Anatomy of Melancholy* describes the "burning fever of the soul," the torment of those afflicted with this intense self-loathing. Practicing self-compassion keeps us from falling into such despair. St. Francis de Sales reminded Renaissance men and women to be "gentle to themselves," advice we can use in our lives today. Self-acceptance means facing our faults with kindness and understanding. Of course, you feel disappointed when you make mistakes, but don't condemn yourself or wallow in what St. Francis would call "a displeasure which is bitter, sullen, fretful, and angry."

Psychologists now realize that "self-compassion" is essential to spiritual and emotional health. It reduces stress, anxiety, depression, and fear of failure, while improving our relationships. Psychologist Kristin Neff's definition of self-compassion includes being gentle and kind to yourself, especially when things go wrong; seeing yourself as human, as part of a larger pattern of life;

and identifying your painful feelings without becoming engulfed by them.[12]

Personal Exercise: Practice Self-Compassion

You can begin practicing self-compassion right now by making a conscious effort to be kinder to yourself. Then when something goes wrong, don't beat yourself up. Instead:

- Treat yourself with understanding, as you would a dear friend.
- See yourself as part of a larger pattern. Realize that you're not alone—you're experiencing what it means to be human.
- Be kind and patient with yourself. You are a unique and worthy individual, here to learn, grow, and become more of who you truly are.

Self-compassion not only makes you feel better, it also makes you a better problem solver by increasing your objectivity. When you accept yourself, you don't catastrophize or blow things out of proportion. Instead, you learn from experience, forging new pathways, and handling your challenges with wisdom and hope.

● ●

Personal Affirmation

You can build self-compassion with an affirmation: a favorite prayer from your own tradition or this loving-kindness affirmation from my friend Shauna Shapiro, a psychologist who blends her background in Vipassana meditation with research on optimal health and wellness. To begin, simply take a deep breath, release it, and say slowly:

May I be filled with loving kindness.
May I be well.
May I be peaceful and be free.

May I be happy.

Then think of someone you know, saying:

May you be filled with loving kindness
May you be well.
May you be peaceful and be free.
May you be happy.

Finally, expand your blessing to include all of life:

May we be filled with loving kindness.
May we be well.
May we be peaceful and be free.
May we be happy.[13]

Spiritual Community

A spiritual community—close friends, shared worship or meditation—will also help you develop greater compassion for yourself and others. I cherish my friendship with Tina Clare, a minister and spiritual counselor who has become like a sister, and I find inspiration in a centering prayer group at my church.

Where is your spiritual community? In a church, mosque, or synagogue? In a meditation group? With a close friend?

Keeping Time in Faith

By enabling you to live more mindfully, your faith can help you deal with time pressures.

My colleague Carolyn used to commute over sixty miles on the busy Nimitz Freeway from her home in Oakland to teach at Santa Clara. When she was running late or caught up in traffic, she would regain her peace of mind by affirming, "I am on God's time."

Like Carolyn, you can build your faith by remembering that you are *not* responsible for everything, that there's a larger pattern in the universe.

To become more mindful, focus on living in the present: where you are right now; not where you're going—looking ahead in worry or breathless anticipation, or where you *were*—looking backward with nostalgia or regret; but here and now in the sacramental present tense.

I've spent lots of time living in anticipation, filled with suspense, my mind racing ahead to the next big project, wondering if I'm going to finish this book on time, get that grant, publish that article, give a successful class, retreat, or workshop. But once I've done my work and made the necessary preparations, I cannot touch the future. Obsessing about it only makes me ignore this present, this gift of time, the only place I really *can* make a difference. When I can still my racing mind to rest in the present moment, I find my serenity and affirm my faith in life.

Moving Forward

Take a few minutes now to reflect on your progress in this chapter, writing your answers and today's date in your Renaissance Notebook.

1. How did the gratitude practice work for you? Did you notice more CS joy, more to be thankful for?
2. What did you learn from spiritual modeling?
3. Are you practicing self-compassion, becoming more accepting of yourself?
4. Now, choose one of these practices to support you on the journey and record it. My faith practice is

   _____.

5. What was your creative victory in this chapter and how are you celebrating it?

RENAISSANCE REMINDERS

When you reach out to follow your calling, the universe supports you with a world of possibilities.
As you move forward into the next chapter of your life, remember to:

~ Be kind to yourself.

~ Practice your faith.

~ Live in the present moment.

CHAPTER 6

Daily Examen

Staying on Course with Your Dreams

The unexamined life is not worth living.
—SOCRATES[1]

You're now moving forward in your personal Renais-sance. But unless you check in with yourself regularly, you could easily drift off course, tossed about by the distractions and diversions of daily life.

Phaedria is a character in Edmund Spenser's Renaissance poem, *The Faerie Queene,* who lured people off course with laughter and idle chatter, taking them drifting in her boat around the lake of idleness.[2] When I was in graduate school at UCLA, my friends and I found our version of Phaedria in the distracting life of Los Angeles, pleasant enough in itself but hazardous when it pulled us off course. Following the delights of Venice Beach or the glitter of Hollywood, some people failed out of the program, while others stayed on course to get a PhD.

Staying in touch with your goal and values not only helps you stay on course, it can awaken your intuition, help you recognize opportunities, and create the life of your dreams. As a corporate manager for an international hotel chain, Guy lived in Chicago but constantly traveled to oversee hotels in his division. Restless and discontent with all the airports, e-mail, and cell phone calls that filled his days, he began reflecting on his life and having long talks with his wife, Anna. They realized they wanted to raise their sons in a rural area and spend more time together as a family, so they began looking for pathways.

Guy found that he could relocate and still oversee his hotels, and Anna was an artist who could work anywhere. A few weeks later he invited her to join him on a business trip to Calgary. When he'd finished his hotel work, they drove their rental car to the hills outside of town to go hiking. As they saw a flock of Canada geese flying overhead, Guy intuitively turned the rental car up a winding road, following the direction of the geese. There, at the crest of the hill, they found a ranch for sale. Guy called the listing number on his cell phone, and within minutes a realtor drove up to take them inside. The ranch was amazing. The house looked out at the magnificent Canadian Rockies, and in the master bath was a stained-glass window with images of Canada geese. Guy and Anna made an offer on the ranch, the first step in their journey to a new life.

Following their pathways, Guy moved his office to Calgary and the family moved to their new home. Their sons loved the ranch, and the family began hiking together in the hills and riding horses on the nearby trails. Two years later, Guy took another step, leaving his hotel job. Today, as a leadership consultant, he has more control of his time and is living the life of his dreams.

By introducing you to your second Renaissance practice, the daily Examen, this chapter will help awaken the power of your intuition, giving you the courage to follow your heart and transform your life.

According to Harvard psychologist Daniel Gilbert, what makes us uniquely human is our ability to think about the future. We can use this ability for good or ill, sabotaging ourselves with worry or reviewing our behavior in a process psychologists call "metacognition." An Examen is a metacognitive practice that deepens your awareness of your goals and values.

This practice requires brief periods of silence and solitude, a contemplative habit contrary to our busy, over-scheduled culture. But checking in with yourself regularly is well worth the effort, for research has shown that it can help you overcome stress, achieve better health, and dramatically improve your life.[3]

Looking Back

People in the Renaissance practiced their daily Examen, or examination of conscience, by reflecting on each day's events, giving thanks for their blessings, confessing their faults, and resolving to improve in the future. While a student at the University of Padua, St. Francis de Sales drew up a daily Examen he followed for the rest of his life. Each morning he would ask for divine guidance, visualize his goals, plan his day, and then focus on living with patience and compassion. In the evening, he reflected on the day's events. As a young man, Francis had been impatient and quick-tempered. The kindness and serenity he was known for in later life were acquired from his daily Examen.[4]

Nicholas Herman grew up in a French peasant family. Joining the army at eighteen, he was captured by the Germans and held as a spy, then wounded by Swedish soldiers in another battle. But one winter, while trudging wearily through the snow, he came upon a barren tree and suddenly realized that God's grace could renew his life as surely as it would renew that tree in springtime. Leaving the army, Nicholas joined the Carmelite order. Assigned to tedious work in the monastery kitchen, he began practicing his daily Examen.

Each morning he would ask for God's grace, then offer his daily tasks as services to God. At the end of the day he would thank God for any good he had achieved, ask forgiveness for his errors, and resolve to improve. Nicholas, now Brother Lawrence of the Resurrection, became known for the quality of his work and his benevolent spirit but even more for the process of self-examination that transformed work into worship, influencing generations with his book, *The Practice of the Presence of God.*[5]

Brother Lawrence's daily Examen gave him a strong sense of inner direction. In the busy monastery kitchen, he could do more alone than two other monks combined. Yet he never rushed, never acted in haste. Giving each task the time it required, he acted with kindness and serenity.

As you go about your own daily tasks, stay focused on your direction, on what is truly essential for you. Don't let your gentle, creative CS be tyrannized by endless to-do lists or bullied by other people's distractions and demands. Remember who you are and the deeper purpose of your life. The daily Examen you begin in this chapter will help you do this.

Know Thyself

It's challenging to find balance in our busy lives today. But the first step is taking the time to know yourself. As the Renaissance poet Sir John Davies wrote:

> *We that acquaint ourselves with every zone*
> *And pass both tropics, and behold the poles,*
> *When we come home, are to ourselves unknown,*
> *And unacquainted still with our own souls.*

The title of this Davies poem, *Nosce Teipsum* (no skay tay ipsoom), means "know thyself" in Latin, a lesson that echoes from the Renaissance to today. Shakespeare's "this above all to thine own self be true" has been quoted out of context for centuries. In our own time, theologian Matthew Fox says that our culture has a desperate need for "inner work," and educator Parker Palmer has written that "the work required to 'know thyself' is neither selfish nor narcissistic" but essential for a meaningful, productive life.[6]

Psychologists see self-knowledge and self-direction as essential to our health, both individually and collectively. The alarming rise in depression and discontent throughout America and Western Europe today reveals that many people feel their actions are futile, that they have no control over their lives. But we are *not* victims of circumstance. Stanford psychologist Albert Bandura has affirmed—with the optimism of a Renaissance philosopher—that "The human mind is generative, creative, proactive, and reflective, not just reactive."[7] By becoming more mindful of the world within you, you can live more creatively in the world around you.

The Power of Focused Attention

Most of what you accomplish in life comes from the power of focused attention. In his research on creativity, psychologist Mihaly Csikszentmihalyi found that the two qualities shared by creative artists, scientists, philosophers, inventors, writers, and political leaders are the vital curiosity of childhood and the attention he calls "inner focus."[8]

For the last few chapters, you have been cultivating your curiosity, increasing your joyous CS energy by using your gifts and experimenting with your Exploration List. In this chapter you can strengthen your creativity with the power of focused attention.

Our attention directly affects our motivation. In one revealing psychological study, preschool children were offered one cookie immediately or two cookies if they could wait for fifteen minutes—a long time for a four-year-old. A researcher sat each child alone at a table with two cookies and a bell, telling them they could ring the bell to summon her and get one cookie or wait until she returned and get both. Some children rang the bell or ate the cookies as soon as she left the room, while others waited until she returned. Videotapes revealed that those who waited directed their attention *away* from the cookies, while those who sat there staring at the cookies simply could not hold out.

Learning to direct our attention has a major impact on our lives. A ten-year follow-up study revealed that, as teenagers, the children who had waited for the cookies had better self-control, greater concentration skills, higher SAT scores, and were less likely to use drugs than the other students. Additional studies have shown that when we know how to direct our attention, plan ahead, and make informed choices, we become healthier, happier, and more successful.[9]

Finding Time to Check In

Focusing your attention on your direction, goal, and values makes the difference between efficiency—cramming dozens of activities into your day—and effectiveness, doing things that really matter. Without time to reflect, you could be distracted, overwhelmed, or pulled in too many directions at once because you can't see the larger patterns. Your Examen will actually *save* you time by keeping you from doing things you don't really care about. Remember: Small actions over time produce monumental results. For your Examen, choose a regular time and place to check in with yourself:

- Ten minutes in the morning as you plan your day
- Ten minutes at the end of the day—perhaps on the bus or train on the way home from work
- A few minutes before going to bed

Now that you've chosen a time for your Examen, the rest of this chapter will show you how to do it.

The Examen: Models from the Past

In the Renaissance, St. Ignatius Loyola asked each Jesuit to pause for a brief Examen three times a day—the first thing in the morning, after the noon meal, and at the end of the day. Their Examens included:

- Praying for the grace of understanding
- Reviewing the day's events for patterns of consolation and desolation

- Expressing gratitude for blessings, sorrow for sins
- Asking God's grace and forgiveness
- Resolving to do better in the future

The Jesuits have practiced a version of this Examen for centuries, sharing it with others in their retreats and spiritual direction.[10]

During the American Enlightenment, Benjamin Franklin practiced a more secular version of the Examen. In his mid-twenties, Franklin resolved to improve his life, developing a system for virtuous living. Taking out his account book, he entered the twelve virtues of Temperance, Silence, Order, Resolution, Frugality, Industry, Sincerity, Justice, Moderation, Cleanliness, Tranquility, and Chastity. When a Quaker friend told him that people considered him too proud, he added a thirteenth virtue—Humility.

Franklin's common sense told him what research in hope psychology has now revealed: that our goals need to be measurable. He added a definition for each virtue, making them more specific, like the goal you set for yourself in chapter four. For him, Temperance meant "Eat not to dullness. Drink not to elevation." Franklin was striving for moderation. Silence, for Franklin, meant "Speak not but what may benefit others or yourself. Avoid trifling conversation," which meant avoiding gossip, negative talk, and idle chatter.

Every week, Franklin used his account book to focus on one of the thirteen virtues. Each morning, he would review this virtue, asking himself, "What good shall I do this day?" In the evening, he asked, "What good have I done today?" and marked any faults in his ledger. When he'd gone through all thirteen virtues, he began another cycle. At first he made many "fault" marks in his ledger, but, as he improved, they gradually diminished.

Franklin kept up his Examen for years. At age seventy-nine, he credited this practice with his success in life, his "evenness of temper and . . . cheerfulness in conversation." His Examen helped him recognize both his strengths and limitations. He knew he had a strong personality and could not overcome his pride: "Disguise it, struggle with it, beat it down, stifle it, mortify it as much as one pleases, it is still alive, and will every now and then peep out and show itself." He concluded that "even if I could conceive that I had completely overcome it, I should probably be proud of my humility." Yet Franklin said that "though I never arrived at the perfection I had been so ambitious of obtaining . . . yet I was by the endeavor a better and a happier man than I otherwise should have been."

Franklin led a remarkable life. Beginning work at age ten, as an apprentice in his brother's print shop, he had little formal education but became a successful printer, writer, philosopher, scientist, and statesman. He wrote *Poor Richard's Almanac,* experimented with electricity, invented the lightning rod, the Franklin stove, bifocals, and the glass harmonica. He was elected to London's Royal Society, served as postmaster of Philadelphia, deputy postmaster of the American colonies, and the first postmaster of the new United States. He read widely, acquired a large library, and taught himself French. A tireless innovator, he helped establish the Philadelphia Fire Insurance Company and the University of Pennsylvania, serving as their first presidents as well as president of Pennsylvania Hospital, the American Philosophical Society, and the Pennsylvania Society for the Abolition of Slavery. As a statesman and patriot, he served as a colonel in the Philadelphia regiment and went on several diplomatic missions to France and England, helped draft the Declaration of Independence, and developed the compromise that produced the United States Constitution. He received honorary degrees from Harvard and Yale as well as honorary doctorates from St. Andrews and Oxford universities.

Franklin's plan—drawing up a list of virtues, or values, reviewing them, setting goals, and checking his progress each day—has been adapted by contemporary management consultants, including Hyrum Smith of the Franklin Covey day planners. His practical approach to virtuous living anticipates many principles in Stephen Covey's philosophy of leadership.[11]

Daily Examens Today

From the Renaissance to today, an Examen generally includes four steps:

1. Focusing attention on your goals and values
2. A daily review to measure your behavior by these guidelines
3. Learning from both successes and failures
4. Planning to improve in the future

Daily Examens have become an important part of coaching and counseling. Sports psychologist Jerry Lynch asks athletes he works with to pause after each event to ask themselves two simple questions—"What went well?" and "What needs work?"—focusing first on their successful performance, then on how to improve their performance in the future. Health psychologist Tom Plante says that his clients need "ongoing assessment and corrective feedback" to support behavior change. In addition to checking in with them during therapy, he works with them to develop ways to monitor their progress. When beginning a new routine, some clients record their progress in daily planners, while others keep spreadsheets or e-mail their pedometer readings to him between sessions. The important thing, he says, is to find a practice that works for each person.[12]

Many people today incorporate Examens into their lives. As a licensed esthetician, Karen pauses to reflect on her goals and values each morning. Then she welcomes clients into her quiet salon, where they relax on a recliner as she gives them facials and skin treatments with gentle, healing herbs. Years ago, Karen became dissatisfied with her job as a hairstylist. Recalling her own skin problems as a teenager, she realized how profoundly our skin is connected to our self-esteem, so she trained as an esthetician. Now she enjoys treating her clients, who often confide in her, telling her about their lives and what's "getting under their skin," as she listens compassionately, feeling a deep spiritual connection to her work.

Gary, a successful scientist, practices his own abbreviated Examen. Rejecting the complexities of planners and electronic organizers, he keeps his priorities on a three-by-five index card, which he reviews each morning. Every Sunday evening he reviews his plans and priorities, keeping two weeks at a time on his card, each week separated by a horizontal line. Anything beyond his ordinary routine—special projects, meetings, veterinary appointments for his horse—he writes on the card. This simple practice also keeps him from over-scheduling himself. "If it won't fit on the card," he says, "then I know I'm trying to do too much."

Personal Exercise: Begin Your Daily Examen

It's time to begin your own Examen. You've already chosen a time to check in with yourself: ten minutes in the morning or evening. Now you can set up your Examen, using this simple formula. Take out your Renaissance Notebook and write down the formula, filling in your direction, goal, and values from Phase One of this book.

1. My direction _____; my current goal
    _____

2. My guiding values:
    _____

3. What brought me consolation (joy, energy, vitality, authenticity, serenity)?

4. What brought me desolation (sadness, confusion, anger, doubt, despair)?

5. What would I do differently next time?

Now write your formula on a three-by-five card to consult as your daily Examen. Each day, review your card. See yourself using these lessons to improve your performance. Make any necessary plans, modifying your pathways or goals if needed.

You may practice your Examen as a silent reflection, as Brother Lawrence did working in the monastery kitchen, or you can record it as Franklin did, using your Renaissance Notebook. The most important thing is to perform it daily. Reflecting on your values, direction, and goal will keep you in touch with your dreams, while focusing on consolations will inspire you. A recent study found that people who recorded each day for a week three things that brought them joy and their causes significantly increased their happiness and well-being.[13]

Shadows on the Path:
Turning from Darkness to Light

As Guy discovered when he grew restless and unhappy with his overextended life, identifying desolations can bring you valuable insights, helping you get back in touch with your dreams. But desolations can also drag you down. The difference is in how you face them.

What psychologists call *ruminating*—worrying, obsessing about negative situations—can drain your energy and lead you into depression, while asking "What can I learn from this?" helps you move into a larger pattern of learning and growth.

The abiding wisdom of many traditions moves people from desolation to renewal, darkness to light. Cutting-edge businesses now focus on employee strengths rather than weaknesses. Anna Miller-Tiedeman, president of the New Careering Institute, Inc., suggests thinking not about right and wrong decisions but "right and *left*," maintaining that we can learn important lessons from both directions in life. She calls our attention to this because, as she says, "You don't make decisions outside the confines of your body. It's all a system and when you stress about your decisions or anything else, your immune system is implicated and this can become a health concern." This linking of decision making to the immune system is a sea change in counseling thought that can light your path today.[14]

RENAISSANCE QUESTION

When you experience desolation—make a mistake or feel restless and dissatisfied—don't ruminate. Think in terms of right and *left* turns, realizing that both hold vital lessons. Ask:

"What can I learn from this?"

Moving Forward

As you use your daily Examen to live your calling and use your gifts more effectively, research has found that this practice will also bring you greater health and happiness, dispelling stress, depression, guilt, resentment, and anxiety.[15] But the effects extend far beyond your personal life. By connecting your creative energies to your deepest values, you will create new possibilities, find new solutions to old problems, doing your part to help heal disease, despair, and the cycles of violence, lighting the world with new sources of energy. By developing a Renaissance within you, you help create a new Renaissance around you, affirming new patterns of hope to inspire and renew our world.

Take a few minutes now to reflect on your progress, writing your answers and today's date in your Renaissance Notebook.

1. Have you begun your daily Examen? If not, begin today.
2. Where did you find your CS joy this week?
3. Have you followed any actions on your Exploration List? What did you learn? If not, review your list and choose one action to explore.
4. What was your creative victory in this chapter and how are you celebrating it?

RENAISSANCE REMINDERS

Your calling is your vocation of destiny that brings greater joy and meaning to your life.

Each day:

- ~ Stay on course with your daily Examen.
- ~ Embrace the light of consolation with joy and gratitude.
- ~ Learn from "left turns."
- ~ Move forward with confidence as a new Renaissance person.

CHAPTER 7

Renaissance Community

Gaining Support from Mentors and Friends

No man is an island, entire of itself;
Every man is a piece of the continent, a part of the main.
—JOHN DONNE, *DEVOTIONS*[1]

In the seventeenth century, John Donne wrote that "No man is an island," and today, psychologists agree that we need a supportive community to develop a healthy sense of self. Renaissance men and women did not develop their callings alone. They benefited from role models, mentors, and supportive friendships. Young people learned their craft from their parents or were sent out to work from age ten through their teens. Boys became apprentices or pages in noble households, working-class girls became household servants, and girls from aristocratic families became maids of honor. Living in their mentors' households, Renaissance young people acquired not only valuable skills but the values and responsibilities of adulthood. Apprenticeships or service generally lasted seven years, after which most young adults moved on to higher positions and married.[2]

Unlike our Renaissance counterparts, you and I live in a fast-paced, compartmentalized culture. Most young Americans have little experience with the world of work and precious little interaction with their parents or other adults, spending most of their time with their peers—an average of thirty-five hours a week outside of school. Longer work hours have curtailed parents' time with their children. On average, teenagers spend only thirty minutes a week alone with their fathers, and only 34 percent of American families now have dinner together regularly.[3]

Jack and Sheila have high-paying jobs and a spacious home with a cleaning service, gardener, two cars, and an SUV. But all this comes at a price: they are almost never home. Their schedules are packed with commitments as they navigate between business and after-school activities for their three children. On most nights, six-year-old Brendan heats up his own frozen dinner in the microwave; teenagers Steve and Jackie eat on the run between school, karate, and soccer practice; and their parents pick up fast food on the way home. Beneath this hectic surface, Sheila hates her job, Steve is having trouble at school, and seventeen-year-old Jackie is worried about her future, but they never have time to talk to each other.

This family's plight is all too common. To pursue our callings as new Renaissance men and women, we need to develop what psychologist Sharon Daloz Parks calls "mentoring communities," relationships that support us in living with greater joy and purpose.[4] This chapter will help you build your own Renaissance community.

Looking Back

To see what such a community looks like, let's go back to the Renaissance, when helping others develop their callings was considered a vital responsibility. When parents failed to support their children's callings, other adults were there to help. Although Michelangelo's father initially opposed his son's artistic calling, Francesco Granacci, a young artist and friend of the family, recognized Michelangelo's talent and took him to visit the studio of artist Domenico Ghirlandaio. With Granacci's encouragement, Michelangelo's father finally apprenticed his son to Ghirlandaio. As a country parson, George Herbert saw support for vocations as part of his ministry, making regular visits to parishioners' homes and shops to encourage them in their callings.[5]

Renaissance culture encouraged people to seek out positive role models. Scholars and artists developed their skills by imitating the masters. As a young apprentice, Botticelli studied the frescos of Masaccio, who had learned from the art of Giotto and classical antiquity. Mature artists learned from one another as well. Despite their rivalry, Leonardo da Vinci made a sketch of Michelangelo's *David* in one of his notebooks.[6]

Did you have a supportive teacher who acknowledged your gifts? Many people in the Renaissance did as well. Astronomer Johannes Kepler found a mentor in Michael Maestlin, his professor at the University of Tübingen, who introduced him to Copernican theory. Kepler went on to discover the laws of planetary motion. While a student at the University of Padua, William Harvey learned about the new astronomy from his professor, Galileo Galilei. When Harvey discovered the circulation of the blood, he followed Galileo's example, comparing the heart to the sun as the center of our circulatory system.

Some people found mentors in their local communities or leaders in their professions. George Herbert was encouraged in his poetry and ministerial studies by John Donne. Young poets Vittoria Colonna and Veronica Gambara found encouragement corresponding with scholar Peter Bembo.[7]

Born a shoemaker's son in Canterbury in 1564, the same year Shakespeare was born, Christopher Marlowe was supported by his local community, which gave him scholarships to King's School, Canterbury, and Corpus Christi College, Cambridge. When Marlowe went to London to seek his fortune in 1587, the father of a college friend introduced him to Thomas Watson, who became his mentor. Seven years older than Marlowe, Watson was a poet, madrigal writer, and bon vivant who brought Marlowe vital connections in the theater. Within months, Marlowe's tragedy *Tamburlaine* rocked the English stage and his "mighty line" set a new standard in English drama.[8]

Some people met mentors while traveling. When visiting Holland in 1618, René Descartes met Isaac Beeckman, a young doctor eight years his senior who shared his interest in mathematics, corresponding with him for years. After finishing his education at Cambridge, John Milton traveled to Italy in 1638, sharing his poetry with eminent scholars there who encouraged him in his calling, a welcome vote of confidence to a young man with a dream.[9]

You can find different mentors in different seasons of your life. Political philosopher John Locke's first mentor was his father, a Puritan lawyer and county clerk who taught him about popular sovereignty and the power of parliament. At Oxford, John found mentors in his professors, and was then influenced by Descartes and Robert Boyle, founder of the Royal Society, with whom he conversed and corresponded for years. In later life, Locke found a supportive friend and patron in the Earl of Shaftesbury.[10]

What Mentors Bring You

Mentors help you overcome challenges and move forward in the new world, or domain, of your calling. As psychologist Mihaly Csikszentmihalyi has found, each field has its own principles, skills, and vocabulary—foundation knowledge—which you must master to do your own creative work.[11]

Today, people are often impatient learning the basics, yet these are the building blocks of greatness. Musicians must learn their way around an instrument, practicing until their brains build new neural pathways and the instrument becomes an extension of themselves. Actors must become attuned to their own instruments of body and voice. To think like scientists, young researchers must learn the scientific method and acquire basic knowledge in their fields.

Renaissance artists gained foundation knowledge in the early stages of apprenticeship. Botticelli, Leonardo, and others began by learning to mix paints: grinding colored stones and blending them with oil or egg yolks. Making hundreds of sketches, they learned to draw from nature and by imitating other artists, with the master coming by to offer advice. Later they were allowed to paint, first filling in a portion of sky or clothing, and next a minor figure in one of their master's paintings. Only then could they begin producing their own work.[12]

Mentors not only provide you with essential foundation knowledge, they also build hope. A good mentor can strengthen your pathways and sense of agency, helping you believe in yourself and your vocation.

The Pygmalion Effect

When someone believes in you, you can do amazing things. In their remarkable 1968 study, psychologist Robert Rosenthal and school principal Lenore Jacobson selected 20 percent of students at random from a California elementary school. They told the teachers that these "special" students would have an intellectual growth spurt later that year, and their predictions came true. By the end of the year, the "special" children increased their IQs and achieved higher grades and test scores than the others. But the only *real* difference between these children and the others was in the teachers' minds. They had seen these students as gifted, expected them to do well—and they did. This result, called the "Pygmalion effect," demonstrates the powerful effect of others' expectations on our lives.[13]

Have you had someone who believed in you, someone who made a major difference in your life? If so, you know this Pygmalion effect first hand. If not, you can experience it by cultivating your own Renaissance community.

Personal Exercise:
Cultivate Your Renaissance Community

This exercise will help you cultivate your own Renaissance community by (1) finding a mentor, (2) being a better mentor to yourself, and (3) becoming a mentor to others.

1. Find a Mentor.

If you don't have a mentor, you can begin cultivating a mentoring relationship right now.

Find an Experienced Guide. If you are entering a new stage of life, an experienced mentor can provide knowledge, advice, and a network of connections. Your guide may be someone in your own or a related field. When I was a young English professor, I found two mentors: Elizabeth, a tenured professor in my department, and Bill, a tenured professor of physics. Elizabeth advised me on teaching and service, while Bill helped with my research agenda. Each gave me strategic advice, wisdom, and guidance as well as the priceless gift of friendship.

Take Positive Action. Your guide may be a senior member of your profession or your community. When you've found a potential mentor, arrange a meeting. Send an e-mail or call for an appointment. Invite this person to coffee or lunch. Ask a short advice question. If you get a positive response, you've found a mentor. If not, try someone else.

Chris was a theology major in college but minored in finance to please his parents. While he found some of his business courses interesting, his theology courses really inspired him, resonating with his Catholic faith. He made retreats to discern his vocation, then worked as a grant writer before going to law school. During his second year in law school he began feeling anxious, wondering if his personal values would really translate into this cutthroat culture. Looking for guidance, he joined the St. Thomas More Society, a group of Catholic judges and lawyers who meet twice monthly for mass and a meal. There he met a prominent lawyer and began a mentoring friendship. His mentor became executive director of the California Commission on the Fair Administration of Justice, inviting Chris to become his assistant. Now Chris works to exonerate people wrongfully convicted of crimes, seeing his values and legal training converging in his vocation. By promoting justice and responding to very real human needs, he feels that he's standing in a long tradition of dedicated people who have made a positive difference in their communities.

Recruit Your Mentoring Team. You may need advice in a variety of areas. Jeanne wanted to be a recording artist, so she recruited a mentoring team of a successful musician she admired, another aspiring musician, and the owner of a recording studio. She meets with her team regularly to brainstorm about their work and has just produced a music video. She's now looking for an agent to add to her mentoring team.

Take Positive Action. Pick your team by asking what skills and information you'll need, then look for people who know these things. Contact them by e-mail or phone and set up appointments. If you feel empowered and energized by them, they're valuable team members. If not, keep looking.

Sometimes we find our mentoring team by following our inclinations. A few years ago I went to a "Spirituality and Health" luncheon organized by psychologist Tom Plante. It was so much fun I kept going back. We have now become the Spirituality and Health Institute (SHI), a group of psychologists, theologians, researchers, and health and counseling professionals from Stanford, Berkeley, Santa Clara, and the surrounding community who meet to share ideas and collaborate on projects. I've been working with my SHI colleagues on four different research projects as well as a book and a national conference. Now that's a great mentoring team!

Now choose one of these ways to find your own mentor and begin experiencing a positive difference in your life.

2. Be a Better Mentor to Yourself

Another kind of mentoring is your relationship with yourself. As psychologist Jon Kabat-Zinn says, "Wherever you go, there you are."[14] We mentor ourselves constantly through our inner dialogue. If you're like most people, you could be a better friend to yourself. Here's how:

- Listen to what you tell yourself. Are you supportive, or do you call yourself names? If so, you are sabotaging yourself, producing the exact *opposite* of the Pygmalion effect. Change your inner dialogue by using your favorite affirmation, or the one from the last chapter:

> May I be filled with loving kindness.
> May I be well.
> May I be peaceful and be free.
> May I be happy.

The next time you hear yourself engaging in abusive self-talk, STOP. Say your affirmation instead.

- Smile at Yourself. Not only do we smile when we're happy, but psychologists have discovered that smiling can actually *make* you happy, causing a physiological change on the left side of your brain.[15] When you see a friend, what do you do, naturally? You smile. When you see yourself in the mirror, do you smile? Many people don't. They scowl and obsess about tiny flaws. If you do this, STOP. Be a better friend to yourself: Smile.

3. Be a Mentor to Others

You complete the mentoring cycle by becoming a mentor to others. Psychologists have recently discovered what Renaissance artists knew as they mentored their apprentices: that there is deep fulfillment in empowering others, great joy in passing it on.[16]

You can mentor most effectively by setting a positive example, pursuing your own personal Renaissance while offering wisdom and support. Mentoring is a relationship of mutual respect, not codependency. Remember to keep your balance, to be a mentor, not a martyr. Don't sacrifice your own creative growth in your desire to help others. Stay balanced by remembering to:

- Listen to your own CS.
- Stay in touch with your energies and what they're telling you.
- Practice discernment, noting patterns of consolation and desolation. True mentoring brings consolation to all.

Some ways to become a mentor are to:

- Acknowledge People's Gifts. Make a positive difference in people's lives by simply acknowledging their gifts. Instead of saying "That's a great outfit," complimenting someone's clothes, say "That's a beautiful outfit. You have such a *gift* for color and design." If your friend has solved a difficult problem, say "You have a real *gift* of resourcefulness." Look for the gift beneath the action.

- Mentor a Younger Colleague. Meet a younger colleague for lunch or coffee and then listen. Point out the person's gifts (as above), offer encouragement, then check back to offer support. One thing I love about my life as a college professor is becoming a mentor to my students. It's one way I can honor the professor who helped me believe in my own gifts—by following his example and passing it on.

- Create an Apprenticeship. Some resourceful individuals are reinventing the Renaissance tradition of apprenticeship. For over twenty years, California veterinarian Dr. David Reed has been creating his own apprenticeships by hiring high school students as veterinary assistants, giving them a chance "to see how an actual hospital works." "They can watch veterinarians on TV," he says, but unless they have "direct hands-on experience," they won't know what it's really like to be a veterinarian. Working part time after school and weekends, they begin with the fundamentals, checking pets in, weighing them, cleaning kennels. If Dr. Reed sees they have a real interest and aptitude, he helps them develop their skills. By shadowing experienced vets, they learn how to give shots and insert catheters, becoming veterinary technicians and finding out "if they want to do this for the rest of their lives." Dr. Reed's apprentices work with him for two or three years, then go on to college and, often, on to veterinary school.

With a smile, Dr. Reed told me of a young man from Israel who wrote every veterinarian in Santa Clara County asking for a job. He said he was willing to start at the beginning, that he'd driven a tank in the Israeli army, and could live with his sister in Santa Clara. Dr. Reed wrote back that if he could drive a tank in the army, he could work in his clinic. The young man worked for him for six years, attending community college part time, then going on to vet school. Today, he is a professor of veterinary medicine at UC Davis, one of the top veterinary hospitals in the country.

Many of Dr. Reed's former apprentices are now successful veterinarians, while others have found careers in business and other professions. Whether or not they become veterinarians, they learn discipline, precision, and responsibility, valuable skills for success in life.

A successful apprenticeship is a win-win experience. You can get help with routine tasks, and give a young person an inside view of your life's work. Could you use a young assistant in your office or organization? If so, set up your own apprenticeship. Place an ad at your local high school or college. You'll be helping to create a new Renaissance in your community.[17]

- Share Your Wisdom in Retirement. If you're retiring, you can share your wisdom by volunteering for a cause you believe in. Join the thousands of active men and women making a positive difference in their communities. The opportunities are many. You can offer your time and talents to your local school, community center, professional organization, church, mosque, synagogue, or favorite social cause. If you have Internet access, the Elder Wisdom Circle welcomes volunteers over sixty at www.elderwisdomcircle.org.

New Renaissance Mentoring Today

Cultivating a mentoring community today takes more initiative than in the Renaissance, but the rewards are worth the effort.

Like his Renaissance counterparts, New Mexico artist R. C. Gorman was encouraged by a teacher who helped him believe in his gifts. He later received a tribal scholarship to study art in Mexico City, where Diego Rivera and other artists helped him develop his foundation knowledge. When he returned home, he began painting people from his Navajo culture with the bold strokes and vivid colors of Mexican art. Throughout his long career, Gorman continued to learn from other artists, visiting Europe to study the works of Michelangelo, Leonardo, Van Gogh, and Picasso, and he enjoyed mentoring younger artists as well.[18]

Some people begin mentoring relationships through correspondence. In her twenties, Denise Levertov wrote a letter to distinguished poet William Carlos Williams. He responded graciously, offering encouragement, friendship, and advice on her work. Their friendship continued as Levertov became a celebrated poet in her own right.[19]

International portrait photographer Michael Collopy actively sought out mentoring relationships. He found his first mentor in his father, a successful graphic artist, but when he decided to become a photographer, he had to arrange his own apprenticeships. After seeing an Ansel Adams exhibit in Oakland, Collopy got Adams' number from Information and called him. The two men met and became friends, with Adams sharing his expertise in black and white photography, love of nature, and dedication to environmental causes. When Collopy realized he wanted to photograph people, he went to New York to meet photographer Richard Avedon. He stood outside Avedon's studio for days, waiting for him to come out. Collopy's patience paid off and he learned more valuable lessons.

Returning to California, Collopy took a job as a yearbook photographer to gain portrait experience, then began photographing entertainers at a local theater and world leaders at a regional lecture series. In 1982, when he went to hear Mother Teresa speak, by serendipity he ran into her in a corridor, which led to a strong and inspirational friendship. He visited her in Calcutta, and published his photographic tribute, *Works of Love as Works of Peace,* in 1996. Collopy's compelling portraits of world leaders appear in his book, *Architects of Peace* (2000). I met him in 2004 when Santa Clara hosted an exhibit of his work. His portraits of Mother Teresa, Jimmy Carter, Jane Goodall, Linus Pauling, and others now grace the halls of our arts and sciences building. Offering personal inspiration, Collopy shares his story with students, encouraging them to develop their callings as well.[20]

Developing your Renaissance community takes courage and persistence. Your potential mentor is probably busy, may not agree to meet, may not even answer you, but you'll never know until you've tried. Years ago, while writing *The Tao of Inner Peace,* I contacted many people for interviews. Some ignored me, others declined, but I had wonderful conversations with Linus Pauling and Norman Cousins, and my interview with Frances Moore Lappé blossomed into friendship. In 2003, when Frankie and her daughter, Anna, came to Santa Clara on tour for their new book, *Hope's Edge,* I met their train from San Francisco and we embraced in celebration.

Shadows on the Path:
Outgrown or Unhealthy Relationships

A mentor can be a tremendous force for good in your life, but the reverse is also true. It's important to recognize when you've outgrown a mentoring relationship or, even worse, when a relationship is toxic. We gain valuable knowledge from our mentors, but at some point it's time to move on. This need not be a hostile break. In the Renaissance, Botticelli became a master with his own distinctive style, while staying in touch with his mentor, Fra Filippo Lippi, later taking Lippi's son as his own apprentice.

There are parallels for moving on in many fields. When I was in my twenties, I took flying lessons. One day, my instructor climbed out of the plane and said, "Now, take it around by yourself." Excited and shaky, I taxied the yellow Cessna up to the runway, got my clearance, and took off. All alone up there, I flew the plane around the pattern, then landed and steered the plane off the runway. I had soloed.

That night, I called my dad, who'd been a flight instructor for decades. After he congratulated me, I asked him, "How do you know when someone's ready to solo?" His answer surprised me. "Timing is essential," he said. "Of course it's dangerous to solo someone too soon, but if you wait too long, that person will never solo."

The lesson holds true in many fields. If we become too dependent upon our instructors, we will never learn to fly on our own.

> ## RENAISSANCE QUESTIONS
>
> If you've been in a long-term mentoring relationship, are you ready to solo? These questions will help you find out:
>
> ~ Have I learned all I can from this person?
> ~ Do I feel confined, fenced in, like I cannot express my own voice?
> ~ Is it time to move on?
>
> Remember, you are here to follow your own calling, not copy someone else. If you're ready to solo, give the person a gift or write a letter expressing your gratitude. You can stay in touch, but you are no longer an apprentice. It's time to follow your own guiding star.

Avoiding Toxic Personalities

Outgrowing a mentoring relationship is one thing, but some relationships are toxic, shaming you and sabotaging your dreams. Unless you're a clinical psychologist, it's no good trying to figure them out. The best thing you can do is recognize them and get away.

There's a world of difference between toxic criticism and the advice of friends and mentors. Constructive criticism helps us improve, while toxic criticism demoralizes us. I once had a toxic colleague at work who would come up with smiles and pleasantries, then launch into verbal attacks. His accusations felt eerily familiar, taking me back to a shaming interaction in my past.

When I was in the seventh grade, the U.S. Air Force sent my father to command a radar site in Nebraska farm country. Each day, the few children living on the base were driven to school in Omaha by an airman in a blue staff car. That January, my brother and I were enrolled in an Omaha parochial school.

I had always been a good student and since I was new I raised my hand to ask lots of questions. Standing over us in her long black habit, Sister Mary Paul expected students to be obedient, not ask questions, and not talk back. If anyone misbehaved, the whole class had to stay after school. This happened twice the first week I was there and the driver in the air force staff car had to wait until my class was dismissed.

Since there was no school cafeteria, my mother packed me a bag lunch every day, with a sandwich, fruit, cookies, or sometimes a slice of pie in a plastic container. I was eating my lunch one day when Sister Mary Paul came up to my desk. "Diane," she said sternly, "good little Catholic girls do *not* wear lipstick!"

I wasn't wearing lipstick. Then I looked at my lunch. "I don't wear lipstick," I said. "I've just been eating this cherry pie."

She stormed across the room, called me a liar, and made the whole class stay an hour after school. The air force staff car with all the other children had to wait outside in the snow, and it was dark when we finally got back to the base. Used to military precision, my father was angry. This was the third time in two weeks the children were late getting home because of my class. In the morning, he called the principal and pulled his children out of that school.

The next week, I went to McMillan Junior High School on the other side of Omaha, where my teacher, Mrs. Striker, praised me for speaking up and asking questions, the same behavior that had gotten me in trouble the week before. Mrs. Striker thought I was a "gifted child," and invited me to wear my costumes from our overseas travels for social studies reports. At home each night, I'd happily spend hours reading about other countries, drawing maps, preparing my costumes and reports.

The McMillan cafeteria had hot meals with pie for dessert, and Mrs. Striker ate lunch with us, sharing her ideas about history, nutrition, and culture. I don't know if I was a gifted child, but she was a master teacher. Her class excelled on all the tests and she took a group of us in costume to the Nebraska State Teachers' Conference for a model social studies presentation.

Two schools, two weeks, two completely different lives. In one school, I was a juvenile delinquent, in the other a genius. I'm grateful for Mrs. Striker and the Pygmalion effect and sometimes wonder what would have become of me if I'd stayed in the other school.

Dealing with Toxic Personalities

Is there a toxic personality in your life: an authority figure from the past, a boss or colleague today? You can recognize them because their criticism is:

- Irrational. They don't listen to reason and seem personally biased against you.
- Unexpected. They may appear friendly, but then—usually in front of other people—they stun you with toxic criticism.
- Destructive. A mentor will point out problems while offering helpful advice, but toxic criticism is meant to sabotage you.

You cannot reason with toxic personalities, you cannot befriend them, and you cannot satisfy them. What you *can* do is recognize and avoid them, protecting yourself from further shaming. New Renaissance men and women support each other's creative growth. Those who sabotage you or block your calling are not your friends.

If a toxic personality has shamed you in the past, free yourself from the negativity by writing about it.

1. Record the incident in your Renaissance Notebook or write the person a letter you will *not* send, saying that you refuse to accept this shame.

2. Then take a walk, buy yourself a present, or do something special to celebrate your liberation.
3. If you're still troubled by the incident, get professional help.

Toxic personalities often attack people they see as "different." My former student, Brian, a gifted actor and poet, works at a blue collar job to pay the rent. Because he reads during his lunch hour, one of his coworkers lashes out at him, questioning his masculinity and the quality of his work.

If a toxic personality has been attacking you at work, try keeping a record of the person's behavior and taking it to your manager. But don't be surprised if the toxic person has infiltrated the system. You may need to get a transfer or look for another job. That's what Brian is doing. Life is too short to spend with toxic personalities.

Our relationships make a tremendous difference in our lives. You deserve a Renaissance community, people who support you in living a healthy, fulfilling life. Don't settle for anything less.

Your Friendship Circle

Psychologists have long realized that friends are good for our health, but only recently have they found that seeking friendship is a natural response to stress. In addition to the familiar "fight or flight" response, UCLA psychologist Shelley Taylor says that we have an equally common tendency to "tend and befriend," to seek out supportive friendships.[21]

This need to befriend explains teenagers' need to "hang out" with their peers, searching for support in their stressful journey to adulthood. It also explains why troops returning from combat often miss the close emotional bonds they formed with their buddies.

Many people develop close friendships in college or graduate school. As the first college graduate in my family, I entered graduate school at UCLA as unknown territory. Anxious before our first exam, I invited other students to my apartment for a pizza and study session. We not only passed that exam but also became close friends, sharing years of laughter, support, and inspiration. Decades later, I realize how much my close circle of friends contributed to the joy of those years. Although life has taken us in different directions, my UCLA friends will always have a special place in my heart.

Personal Exercise: Cultivate Your Friendship Circle

As you move forward in your personal Renaissance, you are entering unknown territory. A close circle of friends can support you on the journey. Sharing goals, pathways, and moral support, you and your friends can enhance each other's creative growth.

- Make a list of your friends—people who support you, listen, are honest without being offensive, and energize you with new insights.
- Get back in touch with a call or e-mail if you haven't seen them lately.
- Meet with your friendship circle regularly, either one-on-one or as a group.

My latest friendship circle came together at our local high school track. Twice a week, my husband, Bob, and I go there for regular workouts, where we meet Tom, a gifted nature photographer, and Michelle, a multitalented psychologist, musician, writer, and consultant. Combining our workouts with insights from neuroscience, psychology, art, and music, we support each other in everything from life's mountains and valleys to our current creative projects, always energized by our time together.

Developing your Renaissance community is a gift to others as well as yourself, making the world a more creative and friendly place.

Moving Forward

Take a few minutes now to reflect on your progress in this chapter, writing your answers and today's date in your Renaissance Notebook.

1. Have you increased your CS joy by being a better friend and mentor to yourself this week?
2. Do you have a mentor or mentoring team? Have you found a way to mentor others? If not, think of one step you can take, write it on your Exploration List, and do it next week.
3. Do you have any toxic personalities in your life? If so, what are you doing to deal with them?
4. Are you in touch with your friendship circle? If not, reach out to a friend today.
5. What was your creative victory in this chapter and how are you celebrating it?

RENAISSANCE REMINDERS

New Renaissance men and women follow their callings and support each other's creative growth.
Remember to:

~ Cultivate your own Renaissance community.
~ Be mindful of small ways to mentor others each day.
~ Smile and be a better mentor to yourself.

CHAPTER 8

Contemplation

Finding Your Inner Oasis of Peace

A paradise within thee, happier far.
—JOHN MILTON, *PARADISE LOST*[1]

As Renaissance philosophers realized, life depends on the dynamic balance of action and contemplation. We all need time for friends, family, and community as well as personal time for reflection and renewal, a balance as essential to health as breathing in and breathing out.

Yet today this balance is hard to find, for technology has blurred the boundaries of our lives, depriving us of *both* companionship and contemplation. A recent UCLA study showed many contemporary families not only lack time for silence and solitude, they rarely speak to each other! They're "plugged in" to computers, cell phones, TV, video games, and iPods. Caught up in frantic schedules, too many of us live mechanically, so busy "doing" that we neglect our essential being.

Susan managed the office for a busy medical group, welcoming patients, handling insurance forms, and juggling dozens of daily tasks. At home she managed the meals, budgeting, and household chores for her husband and two daughters. But despite her work in health care, Susan's life was anything but healthy. She had chronic tension headaches, her neck and shoulders were always tight, and she felt her heart racing whenever responsibilities piled up, she faced a tight deadline, or the people around her had problems.

When Susan attended one of my vocation day retreats with a friend from church, she was so overwhelmed she couldn't come up with an answer to "What brings you joy?" Later, during a guided meditation, she realized how imbalanced her life had become. She left the retreat with two new goals: to begin a meditation practice and balance her own needs with those of the people around her, but she wondered how she'd fit meditation into her busy life.

The lives of Renaissance men and women were much less frantic. Without electricity or advanced technology, they followed natural cycles of action and contemplation. They worked by day and read at night by lamp or candlelight, and most of them went to bed early. Leonardo da Vinci enjoyed regular periods of silence and solitude. Sir Thomas More, Magdalen Herbert, Thomas Traherne, and many others meditated regularly, beginning their days in prayer, pausing for spaces of silence, finding renewal in nature. Their contemplative practice may have even made Renaissance men and women more creative, for psychologists have found important connections between meditation and creativity.[2]

In your own personal Renaissance, the contemplative practice you begin in this chapter will help you balance your life with greater wisdom and serenity.

Contemplative Practice

Contemplative practice or meditation—I use these terms interchangeably—occurs in many faiths, including Judaism, Christianity, Buddhism, Hinduism, Taoism, Native American religions, and Islam. Research has shown that all forms of meditation will focus your attention, producing greater mental, spiritual, and physical well-being. During meditation, you often feel a deep sense of peacefulness, clarity, and relaxation, while the ongoing practice of meditation can subtly transform your life, bringing you greater serenity, clarity, patience, and understanding.

The three major forms of meditation are:

- Concentrative: focusing attention on an object, breath, word, or memorized passage.
- Mindfulness: focusing nonjudgmental attention on your thoughts, feelings, and external sensations.
- Contemplative: opening up to a greater source of inspiration by using a sacred word, asking a question, or reflecting on nature.[3]

Decades of research have shown that meditation can improve your health. It enhances your immune system, relieving stress-related anxiety, asthma, cardiovascular disease, chronic pain, depression, eating disorders, headaches, high cholesterol, hostility, hypertension, insomnia, panic disorders, PMS, skin disorders, stuttering, and substance abuse.

Meditation also affects your brain, producing increased activity in the left frontal lobe, the part of your brain associated with positive emotions. It builds self-compassion, making you less anxious, more mindful. Since it relieves chronic stress, which accelerates the aging process, meditation may even help you stay younger longer.

In addition, meditation makes you wiser. In the Renaissance, philosopher Marsilio Ficino saw it as the road to wisdom, and recent research has connected it with greater self-actualization and self-understanding, joy and serenity, empathy, agency, moral growth, intelligence, clarity, better memory, and improved performance.[4]

Creative individuals from the Renaissance to today have been inspired by meditation, which often brings flashes of insight, new solutions and ideas. Research in neuroscience tells us why. Like the screen on your computer, your conscious mind (or working memory) can contain only so much information. Complex decisions and large-scale projects are too much for its limited capacity. But like a powerful hard drive, your unconscious mind draws upon a vast reservoir of stored memories. Integrating millions of variables into implicit wisdom, it works with larger patterns, revealing complex solutions. Thus, perhaps the best thing you can do whenever you have a complex problem is to review the material, then meditate or rest to let your implicit wisdom emerge.[5]

Looking Back

For centuries, Renaissance men and women gained implicit wisdom from their contemplative practice. St. Ignatius's *Spiritual Exercises* influenced scores of others, including John Donne, George Herbert, Andrew Marvell, John Milton, and Thomas Traherne. St. Teresa of Avila's contemplative practice transformed her life and helped her reform the Carmelite order.

A common Renaissance belief was that everything in life holds spiritual lessons, or, as Shakespeare wrote, there are "books in the running brooks,/ Sermons in stones, and good in everything." English clergyman Joseph Hall wrote meditations "Upon a cloud," "Upon the vision of a lily," and even "Upon the barking of a dog."[6]

Meditation helped many people discover their callings. Excelling as a student at Cambridge, George Herbert impressed court officials and King James with his eloquent Latin speeches. Hoping for a political career, he was elected to Parliament in 1624, but then considered entering the ministry, asking John Donne for advice. Struggling with illness, uncertainty, and his mother's death in 1627, Herbert went to a friend's country retreat in Kent, where he meditated on his vocation. He emerged with greater clarity, becoming pastor of a country parish in Bemerton, Wiltshire, where he lived an inspired life and wrote his book *The Temple*.[7]

Herbert's French contemporary, René Descartes, was a delicate child with a natural curiosity and love of learning. At ten he was sent to boarding school at the Jesuit Collège de la Flèche, where he found a mentor in a kindly priest and excelled in his studies. In

1619, while Descartes was a soldier in Bavaria, he had a dream about reforming human knowledge with a new scientific method. He traveled to Paris, where his friends encouraged him in this new vocation. But he found Paris too distracting, so he moved to Holland, where he wrote his *Discourse on the Method* in 1637 and *Meditations* in 1641.

Descartes began his lifelong contemplative practice in boarding school. Because of frail health, he was given a private room and allowed to sleep late in the mornings, which gave him time for reading and meditation. As an adult, Descartes used the early morning hours to meditate, reflect, and write down his thoughts, beginning each day's work while still in bed.[8]

RENAISSANCE QUESTION

What is my contemplative practice?

If you have one, you need only follow it consistently. As Joseph Hall advised, "Set thine hours and keep them, and yield not to an easy distraction."[9] We each have our own daily cycles or circadian rhythms. Some people meditate in the morning. Others prefer the end of the day. What time works best for you?

If you do *not* yet have a contemplative practice, the next exercise will help you begin.

🌿 *Personal Exercise: Meditate on a Passage*

You can begin meditating or add a new dimension to your practice by focusing on an inspirational passage. The following passage meditation was adapted from the work of Sri Eknath Easwaran, Berkeley professor and founder of the Blue Mountain Center of Meditation. This nonsectarian meditation has been used by thousands of people, from spiritual seekers to busy professionals, and can be practiced within, or outside of, any faith tradition. To begin:

1. Select a short inspirational passage, a traditional prayer or devotional poem. You can find many passages, including the prayer of St. Francis of Assisi, the Twenty-third Psalm, and selections from Jewish liturgy, the Upanishads, the Bhagavad Gita, Native American tradition, and the Tao Te Ching on the Blue Mountain Web site, www.easwaran.org.

2. Easwaran recommends beginning with the prayer of St. Francis, which I use myself and share in my retreats and classes. If we become what we think about, then I cannot imagine better seeds to sow in the depths of our consciousness than this:

> *Lord, make me an instrument of thy peace.*
> *Where there is hatred, let me sow love;*
> *Where there is injury, pardon;*
> *Where there is doubt, faith;*
> *Where there is despair, hope;*
> *Where there is darkness, light;*
> *Where there is sadness, joy.*
> *O divine Master, grant that I may not so much seek*
> *To be consoled as to console,*
> *To be understood as to understand,*
> *To be loved as to love;*
> *For it is in giving that we receive;*
> *It is in pardoning that we are pardoned;*
> *It is in dying to self that we are born to eternal life.*

3. When you've chosen your passage, set aside a regular time to meditate, a half hour when you can be alone and undisturbed. I meditate in the mornings because it's a great way to begin the day and that way I'm sure my meditation will get done. Choose your time and make it a daily ritual.

4. In the beginning, set aside fifteen minutes for meditation, then gradually add five minutes at a time to expand your practice to half an hour. I use a timer so I can close my eyes, relax, and not worry about the time.

5. Sit with your back straight in a chair, on the floor, or on a cushion. (Don't lie down or you may fall asleep.) Your legs, arms, and hands can be in any comfortable position.

6. For your first session, slowly read the passage silently to yourself, letting the words soak into your consciousness. Then repeat this process, focusing on the words, thoughtfully and slowly, until the time is up. The point is to memorize the passage, engrave it into your consciousness.

7. The next time, sit with your back straight as before. You may keep the written passage to refer to if needed. With your eyes closed this time, say the passage silently to yourself in your mind, "*Lord . . . make me . . . an instrument . . . of thy . . . peace.*"

8. If—or rather, *when*—your mind strays, go back to the beginning of the passage and start again. You will have to stop and start again and again. This is normal. Our minds wander off into worries, memories, plans, and other distractions. When this happens, gently pick yourself up and go back to the beginning. "*Lord . . . make me . . . an instrument . . . of thy . . . peace.*"

The point is *not* to beat yourself up when you stray, but train your mind to go where you want it to, gently, as you would train a puppy. Imperfect as it seems, this process is your practice. Some days your mind will be filled with distractions. Other times, you'll find a brief oasis of peace, then more distractions.

That's it. Each day, at your chosen time, repeat this process, gradually expanding your time from fifteen to thirty minutes. At first, you may not feel any different, but you are gradually opening up to a deep reservoir of serenity, wisdom, and peace. As St. Teresa of Avila explained in the Renaissance, "This quiet recollection of the soul makes itself in great measure felt in the satisfaction and peace, attended with very great joy and repose of the faculties, and most sweet delight in which the soul is established."[10]

Personal Exercise: Release Tension

If you find it hard to relax when you sit down to meditate, try this simple muscle relaxation technique I learned from my friend, clinical psychologist David Feldman.

Dave says that we often store stress as tension in our muscles. We can release this tension by repeatedly tensing our muscles, then letting go. The complete muscle relaxation technique addresses muscles in all the major regions of the body.[11]

Here's a brief muscle relaxation exercise I find useful. Try it:

- First tense up the muscles in your hands. Then release them.
- Tense up these muscles again. Then release them with a long, deep breath.
- Now tense up the muscles in your arms. Again, release them.
- Tense up these muscles again with a long, deep breath.

Continue to tense and relax various groups of muscles throughout the body in this way. When you're finished, you should feel less tense, more relaxed. I often use this exercise to release tension before going to sleep.

· ·

Ways to Meditate

Many people today meditate—for inspiration, spiritual growth, stress management, health, and well-being. My friends have a wide range of contemplative practices.

Passage Meditation

Carol Lee Flinders and her husband, Tim, are writers and educators. Carol has taught at UC Berkeley and written books about medieval and contemporary women mystics. When I asked about her practice, she said that she and Tim have practiced passage meditation "every day, morning and evening, for nearly forty years." They began in the 1960s, studying in Berkeley with Eknath Easwaran, founder of the Blue Mountain Center of Meditation.

Carol and Tim sit quietly with their spines straight and eyes closed, repeating to themselves a "repertoire of inspirational passages, drawn from all of the world's great spiritual traditions."

One day this might be "a chapter from the Bhagavad Gita in the morning, a Psalm or poem by Rumi at night." Passage meditation involves repeating the words "slowly and silently, bringing attention to bear on each word with as much concentration as possible but refraining from actually thinking about the words or their meaning."

Redirecting our wandering minds is an essential part of the process, Carol says: "Attention is brought gently back whenever it wanders, over and over *and over!*"

Their passage meditation "has powerful implications for work and relationships, creativity and good health," Carol says. "In addition, when we recite the words of the St. Francis prayer to ourselves day after day, they begin to work their way down into deeper levels of consciousness and start to affect our thoughts and words and even our deeds."[12]

Ignatian Meditation

Bill Rewak is a Jesuit priest. Former president of both Santa Clara University and Spring Hill College, he is now professor of English and minister of the Jesuit Community at Loyola Marymount University. A gifted poet and teacher, Bill has been doing Ignatian meditation for over fifty years. In this form of meditation, you concentrate on a scene from the gospels and use your five senses to make it come alive. "Hear the voices," he says, "smell the odors, taste the food people are eating, touch the rough wood of the boats or the coarse wool of their garments, watch what people are doing, how they move—most especially how Jesus moves, what he says, how he's saying it, what tone of voice he is using." The meditation then moves into a conversation with Jesus. Bill says, "sometimes it's a talkative conversation, sometimes silent."

Bill meditates each morning after breakfast. Sitting quietly in his easy chair, he acknowledges he is in the presence of God, often reflecting on a passage from the Bible. His meditation time varies with the demands of the day, from ten minutes to an hour. The point, he says, is to "sit quietly with the Lord, in communion, in understanding, where words are few and the communion is a loving one." When I asked how his practice supports his vocation, he said, "My life and vocation are one: as a Jesuit priest and teacher I need to be in constant contact with Jesus, whom I regard as a friend. It is because I have been called to his service," he explained, "that I do what I do: my whole life, from head to toe, twenty-four/seven, is a living out of that service." He spends time in conversation with Jesus throughout the day, a conversation that "is both my support and my motivation."[13]

Buddhist Meditation

Juan Velasco, a gifted writer and associate professor of English and modern languages at Santa Clara, has been practicing Buddhist meditation for over fifteen years. A few years ago, he began directing a weekly meditation in our St. Francis chapel for students seeking to deal with stress and find a path to peace.

When I asked about his practice, Juan was on sabbatical in Los Angeles, writing his next book and able to meditate two hours in the morning from 5:00 to 7:00 and another two hours at night. His morning meditations involve bowing, chanting, and meditation, and his evening practice chanting and meditation. He tells me that his contemplative practice "brings discernment, clarity, and wisdom into my life and work," which helps him "transform a bad situation into a good situation, and simply see life as an opportunity for service, transformation, and spiritual growth."[14]

Psychologist Shauna Shapiro practices Buddhist *Vipassana* (mindfulness) and *metta* (loving kindness) meditation. Radiating warmth and positive energy, Shauna is an assistant professor of counseling psychology at Santa Clara University. She has been practicing Vipassana since she was twenty, for over twelve years, studying with Jon Kabat-Zinn, Shinzen Young, and Jack Kornfield, attending silent retreats at the Wat Suan Mok monastery in Thailand and at Spirit Rock in Woodacre, California. A few years ago, she began practicing *metta* meditation with guidance from Jack Kornfield and Sylvia Boorstein.

Shauna says that before she had her first child she would sit for thirty minutes each morning on a *zafu* (meditation cushion) in her bedroom, practicing mindfulness, attending to her breath, then "opening up to a state of choiceless awareness where I attended to whatever arose in my consciousness." She would end her meditation "with a few minutes of loving kindness: 'May I be peaceful, May I be happy, May I be healthy, May I be free, May all beings be peaceful, May all beings be happy, May all beings be healthy, May all beings be free.'" Since the birth of her son, Jackson, she practices mindfulness once or twice a week, but begins and ends each day practicing *metta* while nursing Jackson. As he dozes off, she finds "a beautiful stillness" in her *metta* practice that embraces Jackson, herself, and all creation.

Shauna says her intention is that her practice "become the ground from which all my life is lived." She says it brings her "clarity, peace, and compassion" as well as "a sense of trust in myself." She finds consolation sitting quietly in meditation whenever she's confused and uncertain, sometimes finding answers, sometimes "a certain comfort with 'not knowing.'" Her practice inspires her work as a professor, therapist, and researcher, helping her be more empathic and present. She has also done research on the healing effects of meditation with physicians and health care professionals, college students, and people suffering from cancer, stress, insomnia, and substance abuse.[15]

Centering Prayer

Pastoral minister Jane Ferguson practices Centering Prayer, a Catholic contemplative meditation taught by Fr. Thomas Keating and explained in his book *Open Mind, Open Heart.* Jane meditates for twenty minutes twice a day and attends a weekly Centering

Prayer group at her church. She also did her doctoral dissertation on Centering Prayer and health.

To practice Centering Prayer, you sit in a chair with your back straight, close your eyes, and repeat a "sacred word" (such as "Jesus," "love," or "peace"), opening up to God's presence within. You don't repeat the sacred word like a mantra but use it as a signal. Jane says whenever her mind wanders during meditation, "I ever so gently introduce the sacred word, to reinstate my intention to consent to God's presence within." Then, "There may be some points in the prayer when I do not use the sacred word at all, because I am resting in God." She concludes each meditation by resting in the silence with her eyes closed, before returning to ordinary awareness.

Jane says, "I usually practice the prayer at home, but I can take it with me wherever I go. I have prayed on airplanes, in my car (when I'm parked), at friends' homes, and on park benches." She tried other forms of meditation but found "They didn't quite 'do it' for me because I didn't know what or who I was opening myself to." Centering Prayer showed her "the Christian contemplative path," helping her develop "an experiential relationship with this living Christ, which is very different than 'thinking' about God."

Providing her with a spiritual "home, where I can always go to be loved by God," her practice supports her work as director of pastoral care and community ministry at St. Mary's Church in Los Gatos, helping her "let go" of her concerns and gain deeper perspective on life and work. "I rarely miss a day [meditating]," she says, "because if I do, the day feels disjointed." The effects of her practice are subtle, but unmistakable: "I find myself showing some person a kindness that in the past might have made me resentful. I'm more patient, less compulsive," and her practice has brought a deeper sense of love to her life. All her relationships have improved and she even met her fiancé at a Centering Prayer retreat. Now they often meditate together.[16]

Advice for Your Contemplative Practice

If you are beginning a new contemplative practice, my friend Shauna recommends that you write down your intention and commit to your practice for two months, trusting in the process, then reflect on your experience, deciding if you want to continue this practice or try something else, as "there are many different paths to the same place." Jane adds, "Congratulations for giving this gift to yourself and to the world." She recommends finding a support group to meditate with regularly and make spiritual retreats "where you can meditate in community and experience the blessings of sustained silence." But above all, she says, commit to your practice: "'Just do it' on a daily basis."

Bill offers Ignatian contemplation as "a relaxing way to pray." In Luke 5, for example, when Jesus calls Peter, "You can put yourself in the boat with Jesus and just watch the people around him, look at Jesus and listen to what he is saying. Then stand in the place of Peter. Imagine Jesus saying to you what he is saying to Peter. Ask yourself, 'What is my response to his words?' because our prayer is basically an acceptance of a word, and then a response to that word." Bill also recommends *lectio divina,* a practice of reading and reflecting on a sacred text we will explore more fully in chapter ten.

For Juan, "the most important thing is to develop a practice that helps you slow down," moving beneath the busy surface of life to explore the silent depths within. "Once you are able to do that," he says, "then you can pay attention to the inner movements of the mind, body, and heart. Ultimately, dwelling in the stillness of the transcendent brings peace, joy, and liberation into your life."

Carol and Tim say, "We can barely imagine what our lives would have been without this precious foundation. And we've come to trust implicitly that no matter what kind of challenge confronts us, we'll be able to go into meditation, bring the mind back to the words of the passage, and emerge more at peace, more resourceful, and much better equipped in every way to take it on."[17]

How Meditation Can Change Your Life

Susan, the woman you met at the beginning of this chapter, experienced some of these results for herself. She was surprised by her family's support when she first told them she wanted to attend a weekly meditation group at her church and meditate for a few minutes each morning. When she first began meditating, endless "to-do lists," plans, and responsibilities would float through her mind. But with the support of her meditation group, she continued. There she met a young woman who meditated in her car each morning after dropping off her children at school, another woman who said meditation had relieved her arthritis symptoms, and a lawyer who felt his meditation practice had helped him become a more patient listener with his clients.

As she continued meditating, Susan began feeling less anxious. Now she has less tension in her neck and shoulders and her headaches have disappeared. She has also developed greater compassion for herself, no longer feeling so responsible for everything and everyone around her, and, surprisingly, her relationships have improved. She can listen to her family and people at work with compassion without getting caught up in their dramas. On a stressful day, she often meditates for a few minutes at noon in the gardens of the medical complex, returning to work more centered and peaceful. Susan's meditation practice has expanded her concept of health to mean not just the absence of symptoms, but greater energy, peace of mind, and overall well-being. Susan considers her morning meditation her spiritual vitamin that fortifies her for the day and keeps her in touch with her core self (CS).

As Susan found, the simple practice of meditation can subtly transform your life, bringing you greater peace of mind and illuminating your world with new insight. You will know the joy expressed in my favorite lines from William Blake:

> *To see a world in a grain of sand,*
> *And a heaven in a wild flower,*
> *To hold infinity in the palm of your hand,*
> *And eternity in an hour.*[18]

❧ Personal Exercise: Make Time for Your Practice

To discover this inner source of peace, to make time for your practice, you'll need more of the detachment you began in chapter two.

Creating margins in your days for peace and renewal means eliminating the nonessential. One way to do this, according to Eknath Easwaran, is to list everything you do—your commitments at home, at work, in the community—then cross out everything that's not really necessary. Try it.

- Take out your Renaissance Notebook and list all your commitments and responsibilities: at home, at work, in your community. Then close your notebook.
- Tomorrow, review your list, crossing out whatever is unnecessary or doesn't bring you joy or meaning.
- Now begin eliminating these things from your life. You may be surprised by the results.

• •

When Eknath Easwaran was a busy college professor, he belonged to several campus committees. When he asked himself what was really necessary, he stopped going to many of them. He was surprised to find that no one even noticed.[19]

Shadows on the Path: Dealing with Boundary Violators and Mental Debris

As you pursue your practice, you will become more mindful of other people's attitudes and expectations. When I was in college, just beginning to meditate, I had a double major, a part-time job, and a boyfriend. The weekend before a big English paper was due,

I told my boyfriend that we could see each other for a study break but that I needed to spend most of the weekend writing my paper. He frowned and said, "Can't you do that on your own time?"

What a weird question, I thought. Did he really think my time on weekends belonged to him?

No one owns your time. Renaissance philosophers saw time as a precious gift from God, yours to use and to share. Anyone who pretends to own your time is a boundary violator. These people are trying to control you. Don't let them. Take care of your CS, stay on the path, and follow your heart.

Your meditation may also bring up feelings of restlessness, boredom, old resentments, fears, and doubts, feelings that have been there all along, but were covered up by surface commotion. If you are experiencing deep-seated fear, depression, or anxiety, please take care of yourself by getting professional help. But for ordinary garden-variety mental debris, you can use another meditative practice recommended by Eknath Easwaran: the mantra.

The mantra (or mantram) is a symbolic word or phrase. The practice of repeating a holy word or name occurs in many faith traditions. Some familiar mantras are "Jesus," "Ave Maria," "Barukh attah Adonai," "Om," "Allah," and "Rama" (Gandhi's mantra). Some contemporary researchers have used nonsectarian mantras like "harmony."

Choose a mantra that appeals to you, setting it in your consciousness by silently repeating it to yourself when you're relaxed, drifting off to sleep, or performing a routine chore like pulling weeds or washing dishes. Then you can use your mantra to clear mental debris, unwanted thoughts, or negative feelings. In 2006, researchers introduced the mantra practice at the VA hospital in San Diego, where it helped veterans and health care professionals manage unwanted thoughts, stress, insomnia, anxiety, frustration, impatience, and anger. Researcher Jill Borman, RN, PhD, says the mantra is "portable, invisible, nontoxic," a welcome alternative to medication that requires no technology and can be used any time, anywhere. In the Renaissance, St. Francis de Sales recognized the power of such a brief meditative practice, reminding people to "make many withdrawals into the solitude of your heart, whilst you are outwardly in the midst of . . . business."[20]

Taking Action: Exploring Resources for Your Practice

There are many resources to support your contemplative practice. Some of them are:

- Classes and meditation groups at your community center, church, or synagogue. If you've never meditated before, an experienced teacher can offer valuable advice. If you're more experienced, meditation retreats will bring new depth to your practice.
- For more on the passage meditation, the foundational tool of Sri Eknath Easwaran's Eight Point Spiritual Program, see his book *Meditation* (Tomales, CA: Nilgiri Press, 2006) or visit the Blue Mountain Center Web site, www.easwaran.org.
- For more on Ignatian meditation, see William Barry's *Finding God in All Things* (Notre Dame, IN: Ave Maria Press, 1991). You can find an online Ignatian retreat at www.creighton.edu/CollaborativeMinistry/Cmo-retreat.html.
- For Buddhist mindfulness meditation, some helpful guides are *Peace is Every Step* (New York: Bantam, 1992) and other books by Thich Nhat Hanh. For Vipassana, see Jack Kornfield's *A Path with Heart* (New York: Bantam, 1993), his audio guide, *The Inner Art of Meditation* (Boulder, CO: Sounds True, 1993) and the Spirit Rock Web site, www.spiritrock.org.
- For more on Centering Prayer, see Thomas Keating's *Open Mind, Open Heart* (New York: Continuum, 1994). Information on Centering Prayer books, videos, and retreats is available at www.contemplativeoutreach.org.

- For more on the mantra, see Eknath Easwaran, *The Mantram Handbook* (Tomales, CA: Nilgiri Press, 1998) and the Blue Mountain Web site, www.easwaran.org.

Moving Forward

Take a few minutes now to reflect on your progress in this chapter, writing your answers and today's date in your Renaissance Notebook.

1. Have you been following your own contemplative practice? How was it? If you have *not yet* begun your practice, choose a time to begin this week.
2. How have you simplified your life to make room for meditation?
3. Have you been using a mantra? If not, choose one and begin using this simple but powerful tool.
4. Where have you found CS joy in your life this week?
5. What was your creative victory in this chapter and how are you celebrating it?

Your contemplative practice will bring greater balance to your life, offering you the keys to your own inner garden of peace and renewal, what John Milton called the "paradise within."

RENAISSANCE REMINDERS

Detach from the noisy world around you to discover the deepest values of your heart.
Remember to:

~ Cultivate greater balance with daily meditation.

~ Realize that time is your most valuable resource. Anyone who pretends to own your time is a boundary violator.

~ Use your mantra to bring greater peace to your life.

CHAPTER 9

Creativity

Making Your Life a Work of Art

And as imagination bodies forth
The forms of things unknown, the poet's pen
Turns them to shapes, and gives to airy nothing
A local habitation and a name.

—WILLIAM SHAKESPEARE, *A MIDSUMMER NIGHT'S DREAM*[1]

Do you have a creative practice? Creativity, for most people, was the hallmark of the Renaissance, when people like Leonardo da Vinci, Michelangelo Buonarroti, and William Shakespeare changed forever the way we see ourselves and our world.

Renaissance philosophers saw life itself as a work of art, and people throughout Western Europe pursued creative practices. In England, Sir Philip Sidney and Sir Walter Raleigh were poets as well as soldiers and courtiers. Queen Elizabeth wrote poetry, played musical instruments, and loved to dance. Music filled the households of merchants, craftsmen, farmers, and their families, who sang or played in consort after meals. John Milton's father worked in the London law courts but was also an accomplished musician, and Milton himself played the organ all his life. Michelangelo wrote sonnets, Leonardo sang and played the lyre, and Galileo played several musical instruments and was skilled in drawing and painting.[2]

Research has found that art and beauty can bring greater health and harmony to your life today. In this chapter, you'll experience this for yourself by developing your own creative practice.

The Power of Beauty

Beauty, for Renaissance philosophers, was not a luxury but a necessity. In *The Courtier,* Baldassare Castiglione explained that our souls are naturally drawn to beauty, the light of divine goodness reflected in this world. If we respond to beauty with appetite, we become like animals, driven to consume, but if we respond spiritually, beauty will inspire us to virtuous action. The ideal "Renaissance man" described by Castiglione was inspired by beauty, combining action and contemplation, valor and virtue, intellect and grace. A soldier, scholar, and diplomat, he could speak and write eloquently, compose poetry, sketch, dance, sing, and play musical instruments.[3]

Castiglione was born in 1478 to an old family from Lombardy. Growing up with his cousins, the Gonzaga princes, he studied the classics, fencing, horsemanship, and jousting. At eighteen, he became a courtier to the Duke of Milan, where he met Leonardo da Vinci. He later served at the court of the Marquis of Mantua, becoming friends with the artist Raphael, and meeting Guidobaldo da Montefeltro, Duke of Urbino, whose court was a brilliant center of Renaissance culture. Guidobaldo's father had built a grand palace in Urbino, filling it with beautiful objects—classical statues, silver vases, silk tapestries interwoven with gold, rare paintings, and musical instruments. His greatest treasure was his library of rare books in Greek, Latin, and Hebrew, bound in crimson with clasps of silver and gold. In 1504, Castiglione moved to Urbino, where he served for many years as a courtier and ambassador to France, England, and Rome.

In his later life, Castiglione's early years at the court of Urbino remained with him as a golden memory, an idealized Camelot. Although Duke Guido had been chronically ill, he had borne his infirmity with fortitude, watching the jousts he could no longer join and welcoming eminent scholars to court. His duchess, Elisabetta Gonzaga, had presided at their evening soirees of music and sparkling conversations about literature and ideas, linking the courtiers in such love that they seemed a band of brothers.

Growing weary of the wars and petty politics that filled his days after Guidobaldo's death in 1508, Castiglione began writing *The Courtier,* describing a world that seemed a distant dream. He shared his manuscript with friends, who urged him to publish it, but for nearly twenty years he carried it around in his travels, as Leonardo did the *Mona Lisa,* unwilling to release his masterpiece, unwilling to relinquish the dream. Finally, in 1528, Castiglione sent his beloved book to press. A few months later, he died.[4]

Castiglione's *Courtier* was translated into English by Sir Thomas Hoby in 1561, early in Queen Elizabeth's reign. Setting a standard for the English Renaissance, it influenced William Shakespeare, Ben Jonson, and Sir Philip Sidney, the charismatic young courtier, poet, and patron of the arts. When Sidney died in 1586, wounded in battle after lending his armor to a friend, he was memorialized as the ideal English courtier.

Why We Need the Arts in Our Lives

The Renaissance reverence for the arts has been validated by modern psychologists who have discovered that a creative practice can improve your health and bring greater meaning to your life. Abraham Maslow associated creativity with being "healthy, self-actualizing, fully human." Positive psychologists regard it as a key character strength, and studies have shown that pursuing a creative practice helps young people develop essential skills and older adults to maintain a sense of purpose.

High school and college students who write poetry or are involved in music, drama, or the visual arts develop a stronger sense of identity than their peers. In a study of 25,000 high school students, those involved in the arts had higher grades and test scores, more community service, and lower drop out rates. Listening to music enhances our intellectual performance, and performing it produces even stronger results. Researchers believe that focused attention on musical patterns strengthens our brain's neural connections for spacial-temporal reasoning. Music lessons have been associated with stronger math, spelling, reading, and spacial skills in elementary school children, and many of the best engineers and technical designers in California's Silicon Valley are also musicians.[5]

Your creative practice can bring you greater clarity in pursuing your calling. After a hectic day as a software engineer, Dan would relax by playing the piano, a practice he'd enjoyed since childhood. The musical patterns calmed his frazzled nerves and brought him back to himself, helping him work through his restless discontent with his job. When a community college catalog arrived in the mail, he signed up for a music theory class. He eventually earned a master's degree in music from the local university, while taking a few courses in environmental science. For his master's recital, Dan gave a magnificent Chopin concert. I still remember his smiling face as he bowed to resounding applause. Developing his musical practice brought a new dimension to Dan's life, helping him change careers and find his calling. Following his interest in environmental science, he's now a middle school science teacher, teaching his students about the complex harmonies of the natural world. He plays the piano at home and at church on Sundays and enjoys creating performance CDs for his friends.

Dan's experience reflects Renaissance scholar Robert Burton's belief that music cures depression and anxiety, and recent studies have revealed that performing music actually does reduce stress. In 2005, researchers asked a group of men and women to spend an hour performing a stressful task—assembling a jigsaw puzzle while an experimenter interrupted and criticized them. For another hour, some people continued working on the puzzle, others relaxed with magazines, and a third group played a simple keyboard instrument. In only one hour the stress level in the musical group was significantly reversed.

Creation is re-creation. The positive effects of performing music along with expressions of joy, beauty, and creativity produce what psychologists call the "broaden and build" positive emotions that provide you with new insights on your life while strengthening your health, social bonds, and resilience.[6]

Personal Exercise: Cultivate Greater Beauty in Your Life

You can begin experiencing these "broaden and build" effects for yourself by becoming more conscious of the beauty in your life.

How do you find beauty? I find it walking on a nearby nature trail or working in my garden, listening to my favorite music, or watching the sky at sunset. Sometimes beauty means taking a rose from my garden to a friend, working on a creative practice, or just slowing down to be fully present.

Each day this week, slow down and ask yourself:

- "How can I find more beauty in my world today?"
- "How can I create more beauty in my world today?"

The Power of Harmony

In the Renaissance, poet John Milton wrote of music "untwisting all the chains that tie the hidden soul of harmony." Thomas Browne wrote that "I can look a whole day with delight upon a handsome picture, though it be but of a horse," finding harmony in the composition of Renaissance art. Browne also loved music—from church hymns to tavern songs—and wrote, "There is music wherever there is a harmony, order, or proportion." With Renaissance philosophers, he believed the human soul was set into harmony by music and that the universe itself resonated with the "music of the spheres," in which the very stars made music.[7]

In our own time, psychologist Mihaly Csikszentmihalyi has also seen beauty as harmony, defining art as the orderly patterns that human beings have "imposed on chaos," framing our experience in music, poetry, drama, dance, and the visual arts. He found that unless teenagers can find order and beauty in life they become disillusioned and depressed, chasing after short-term pleasures. Harmony around us promotes harmony within. An orderly home can help young people transcend poverty and misfortune to lead healthy, productive lives, and the beauty of nature can heal many ills. When New York inner-city neighborhoods planted community gardens in the 1960s, the children there played together more harmoniously and there was a dramatic reduction in litter, vandalism, street crime, and domestic violence.[8]

Personal Exercise: Create Harmony Around You

Could an area of your life benefit from greater harmony?

Could you clear a disordered table, desk, or closet at home? Clearing years of accumulated clutter can be overwhelming, but breaking it down into small steps makes it manageable. Here's how.

- Give yourself thirty minutes (set your timer) to focus on one area—such as a drawer or shelf.
- Bring out a trash can and two paper bags. Then sort the items, putting junk into the trash and other items into three piles: yes, no, or undecided.
- Wipe the drawer or shelf clean and replace the "yes" items.
- Put the "no" items into a bag to donate to Goodwill, The Salvation Army, or your local shelter.
- Put the "undecided" items into the other bag.

- By now your timer should have gone off. Congratulate yourself for creating one small area of harmony and set your two bags aside.
- Repeat this step until you've cleared this area (the chest of drawers, bookshelf, or closet). Then go through the "undecided" bag, deciding which items to keep or donate. Put the donation bag in your car to drop off when doing errands.

Could you bring greater harmony to your work environment by:

- Sorting and discarding old books and papers? (As above, set a timer and do this task one step, one area at a time.)
- Adding beauty with cut flowers or a tropical plant?
- Taking five minutes at the end of the day to clear off your desk, put away files, and leave yourself a note about where to pick up tomorrow?

• •

This week, perform one small act of harmony, not to please others—remember, this is *your* personal Renaissance. Do something your own creative self (CS) enjoys.

Coping with Adversity

On a cold November day in 1588, a young woman rode into London, surrounded by eighty courtiers and servants in gold chains and blue livery. It had been two years since her father, mother, and brother Philip had died. For months, she herself had been near death with illness and grief. Now she returned to court, strengthened by a new sense of purpose.

Mary Sidney, Countess of Pembroke, was classically educated, fluent in French, Italian, and Latin, as well as in singing and playing the lute. With her golden curls and strong will, she had been invited to Elizabeth's court at thirteen, then married at fifteen to the Earl of Pembroke, a widower in his midforties. Their arranged marriage was by all accounts a happy one. The Earl was delighted

with his sprightly young wife, who filled his household with poetry, music, culture, and four children, beginning with his son and
heir, William Herbert. Her brother, Sir Philip Sidney, was a fre-
quent guest in their home, and together they began translating the
Psalms and setting them to music.

Embracing art as both a personal solace and a tribute to her
brother, Mary returned to London, determined to carry on his
legacy as a poet and patron of the arts. She supported the work of
many poets, including Samuel Daniel, Edmund Spenser, and
Nicholas Breton, who compared her to Castiglione's Duchess of
Urbino. She edited her brother's poetry, wrote her own poems,
translated works by French and Italian writers, and completed the
Sidney translation of the Psalms that influenced John Donne and
George Herbert. Transforming her grief into art, she became a
model for later women writers, earning the praise of John Donne,
George Herbert, Edmund Spenser, and William Shakespeare.[9]

The arts also help people cope with adversity today. When
Clare moved from the Midwest to her new job in San Francisco,
she loved everything about the city—Fisherman's Wharf, the cable
cars, the international restaurants, the lively arts scene, and Alex.
She'd met Alex at lunch at the little Italian restaurant near work
where he waited tables as his day job. Alex was an aspiring actor
with dark curls, a flashing smile, and, like the city itself, filled with
surprises. He'd meet her after work in his jeans, turtleneck, and
brown suede jacket, taking her for dinner in Chinatown, plays at
the Presidio, or to meet other actors and artists at the City Lights
bookstore. The two became inseparable and moved in together,
planning to marry. Clare was so swept up in Alex's charisma that
she didn't see the signs, his moods that vacillated from euphoria to
despondency.

One day after work, Clare stopped by the restaurant but Alex
wasn't there. He'd gone for an audition, but he didn't come home
that night. Or the next. Then there was a loud knock at the door.
The police had found his car parked near the Golden Gate Bridge
with his jacket, wallet, and a note inside. Clare cried herself to

sleep, clutching his jacket, hoping against hope he'd come back. They never found him. A week passed, then a month, then longer, until she finally realized Alex was gone. She went in for counseling. To fill the empty nights, she signed up for a creative writing class, joining a local writers' group. As she began writing, the words came pouring out—poems, short stories, the beginnings of a memoir. It helped, somehow, to write it all down. Perhaps some day she'd understand.

Writing puts our emotions down on paper, helping us express the inexplicable. Psychologists have found that writing about adversity strengthens our sense of agency. Affirming our own active artistry helps us cope with misfortune and make creative sense of our lives.[10]

The Power of Play

Today's technology has distanced us from active artistry, while paradoxically increasing access to art through television, recordings, movies, video, computers, and the Internet. As behavioral psychologist B. F. Skinner wrote, we've lost our inclination to act. "People look at beautiful things, listen to beautiful music, and watch exciting entertainments, but the only behavior reinforced is looking, listening, and watching."[11]

Research has revealed that passive entertainments do not bring us joy. Psychologist Mihaly Csikszentmihalyi gave people electronic pagers and questionnaires, asking them to record what they were doing and how they felt whenever the pager went off. He discovered that people were happiest experiencing "flow" (when their "consciousness is harmoniously ordered and they want to pursue whatever they are doing for its own sake"), when they were engaged in productive activities—participating in the arts, work, hobbies, or sports. They felt the least amount of flow while watching television.[12]

Flow states are filled with deep presence and playfulness, and play has long been associated with creativity. The joy of your child self (CS) and capacity for creative play belongs to all of us, regardless of age or culture. Throughout history people have painted pictures, recited poetry, created crafts, and celebrated life in music, drama, and dance.

Neuroscientists have found that not only children but most young mammals play. When researcher Jaak Panksepp put two young male rats together in a cage, they immediately began "play fighting," chasing each other, pouncing, and wrestling. For four days, whenever he put the rats together in the cage, they began to play. But on the fifth day, when he put some cat hair in the cage, all play ceased. The rats sniffed and looked around nervously, sensing danger. He then removed the cat hair, but for the next five days, the rats' play was inhibited by their earlier fearful experience.

We, too, stop playing when we're blocked by fear. When psychologist Michelle Chappel gives creativity workshops, she says it's hard to get people to play, to take time to do something fun to release their inner creativity. "They see creativity as a serious business," she explains. "They push to achieve their goals, put all this pressure on themselves and get blocked." The pressure, she says, comes from judging themselves, which "keeps them from being in the moment. They're filled with 'shoulds,' petrified, afraid they'll make a mistake."[13]

RENAISSANCE QUESTION

Your creative self (CS) can be shut down by fear—fear of failure, fear of being "wrong," fear of criticism, fear of making a fool of yourself. If you've had trouble doing the play activities on your Exploration List, ask yourself:

"What am I afraid of?"

To nurture your creativity, you must be brave enough to be foolish, to explore, to make mistakes. Giving yourself permission to play will boost your energy and open you up to a new world of possibilities. The following exercise will show you how.

Personal Exercise:
Begin Your Own Creative Practice

This week, begin reclaiming your CS sense of play by choosing a creative practice.

When you were a child, what creative activities did you enjoy? Do you remember finger painting, modeling with clay, cutting out paper pumpkins and snowflakes for the holidays? Did you enjoy drawing, painting, ceramics, singing, playing a musical instrument, writing poetry, dancing, or working with wood?

Many people today benefit from the power of play. My friend Shu-Park Chan balances his life by painting Chinese watercolors. As a busy professor, engineer, and founder of the International Technological University in Silicon Valley, he told me, "Whenever I'm troubled by something, I set aside time to paint." By concentrating on the strokes and making the painting beautiful, he finds a deep sense of peace, returning to work relaxed and energized. For years, former president Jimmy Carter has worked in his wood shop making furniture, while working with the Carter Center to create new patterns of peace, health, and understanding. He has also written many books of nonfiction, fiction, and poetry.[14]

Do you have a craft that gives you a sense of active play: knitting, weaving, quilting, working with wood, refinishing furniture? Something else? My sister-in-law Marilyn Numan, who does neuroscience research, enjoys knitting, a popular practice today for busy professionals and college students. Marilyn calls it "a productive form of relaxation." The rhythmic, repetitive motions, colorful yarns, and the joy of seeing what looks like a ball of string take shape as a warm scarf or sweater make knitting a popular creative craft.

What is your creative practice? Something you do for its own sake, something fun that engages and energizes your CS, the creative child within you?

- This week choose one creative practice and begin cultivating it.
- Write this practice on your Exploration List and take one action to begin pursuing it. Get out that old guitar; join a

church choir; sign up for a class in art, creative writing, music, or dance at your local community center; check out a library book on your favorite craft; get refinishing supplies from the hardware store; or visit an art supply store and buy yourself a sketch book, pencils, and art gum eraser.

• When you've taken one positive action, think of the next step, write it on your list, and begin making your creative practice a regular part of your life.

Art and Agency

Renaissance philosophers believed that we reach our highest potential by using our capacity to create. The arts give us what psychologists call "a language of agency," helping us focus our attention, recognize patterns of cause and effect, set goals, make plans, and overcome obstacles—valuable tools for success in life.

Since 1994, the Hilltop Artists in Residence program in Tacoma, Washington, has used this creative power to help thousands of teenagers overcome poverty, homelessness, learning disabilities, academic failure, and substance abuse, transforming their lives as they create breathtaking glass art. In a stimulating, caring environment, they exchange life on the streets for the chance to make glass mosaics and beads, or work with 2,000-degree molten glass in the challenging art of glassblowing. From master artists, mentors, and the process itself, they learn self-discipline, responsibility, precision, and teamwork, creating work they are proud of while developing new visions of themselves, for the program includes alternative education and tutoring. "The primary goal is to get them through high school," Luana Welch, Hilltop's executive director, told me. To participate, young people must be enrolled in school and passing their classes. Hilltop has many stunning success stories. Some participants have become professional glass artists. One young man earned a scholarship to the Rhode Island School of Design and is now a successful architect. Others have gone on to jobs or college. Inspired by the power of beauty, the challenge of creating, they have become artists in their own lives, awakened to new possibilities by the creative process.[15]

New Renaissance Patrons of the Arts

In Renaissance England, men and women of means like the Sidneys became patrons of the arts. In Italy, the quintessential patron was Lorenzo de' Medici. Raised in a wealthy banking family, Lorenzo loved music, dancing in festivals, composing carnival music, and directing his servants in a household choir. As political leader of Florence, he balanced public duties with devotion to scholarship and art, composing songs, writing poetry, and studying the classics. But he made his greatest contribution as a patron, supporting scholars such as Ficino and Pico della Mirandola and artists Leonardo, Michelangelo, Ghirlandaio, Filippino Lippi, Verrocchio, and Botticelli.[16]

New Renaissance man and patron of the arts Carl Djerassi was born in Vienna to a family of physicians. He fled the Nazis in 1938, arriving in New York at sixteen with no money or prospects. Placed in the home of a New Jersey chemist by a refugee organization, Djerassi attended Kenyan College on scholarship, graduating summa cum laude and Phi Beta Kappa at eighteen. He got his PhD from the University of Wisconsin and became a leading research chemist, receiving the National Medal of Science for developing the oral contraceptive, the National Medal of Technology for his work in insect control, the Priestly Medal in chemistry, and twenty honorary doctorates. In 1959, he joined the faculty of Stanford University as a chemistry professor, while serving as president of Syntex Research.

At sixty, Djerassi found a new calling. Drawing upon his scientific background, he has written five novels, an autobiography, and six plays, which have been performed in New York and internationally. In 1982 he and his wife, writer Diane Middlebrook, founded the Djerassi Resident Artists Program, their creative response to the death of his daughter Pamela. Every year visual and media artists, writers, composers, and choreographers come to a redwood forest south of San Francisco for private residences, studio space, and meals—the freedom and solitude to create balanced by vital companionship with other artists. Over 1,500 artists have benefited from the program.[17]

🌿 *Personal Exercise: Support the Arts in Your Area*

You don't need to be a Medici prince or millionaire to support the arts. There are many opportunities in your own community.

A few summers ago, a group of actors set up an Elizabethan theater in the park near our house. My husband and I attended a magical production of *Twelfth Night* in the open-air theater as the sky gradually filled with stars. Every summer since, the theater has reappeared with new offerings. Recently, the actors added Camp Shakespeare, two weeks of dramatic games for children, along with stage combat and classical acting classes for teens.

Last summer, as Bob and I enjoyed a picnic dinner before the performance, we decided to make an annual donation to this festival that brings such joy to our community.

Does your community have a local theater or art program you'd like to support? If so, give them a call. Even a small donation of time, materials, or funds will help. You can be a modern Medici, making a positive difference in your community.

• •

Shadows on the Path: Being Creative, Not Reactive

Too many people feel powerless in their lives when they react instead of living creatively. When you think of an important situation in your life, which response best describes how you feel about it?

1. You're acting from
(a) inspiration (b) obligation

2. You
(a) make things happen (b) feel like things are always
    happening to you

3. Most of the time you feel
(a) expansive (b) diminished

4. You feel like
(a) reaching out (b) withdrawing, collapsing into yourself

5. You feel
(a) energized and renewed (b) exhausted and drained

If most of your choices were *a*, you approach this situation creatively. If many of your choices were *b*, you feel reactive, controlled by externals. The next personal exercise will help you take creative charge of your life.

Creativity Killers and Catalysts

After two decades studying creativity in the workplace, psychologist Teresa Amabile has found that some conditions kill creativity while others foster it.

In your current situation, how many creativity killers can you identify?

Creativity Killers

Urgency, extreme time pressure.
Days fragmented by too many tasks and demands.
Interruptions, distractions.
Days filled with busywork.
Many meetings.
Your schedule and projects subject to last minute changes by
    others.

Creativity Catalysts

Low time pressure, opportunity to explore.

Focusing on one project for a significant block of time.

Freedom from interruptions.

Finding meaning in your work.

Few meetings.

Sense of agency, personal control of projects and schedules.[18]

(Adapted by permission of the *Harvard Business Review* from "Creativity Under the Gun" by T. M. Amabile, C. N. Hadley and S. J. Kramer, *80*, (August 2002), p. 56. Copyright © 2002 by the Harvard Business School Publishing Corporation. All rights reserved.

Personal Exercise: Eliminate Creativity Killers

If you have creativity killers in your life, write them in your Renaissance Notebook and begin transforming them.

- If your work days are filled with interruptions, can you reclaim time to concentrate by closing your office door, posting a sign that you will be available at ____ (two hours from now), and letting calls go into your voice mail?
- Can you work at home one or two days a week?
- If your days are filled with meetings, can you have them less often and work with a definite agenda?
- If you're subject to last-minute changes in plans and schedules, can you address the cause and encourage more long-range planning?

Can you make some of these changes? You won't know unless you try. Many productive people I know now work at home two days a week. Their colleagues know where to find them in an emergency and they get more done, experience less stress, and put less stress on the environment by driving to work less often.

Moving Forward

Creativity brings us new harmonies, new possibilities. Sir Philip Sidney wrote that art transcends "what is" with "the divine consideration of what may be, and should be."[19] Whenever we create anything, we combine our personal gifts with some ineffable power that transforms them into art. We cannot know where our work will go or how far it will reach.

In the fall of 2006, as I was preparing for another school year, haunted by news of war between Israel and Hezbollah, I was surprised by an e-mail from the other side of the world. Josepha Edman wrote from Haifa to say that as she was wandering from city to city to escape the bombing, she read my book, *The Tao of Personal Leadership,* which gave her hope for the future. I was humbled by the recognition that when we least expect it, our efforts can ripple out, touching others in the larger world around us.

Affirming her own creative vision, Josepha and a friend have developed a company that combines the wisdom of East and West in a new model of leadership. Courageous and resourceful, she is committed to seeing beyond polarities, to developing a "dialogue of a different kind" to promote greater harmony and understanding in her community.

For Josepha, her neighbors throughout the Middle East, and all of us who long for a better life, there is enduring hope in the power of creativity that transcends "what is" with new visions of "what may be, and should be." Lighting the darkness with the promise of new possibilities, we can create a new Renaissance within and around us.[20]

Your own creative power can transform your life and your world in remarkable ways. Take a moment now to review your progress in this chapter, writing your answers and today's date in your Renaissance Notebook.

1. What have you done this week to create more beauty in your life? Has it brought you more CS joy?
2. Have you taken one small step to create harmony around you?
3. What is your creative practice? Have you begun to follow it? If not, take action tomorrow!

4. Are you becoming more aware of the arts in your community? Your own creative energies in your life and work?
5. What was your creative victory in this chapter and how are you celebrating it?

As you develop greater creativity in your life, you participate in a transformational process that extends far beyond what your mind can fathom or your eyes can see. The Renaissance within you inevitably creates a Renaissance around you, producing new possibilities to heal and transform our world.

RENAISSANCE REMINDERS

There is a part of you that is forever young, playful, curious, and true that leads you to your calling.
As you live more creatively, remember to:

~ Ask "How can I create more beauty in my world today?"

~ Follow your own creative practice.

~ Trust in the power of creativity to transcend "what is" with "what may be."

CHAPTER 10

Reading and Reflection

Exploring New Worlds Within and Around You

Books are not absolutely dead things,
but do contain a potency of life in them to be as
    active as that soul
whose progeny they are.

—JOHN MILTON, *AREOPAGITICA*[1]

Now that you've begun living more creatively, this chapter will help you move forward in your calling with the skills you're using right now: reading and reflecting.

Today, we tend to take reading for granted. But in the Renaissance, reading created a revolution in consciousness. Throughout the Middle Ages, books were hand lettered, rare, and costly, and few people could read outside the clergy. After 1450, when the invention of the printing press made books more accessible, generations of men and women began to read and think for themselves.

As the Bible was translated from Church Latin into the vernacular and printed in affordable editions, thousands of people began learning to read—from aristocrats to commoners, farmers, shopkeepers, servants, artisans, apprentices, wives, and mothers. In addition to the Bible, people read devotional guides, collections of poetry, cookbooks, and books on education, moral development, health, science, history, law, and geography. Between 1500 and

1557, the number of books published in England increased from a mere fifty-four to over five thousand.[2]

For Renaissance philosophers reading was a path to moral growth, for Christians a vital aid to salvation. While in the Middle Ages priests would read to their congregations from a hand-lettered Latin Bible, now members of these congregations were reading the Bible for themselves and drawing their own conclusions. A catalyst for dramatic change, reading gave rise to the Reformation and new developments in science, politics, and the arts.

John Milton wrote in 1644 that books "contain a potency of life in them to be as active as that soul whose progeny they are." When you read, your mind entertains another person's thoughts, transporting you into other lives and other worlds, helping you discover significant patterns in your life. Experts call reading "one of the most complex and uniquely human of cognitive activities," awakening "things inside us that make our lives more vivid and active." A 2004 study found that readers are up to three times more likely to exercise and become involved in their communities.[3]

Reading can help you transform your life. While people ordinarily remain on the same social and cultural levels as their parents, books move us beyond this status quo by providing visions of other worlds.[4] In the Renaissance, reading a book of saints' lives inspired an injured Spanish soldier to become St. Ignatius Loyola. Although Shakespeare's formal education ended when he left Stratford grammar school, he would read by candlelight after a busy day in the London theaters. Poring over two favorite volumes, Plutarch's *Lives* and Holinshed's *Chronicles,* he brought Julius Caesar, Marc Antony, Cleopatra, and Henry V to life on the English stage.[5] Reading also influenced philosopher John Locke, who studied books of medicine on his own, becoming a capable physician. In 1668, he operated on his friend and patron, Lord Ashley, successfully removing a cyst from his liver—a remarkable medical achievement for the time. Locke developed his political philosophy by reading voraciously in Cicero, Plato, and Descartes, as well as treatises on ethics, logic, epistemology, economics, politics, theology, science, and medicine. His biographer says that probably "no book of any worth published in England during his adult years passed unnoticed by him."[6]

But perhaps the most compelling example of the power of reading occurred during the American Renaissance. In nineteenth-century Baltimore, an African American slave boy overheard his master reprimanding his wife for giving him reading lessons. "Learning will spoil the best nigger in the world. If he learns to read the Bible it will forever unfit him to be a slave," he said, and the boy realized that reading was his path to freedom. Out on the street running errands for his master, he would ask white boys for help deciphering words in the spelling book he kept in his pocket. With money earned shining shoes, he bought newspapers and books on the sly. He taught other slaves to read, fought back when beaten by a brutal master, and ultimately escaped to freedom. "Unfit to be a slave," Frederick Douglass became one of the most eloquent speakers, writers, and abolitionists of his time, a testimony to the power of reading to liberate the human spirit.[7]

Reading can liberate your spirit and support your own personal Renaissance today. It can introduce you to other lives, like the people you're meeting in this book, and help you develop new skills and pathways for moving forward in your calling. Reading can also lead to reflection, revealing new insights about yourself and the patterns of your life.

Personal Exercise: Lectio Divina

Renaissance men and women found inspiration in *lectio divina,* or "holy reading," meditating on a biblical passage, a saint's life, or other devotional work. You can do this, too, by reading a passage reflectively.

- Set aside a half hour in a quiet place where you won't be disturbed. Bring along your Renaissance Notebook and a passage that appeals to you, from the Bible, a devotional work, or one of the Renaissance lives from this book.

- Read the passage over slowly, *very* slowly, pausing to consider each word or phrase.
- If you feel yourself responding emotionally to a word or phrase, focus on this feeling. Repeat the words like a mantra, seeing where they lead—to a significant memory, a lesson, a flash of insight into your life's journey.
- Write the new insight in your Renaissance Notebook.
- Ask yourself, "How can I relate this insight to my life today?"[8]

Reading and Your Brain

You're probably so accustomed to reading that it's become second nature. But there's a reason why reading affects you so profoundly: it is a complex cognitive process of attention, vision, memory, and emotion, involving many regions of your brain. Since the 1990s, declared "the decade of the brain" by the U.S. Congress, scientists have been charting this vast inner territory with sophisticated technology—positron emission tomography (PET) scans and functional magnetic resonance imaging (fMRI). Computer images light up in vibrant colors, revealing new insights into that vast frontier within us, signaling increased oxygen and blood flow to active regions of the brain. Displays of these images at neuroscience conferences resemble modern art, conveying the remarkable inner artistry of our cognition.

Scientists are still investigating exactly what happens in your brain when you read, acquiring new insights into this "most complex and uniquely human of cognitive activities." We now know that regions all over your brain are involved. As you read this paragraph, you are concentrating, activating your prefrontal cortex, the source of focused attention, planning, and executive control, as well as your thalamus, a subcortical brain region that relays information to and from the cerebral cortex. The reticular activating system, a structure in the midbrain, also plays an important role in focused attention. Looking at the individual letters on the page sends a message to the visual cortex in your brain's occipital lobes. But to comprehend these printed symbols as words, you must draw upon the language centers in your left temporal and frontal lobes. Understanding these words in a larger context of meaning activates corresponding areas in your brain's right hemisphere. The more complex the texts you read, the more intensely these regions are activated.

Reading is a delicate balancing act, requiring you to keep in mind not only the sentence you are reading now but earlier sentences, along with your own personal experience, all woven together in a complex cognitive interaction. To do this, you use brain areas involved with working memory—such as the prefrontal cortex and hippocampus, and the cingulate gyrus—as well as long-term memories, which are most likely stored throughout the cerebral cortex.

Drawn into the imaginative world of a book, especially a work of fiction, you can feel intense excitement, sadness, or joy, for reading activates your emotions through your limbic system, which includes the hippocampus, amygdala, septum, certain regions of the thalamus, and the hypothalamus, which regulates your autonomic nervous system, including your breathing and heart rate. The earliest studies of pleasure centers in the brain involved the septum.[9]

My point here is not to give you a course in neuroanatomy but to demonstrate just how much of your brain is involved—right now—in reading and comprehension. In what literary theorist Wolfgang Iser calls "a dynamic interaction between text and reader," if you and I read the same book, your experience is necessarily different from mine. Each of us brings the text to life, filling in the gaps by adding something of ourselves. Drawing upon your own emotions and past experience, your brain takes the information from the printed page and processes it with your working memory and imagination to give form and meaning to everything you read. This dynamic synthesis of reader and text is why many people are disappointed when their favorite novel is made into a movie: the actors playing the roles don't measure up to the heroes of their imagination.

Because reading exercises so many regions of your brain, it strengthens neural connections and brings vital oxygen and nutrients to millions of brain cells. Studies have connected reading with greater self-awareness, enhanced listening and speaking skills, the experience of active engagement known as "flow," healthier adolescent development, and a dramatic reduction in the risk of Alzheimer's disease. Dr. David Snowdon's longitudinal study of the School Sisters of Notre Dame (the "nun study") found that those sisters who remained active and vital in their nineties, some even into their hundreds, regularly exercised their minds and bodies, walking several miles a day, working crossword puzzles, reading a variety of books and the daily *New York Times*.[10]

Rediscover Reading

Yet many people fail to reap these benefits. To Dennis and his friends, reading isn't "cool." Like many high school students today, he grew up with video games, TV, cell phones, and the Internet. When he tries to read, his mind jumps from one thing to the next and he can't concentrate. Easily bored, he craves constant entertainment, doing his homework while listening to his iPod, checking his MySpace page, and instant messaging his friends. Restless and reactive, he drifts through the days with no real interests or direction, getting through another boring class by sending messages on his cell phone. His grades have been slipping, his parents are worried, and he doesn't seem to care.

Dennis's story is not unusual. Studies have revealed a dramatic decrease in reading in America today, a mirror opposite of the Renaissance. A recent UCLA study revealed that 52 percent of entering college students spend less than one hour a week reading for pleasure. After SAT verbal scores fell precipitously between the 1960s and the 1990s, the Educational Testing Service "re-normed" the test in 1994, adjusting the numbers to make the scores seem more acceptable. In a 2004 National Endowment for the Arts study, Director Dana Gioia declared that "for the first time in modern history, less than half of the adult population now reads literature." The study found that, unlike people who select only passive electronic entertainment (television, videos, and recordings), readers are more active in their communities, volunteering, attending concerts and plays, and participating in local politics. Since the reading decline is most dramatic among young adults from ages eighteen to twenty-four, Gioia warned of "an imminent cultural crisis," seeing Americans becoming "less informed, active, and independent-minded . . . not qualities that a free, innovative, or productive society can afford to lose."[11]

Reading awakens a creative spark within us, offering inspiration and the power to transform our lives. Devastated by his brother's assassination in 1963, Robert Kennedy found consolation reading Edith Hamilton's *The Greek Way,* a book that helped him cope with personal tragedy, renewing his sense of purpose.[12]

Scientific studies have shown that reading a good self-help book can significantly reduce depression, often as effectively as psychotherapy or antidepressants.[13] Andrea, a wealthy woman in Switzerland, was resentful and unhappy until a friend gave her a copy of Jerry Jampolsky's *Love Is Letting Go of Fear.* The book affected her so deeply that she began forgiving herself and others. Celebrating life with a new sense of calling, she began sharing her wealth through philanthropy and changed her name to Happy, remaining vital and exuberant into her nineties.[14]

Affecting us more subtly but just as powerfully as these dramatic examples, reading as a regular practice strengthens and inspires us. For over seven years, Anne has participated in a book club, a supportive community of women who meet one evening a month at each other's homes. She shares her love of reading with her children, helping them develop their gifts. Anne's nine-year-old daughter Madeleine reads everything from children's books to history and nonfiction, incorporating books into her imaginative play and writing her own books on pages of computer paper stapled together. Each week, Anne takes her children to the local library and bookstore, where Madeleine gets biographies of notable women or classic novels adapted for children her age. Some afternoons, they read together, with Anne reading the original and Madeleine the children's version. Reading helps Anne's twelve-year-old autistic son, Mike, learn valuable life skills that help him to deal with the world around him. Because autistic children are overwhelmed by unfamiliar events, books help him cope. When Mike became anxious about thunderstorms, Anne got him a book describing cloud formations that helped him learn about the weather. Every night she and her son read together, a routine that is comforting as well as educational.

Psychologists have identified reading as an empowering practice for adults and a vital developmental asset for young people. By sharing her passion for reading with her children, Anne is helping them develop a stronger sense of themselves, as they become happier, healthier, and more engaged with the world around them.[15]

Telling Our Stories

Studies have shown that people with lives of meaning and purpose were read to or told stories as children. Conveying our culture's archetypal patterns through fairy tales, heroic legends, biblical tales, family history, and literature, these stories offer affirmations of hope. My colleague, novelist Ron Hansen, sees fiction as a source of archetypal stories, bringing us greater self-understanding through "analogies of encounter, discovery, and decision that will help us contemplate and change our lives."

Doug Oman and Carl Thoresen, two researchers in Santa Clara's Spirituality and Health Institute, call this process of learning from other lives "spiritual modeling." In chapter five, you discovered how spiritual models can build your faith and strengthen your values. Books can bring you a wealth of spiritual models, introducing you to people from other centuries, other worlds, strengthening your sense of agency and inspiring you to live more courageously.[16]

🌿 *Personal Exercise: Get Inspired by Characters*

Take a half hour to reflect by yourself with a pen or pencil and your Renaissance Notebook. Relax, clear your mind, then answer the following questions:

- Is there someone you've read about whose courage or agency inspires you? A historical figure or a character in a novel?
- Write down this person's name and ask yourself, "How did this person demonstrate agency?" Write this down.
- Now visualize yourself following this person's example. What does it look like? Feel like?
- Think of one action you can take to express greater agency in your life and write it on your Exploration List.

Reflecting on the Patterns in Your Life

In many ways, reading strengthens your self-awareness, helping you understand the intricate patterns of your life. One of my favorite books of Renaissance scholarship, Caroline Spurgeon's *Shakespeare's Imagery,* was written long before the advent of computers. Like a prospector panning for gold, Spurgeon read through all of Shakespeare's works, searching for images that revealed his personal themes. A major theme she discovered was his deep love of nature. Growing up in the English countryside, Shakespeare developed an intimate love of gardening, knew the life cycles of trees and crops, remembered the fragrance of roses and the wild flowers of early spring. He recalled visions of sunrise and sunset, cloud formations, sunlight and shadow, wind and rain. His images reveal a deep sympathy with all living things, especially birds and horses, and he noted all the rituals of daily life—eating and drinking, hunting, cooking, dressing, washing, sleeping, and dreaming. All this was embedded in his long-term memory, recalled in colorful imagery woven through his poetic lines.[17]

You, too, have recurrent patterns stored in your long-term memory, recalled by a familiar song or an old photograph, brought to life as a flashback from regions deep within your brain. Revealing your values, as Shakespeare's imagery revealed his, these patterns frame your experience, shaping the ongoing story of your life.

As a career counselor, Elizabeth helps people discover their callings by uncovering the major themes in their lives. She herself tried several paths before finding her calling. Because she loves working with people, she thought she'd enjoy her first job as an elementary school computer instructor. But teaching computer skills to twenty children at a time in half-hour back-to-back sessions left her frustrated and exhausted. When she went for a walk one day to clear her head, she realized that this job was too rushed, too centered on computers instead of people. It didn't fit her personal themes of creativity and working with people. She tried a public relations job that drew upon her creativity but was frustrated until she realized that she wanted to help *people* grow, not businesses. Combining her creativity with personal interaction and growth, Elizabeth now enjoys meeting with others to help them find their callings.[18]

RENAISSANCE QUESTION

Like Shakespeare and Elizabeth, you, too, have personal themes that can bring greater joy and meaning to your life. Ask yourself:

Do I know my personal themes?

What's your life story? Finding and reflecting on your recurring themes can light your life with greater understanding. According to psychologists, we tell ourselves stories to make greater sense of our lives. Telling your story can also be a spiritual exercise, a source of inspiration. My friend Ann Wittman, a Holy Cross sister in Wisconsin, believes that "God is every bit as present and active in our own stories" as in the lives of biblical saints and prophets. Ann says that "to some extent all families are dysfunctional." Yet even in the darkness, the times we feel "abandoned by God," contemplating our story can help us "see God's presence in it," connecting with a larger sense of meaning.[19]

With all the demands of daily life, it's hard to see the larger patterns, but you can find them by looking back in time. Can you see the patterns in my story?

I grew up as the daughter of an air force colonel, which meant my family was always moving. Packing up and traveling from one base to another, back and forth across the United States, to the Far East and Europe, I attended at least twelve different schools. At each new assignment, I'd find my way to the local library, reading books that brought me new friends and made me feel deeply at home. A small girl in pigtails, I wandered through the stacks, looking up at the endless rows of books that connected me with other lives across oceans of time and distance. Looking up, I promised myself that some day my books would be up there, too.

In high school, I read English novels in bed at night with a flashlight. In college, the writers in my literature classes made me dream of other worlds. But like many young people, I found it confusing to navigate around the demands and expectations of others, especially those I loved. For my first two years at the University of California Riverside, I was a commuter student. Eager to venture out on my own, I applied to a prestigious junior year abroad program. But when I was accepted, my parents said, "There is no good reason for you to study that far from home."

I learned a vital lesson: that dreams are only wishes without the power to make them come true. I had no agency or pathways because I was still a child, still financially dependent upon my parents. That summer I got a job at the local newspaper and in September moved into the college dormitory, paying the fees myself. While other students complained about dorm rules and cafeteria food, I rejoiced in my newfound freedom.

That spring, on a night filled with stars, my boyfriend asked me to marry him. He was graduating in a few weeks and said, "If you love me, you'll drop out of school and work so I can go to grad school." I loved him but couldn't imagine dropping out of school. "You're being selfish," he told me, and we broke up. For the next few nights, I wandered through the stacks in the college library, wondering what I was doing with my life. Then my favorite aunt died, leaving a gift in her will for me to study Shakespeare in Stratford-upon-Avon.

That summer I took a charter flight to London, boarded a train for Stratford, and began my first personal Renaissance. The other students and I lived in local inns. We walked down the cobblestone streets to the Shakespeare Institute for lectures and tutorials, went to Royal Shakespeare performances at night, and had picnics in my room after hours, talking, singing folk songs, and sharing our dreams. When classes were over, we explored the wider world around us. At a London street fair I found an antique seal, a red jasper stone with my initials engraved on it, used many lifetimes ago when letters were sealed with red sealing wax. I bought it with my food money and wore it for years on a chain around my neck, a connection with the mythic past and my imagined future. That fall, I returned to California to complete my senior year and received a graduate fellowship to UCLA to study Renaissance literature.

Books, libraries, journeys, and discovery—these are some of my personal themes. Now it's time to look for yours.

Personal Exercise: Tell Your Story

1. Set aside an hour by yourself in a place where you won't be disturbed, taking along a pen or pencil and your Renaissance Notebook.

2. Take a deep breath, relax, and clear your mind.
3. Then think back on your early life, using these questions to recall key memories.

   Questions:

   - What did you love to do as a child?
   - Did you have a favorite place to go?
   - Was there a special person in your life?
   - Was yours a dysfunctional family? If so, what challenges and gifts did it bring you?
   - What was the most influential event in your childhood?
   - Did a turning point change the way you looked at life? If so, what were you like before and after this event?
   - What was something you were proud of?
   - Were you a pathfinder, "the first person in my family to . . . "?

4. When a memory comes to mind, jot it down in your notebook.
5. Then read the questions again, recording another key memory.
6. When you have recorded two or three key memories, read over your descriptions, noting recurrent patterns.
7. Write them in your notebook.
8. Now complete this sentence and write down your answer: I am the kind of person who_____.
9. Finally, ask, "How do these themes connect with my calling today?"
10. Record your insights in your notebook.

Knowing your personal themes will strengthen your discernment, helping you make wiser choices in the ongoing story of your life.[20]

Shadows on the Path: Reframing Your Story

Sometimes this exercise dredges up past mistakes or shaming experiences that make you feel bad about yourself. But by reflecting, then reframing these experiences, you can move into a better future.

Reflecting on Negatives. Take a few moments to reflect on any negative memories and the feelings that come up.

- Name the feelings. ("I am feeling angry . . . hurt . . . sad . . . ashamed . . . afraid . . . ")
- Don't let the feelings overwhelm you. If you're dealing with memories of abuse or experiencing depression, don't go through this process alone. Seek out a trusted friend, therapist, or spiritual counselor.
- Note the feeling and name it. Naming does not mean approving of these emotions of anger, hurt, or fear, but simply acknowledging their existence. Notice how your body feels. Are you feeling tight? Tense? Focus on the feeling.
- Noting your feelings may cause them to change, increase, or diminish. Ask, "What is this feeling telling me? What do I need to know?"
- When the feeling subsides, bringing relief or new insights, breathe deeply and smile to yourself, feeling a new sense of compassion for the person you were and the person you are now.

Reframing Negatives: Learning and Forgiveness. Instead of feeling like a tragic hero, seeing your life as a failure because of a negative event in your past, ask what your life would look like if you could:

- See this experience as an exploration, not what you planned but an alternate path with a valuable lesson. How can you reframe your own experience from what went wrong to focus on the strengths you discovered, what you learned, and how to move forward into the future?
- See this event as an opportunity for grace, as St. Francis de Sales would call it. Can you pause for a moment of prayer or meditation, forgive yourself and others, and release this experience to move forward in life?

Reframing Your Life from Passive to Active. Our culture often reinforces us for passivity. Many advertisements make us feel inadequate, needing their products to feel okay. Some girls still grow up reading fairy tales—*Snow White, Sleeping Beauty, Cinderella*—about women who waited, often asleep for years, for a prince to come and make their dreams come true. If your old life pattern was passive, reframe your experience.

- Instead of waiting for good things to happen, see your life as an archetypal hero's journey.
- The negative experience can be a summons, a call to leave behind the old pattern to travel into the great unknown, face new challenges, and return with a treasure to grace your life and your world.
- What would your life look like if you were a mythic hero solving the mystery of identity in a struggle against the darkness? Or Dorothy in *The Wizard of Oz* who faced the unknown with courage, compassion, and friendship, finding her way home with a treasure of new awareness?[21]

By reframing your life within a larger pattern of meaning, you will see the light beyond the darkness, living a personal Renaissance of discovery, grace, and renewal.

. . . .

Moving Forward

Now take a moment to review your progress in this chapter, writing your answers and today's date in your Renaissance Notebook:

1. What insight did *lectio divina* bring to light your path?
2. If you found a spiritual model in your reading, what did this person inspire you to do?
3. If you reframed a negative event from the past, how do you feel now?
4. What are your personal themes that bring you CS joy? How can they support your calling today?
5. What was your creative victory in this chapter and how are you celebrating it?

Reading and reflection open up new worlds within and around you. As you see your life story taking shape before your eyes, you become, more than ever, a new Renaissance person, bringing your own creative pattern to the world.

RENAISSANCE REMINDERS

Your daily choices shape your life and inform the world.
As you read and reflect on the patterns in your life, remember to:

- Expand your world through reading.
- Look for meaningful patterns in the story of your life.
- Live your own hero's journey.

CHAPTER 11

Physical Exercise

Building Strength and Wisdom

. . . and by small,
Accomplishing great things.
—JOHN MILTON, *PARADISE LOST*[1]

How much physical activity do you do during the day? Do you go to the gym, practice yoga, play a sport, or take walks? Many people don't have an exercise practice. Like Doris, they think they're too tired or too busy. Bogged down in a job she considers beneath her, Doris goes from one mindless task to the next, filling out order forms, stocking the shelves, and waiting on customers in an arts and crafts store. She resents selling costume jewelry to teenagers and helping housewives with their quilting projects when she dreams of becoming a famous artist. Downcast and lethargic, she also resents her two coworkers. While they take art classes after work and walk to a nearby park to sketch during lunch, Doris only shuffles over to the shop next door for a burger and doughnuts. After work, too tired to even pick up her sketch pad, she sits at home watching television, letting her dreams of a better life fade into the distance.

Don't let inertia drain your energy and drive away your dreams. You can develop greater strength and stamina for your personal Renaissance through a regular exercise practice. Studies have shown that exercising regularly can increase your vitality and motivation and open you up to creative new insights.

Exercise came naturally to people in the Renaissance. In what was still largely an agrarian society, most men and women spent their days plowing, sowing, weeding, harvesting, shearing sheep, tending dairy cows, and taking their goods to market. Before cars, telephones, and computers, our Renaissance counterparts walked miles to do errands and visit friends. While today most families cook with microwave ovens, preparing meals back then involved chopping wood, carrying water, building a fire in the kitchen grate, baking bread, roasting and carving meat, harvesting vegetables and herbs from the garden, then chopping them for soups and stews. Even their recreation was more active. Men and women from all social classes danced, sang, and played musical instruments. Aristocrats rode horses, hunted, and trained hawks. Renaissance courtiers balanced expertise in the liberal and the martial arts, maintaining their physical prowess by hunting, swimming, jumping, running, dancing, and playing tennis. To clear her mind and maintain her stamina, Queen Elizabeth I began each day with a brisk walk around the palace courtyard.

Modern technology has gradually eroded regular exercise from our lives. In today's developed countries, most people no longer do manual labor, farm, hunt for food, or walk to market, and most domestic chores have been mechanized. With convenience has come a chronic lack of physical activity that undermines our health. By adding more activity to your days, this chapter will help you improve your energy, stamina, and overall health.[2]

Looking Back

During the Renaissance, the most common form of transportation was walking. For longer trips, wealthier people rode horses or mules, and some aristocrats rode in coaches. Passenger boats and barges carried people, produce, dairy products, sheep, and cattle on local rivers to London and other major cities. But for daily errands, people walked. Children walked to school. Men and women either worked at home or walked to work; they walked to church, to visit friends, and to buy goods at the local market, generally five to nine miles away. Most people walked during the day, when roads were reasonably safe from highway robbers. In good weather, they covered three to four miles in an hour.[3]

Every afternoon in early seventeenth-century England, a slim, dark-haired young man set aside the manuscripts on his desk to take his daily walk through the village of Bemerton. It was not enough to see his parishioners on Sundays. He wanted to meet them where they lived and worked, greeting farmers in their fields, shopkeepers in their shops, and the blacksmith going about his work. He blessed children as they read their lessons, offered men and women encouragement in their vocations, and shared his money with the poor. Each day, George Herbert comforted the sick, consoled the troubled, and listened to people's hopes and fears with his simple walking ritual.

Herbert also loved music. Twice a week he walked down the country road to Salisbury to attend evensong services in the cathedral. Afterward, he met with friends to play sacred and secular music. He then walked back to Bemerton, his soul refreshed and composed by the music he called his "Heaven upon Earth."

His first biographer tells how Herbert continued his ministry on these walks. One day he came across a poor man in ragged clothes standing in dismay beside his horse, which had fallen, too exhausted to carry his heavy load. Herbert helped the man unload the poor animal, giving him money to feed himself and his horse, and told him to be kind to the animal as one of God's creatures. After they'd let the horse rest, then carefully loaded him up again, the man gently led his horse down the road, thanking and blessing Herbert. When Herbert arrived in Salisbury, his friends were surprised to see him so soiled and rumpled from his journey. One man said that as a clergyman, Herbert "had disparaged himself by so dirty an employment." Herbert replied that he had simply been practicing his faith, "for if I be bound to pray for all that be in distress, I am sure that I am bound so far as it is in my power to *practice* what I pray for." Herbert's walks became a spiritual exercise, as he lived his calling one step at a time.[4]

The Advantages of Walking Today

Walking is the simplest, most natural form of physical exercise. Exerting low impact on your joints, walking builds bone density, promotes better circulation and cardiovascular health. It also stimulates your immune system, helping ward off colds and flu. Walking slows you down, helps you feel the earth beneath your feet, restoring your awareness of the present moment. Returning you to your own natural rhythms, it brings you more deeply in touch with yourself, repairing the stress and fragmentation from rushing, multitasking, and information overload.

As Herbert realized, regular walks build our relationships with others. Walking around my neighborhood with my dachshund, Heidi, helps me stay in touch with my neighbors. Children run up to play with Heidi and tell me about their sports and school. I see Les building a new fence, while Judy sets out a basket of home-grown tomatoes for neighbors passing by. My walks connect me to the seasons as the blossoms on the tree in Kari's front yard turn to tiny apples and the pepper trees become an autumn symphony of red and gold—small rituals, greetings, and gifts marking the changing seasons of our lives.

By simply walking around, you and I can add human warmth to our busy lives. When my husband, Bob, chaired Santa Clara's psychology department, he made what colleagues called his "daily rounds." Walking around the department at the beginning and end of the day, he'd drop by people's offices, ask how they were doing, seeing if there was anything he could do to help. Morale flourished as people felt validated by this simple ritual.

Our technology has given us new methods of communication—e-mail, voice mail, and cell phones—but these are no substitute for human contact. Harvard psychiatrist Edward Hallowell has described the anxiety, confusion, and alienation that arise when professional interactions are limited to e-mail and voice mail. Without human contact, electronic communications are easily misunderstood, making people feel insulted or discounted. Morale plummets, productivity suffers, and people start looking for other jobs. Many problems can be prevented by personal contact, what Hallowell calls "the human moment at work."

This "human moment" is equally vital for families. A recent University of Wisconsin study of over 1,300 families connected habitual cell phone use with psychological distress and decreased family satisfaction. Availability 24/7 and urgent interruptions are no substitute for personal contact.[5]

Personal Exercise: Take a Mindful Walk

You can improve your life by simply walking more mindfully. Here's how:

Walk more at work. When I first came to Santa Clara, many of us met for lunch at the faculty club or saw each other walking through the mission gardens on our way to class. In a small-town atmosphere, we conducted business informally, solving and preventing many problems. Over the years, technology has transformed our college. The faculty club has been replaced by a cafeteria and I rarely see my colleagues around campus. Most of us spend lunch hours at our desks answering e-mail. We even e-mail people in our own departments instead of walking down the hall to talk with them.

If your workplace has been feeling cold and impersonal, try these simple steps to restore what Edward Hallowell calls "the human moment at work":

- Walk down the hall to talk with a colleague instead of just sending another e-mail. Communicating in person is clearer and may even *save* time by preventing electronic misunderstandings and a long succession of explanatory e-mails.

- Don't stay chained to your desk. Prevent chronic tension and repetitive stress injury by getting up periodically to walk around.
- Take a walk at lunch. Take your lunch outside for an impromptu picnic or meet a friend for a light lunch and relaxing walk. A midday walk, even if only ten or fifteen minutes, will add more energy to your days.

Keep Track of Your Steps. Some time ago, a busy engineer saw health psychologist Tom Plante with doctor's orders to lose weight. Oscar had tried many diets and weight loss programs but was always unsuccessful. Because Oscar liked working with charts and computers, Tom asked him to wear a pedometer on his belt, count his steps, and work up to ten thousand steps a day. Oscar entered his daily step count on a computer spreadsheet to track his progress. He lost thirty-five pounds and has maintained the weight loss for over three years.[6]

- One way to walk more is to simply *pay more attention to it.* Attention is power.
- Get yourself a pedometer to keep track of your steps. Make this a game with yourself. By simply paying attention, you will find yourself adding more steps—and more life—to your days.

Work More Active Choices into Your Life. Small changes can make a major difference in your life, while conserving energy and combating global warming.

- Take the stairs instead of the elevator. In my husband's building, these days the faculty climb the stairs, while most students take the elevators. We've built a new campus fitness center for students who want to look fit. But they wouldn't need to work out on the Stairmaster if they took the stairs to class.
- Park your car farther away. At shopping centers, many people burn up fuel waiting for a car to pull out of a nearby space when there are plenty of spaces farther away. Save time and energy—your own and our planet's—by using these spaces.

- Do local errands without a car. If you live or work a mile or two from town, walk or cycle instead of always taking the car. Carry groceries in bicycle saddlebags or a rolling cart from the hardware store. Make your commutes or shopping trips into regular exercise, while doing your part to reduce greenhouse gasses.
- Meet friends for regular walks. Combine exercise with time for family or friends. Two women I know meet for walks on a nearby trail, and a retired couple takes daily walks around my neighborhood.

Now take positive action. Beginning this week, choose one of these steps to add more energy to your life.

The Way to Greater Wellness

Congratulations! By simply walking more, you are on your way to greater wellness. Health psychologists see wellness as a combination of physical, mental, and emotional health, and regular exercise supports all three. Physically, it reduces the risk of heart disease, diabetes, high blood pressure, and some forms of cancer, as well as controlling weight, reducing blood pressure, strengthening bones, muscles, joints, and your immune system. It even helps you fall asleep faster and improves the quality of your sleep.

Exercise stimulates your brain, helping you stay alert, and promotes better cognitive functioning, memory, reasoning, and spacial ability. In 2002, a California Department of Education study related physical fitness to higher academic achievement in thousands of students from elementary school to high school. A chronic lack of exercise has been linked to attention deficit hyperactivity disorder (ADHD), and studies have found that aerobic exercise can relieve its symptoms. Exercise also helps prevent age-related mental decline, reducing the risk of Alzheimer's disease.

Exercise strengthens your emotional well-being, improving your mood and making you feel better about yourself. Regular exercise is one of the major sources of "flow" for young people. Research has shown that exercise improves your mood both immediately after a workout, because of endorphins in the brain, and over the long term, by reducing anxiety and relieving tension, stress, depression, and fatigue.[7] Today's psychologists are rediscovering what Robert Burton knew in the Renaissance when he prescribed moderate exercise to maintain health, build strength, and relieve depression. Burton recommended gardening, tennis, hawking, hunting, fishing, and riding, but, above all, walking in a natural country setting, where men and women could lift their spirits by enjoying fresh air, bird songs, and visions of trees, meadows, and flowers. Nearly four centuries later, research has shown that exercise does indeed dispel depression and that sedentary people are much more likely to become clinically depressed. Psychologists now use exercise to treat a wide range of diseases and disorders, including anxiety, depression, autism, attention deficit disorder, conduct disorders, alcoholism, and substance abuse.[8]

Personal Exercise: Begin Your Physical Exercise Practice

You've already begun to add more walking to your days. Now it's time to develop your own personal exercise practice, an enjoyable activity that will nurture your joyous CS energy, relieve stress, restore your natural vitality, and bring more sense of play into your life.

If you're just beginning to exercise, move into your new practice gradually. Don't do too much too soon. If you have been *very* sedentary, check with your doctor before beginning your new practice. Current health guidelines recommend at least thirty minutes of moderate exercise (brisk walking, hiking, or swimming) three times a week. You can also break this into smaller units—two fifteen-minute walks or three ten-minute walks a day.[9]

1. First, find an exercise you enjoy. Yes, your exercise practice should be fun! What do *you* like? After working all week at a title company, Tom runs after work and rides his mountain bike on weekends. Jerry runs and cycles, Nikole swims, Bob trains his horse, walks on the track, and works out on an elliptical trainer. Michelle takes walks, dances, and does yoga. I walk around my neighborhood, on the trail and track, and do Pilates. After being inside teaching or writing, it feels great to get out and *move* at the end of the day. What exercise do *you* like to do?

2. Make your workout a regular part of your life. Begin your new habit by taking a first step: buy a pair of running shoes, sign up for an exercise class at your community center, or join a gym. Then find a schedule that works for *you*. Diana takes a brisk walk at noon, carrying a light lunch in her pockets. Bob unwinds with workouts at the end of the day. Tracey begins her day with exercise, walking in the woods before going to work.

3. Begin your workouts gradually, increasing their time and intensity as you build your stamina. Begin walking for ten to fifteen minutes, then build up in five-minute increments to reach a thirty-minute goal. Begin running by jogging a short distance then walking the rest of the way, gradually increasing your jogging time. Or take a short bike ride around the neighborhood and gradually build time and distance. Remember: small actions over time produce monumental results.

4. Record your workouts. Make appointments with yourself. Schedule regular workouts on your calendar, then record your progress. For fun, I keep track of my walking mileage, recording my four-mile track workouts, trail workouts, and daily walks with my dog, adding up my score at the end of the month.

● ●

You'll find your workouts improving your life in unexpected ways. After a recent merger, Melanie's banking job had become stressful and exhausting. Worried about the next round of layoffs and dealing with increased work, she felt anxious and unhappy.

On the advice of a friend, Melanie signed up for a weekly Pilates class at the local community center, although she wondered if she'd have the energy or time for class. The first night was a pleasant surprise: a supportive group of women and an upbeat instructor who encouraged her to exercise at her own pace. The exercises made her feel like a child again, lying on the mat kicking her feet in the air, and she left feeling more relaxed. Gradually, Melanie's exercise practice helped her overcome her inertia and develop positive forward momentum. After a few weeks, she was standing taller, had lost five pounds, had more energy, and could cope better with work. On stressful days, she began taking brisk walks during lunch to clear her head. She made it a point to leave the office on time for class or to join friends for a walk after work. Although she's still working at the bank, she's now moving into a new career, going to school two nights a week to get a degree in counseling to begin a healthier new direction in life.

Building Wisdom and Strength

As Melanie discovered, your exercise practice can help you move forward on many levels. First of all, since you've chosen a practice you enjoy, you'll have more fun, nurturing your creative CS. Psychologist Rick Snyder found that regular exercise will also help you develop greater energy, willpower, and hope.[10] You'll become more creative and resourceful, able to see new possibilities for your life.

One person who models these strengths for me is sports psychologist, personal coach, and former national champion distance runner Jerry Lynch. With his ready smile, upbeat attitude, and Brooklyn accent, Jerry radiates positive energy. Working with NCAA champions, world-class athletes, and CEOs, he applies lessons of courage, integrity, and perseverance from competitive athletics to help people become champions in every area of their lives.

Last summer, as we sat on the porch of his seaside home in Santa Cruz, California, Jerry shared the wisdom he'd gained from exercise. "I believe that exercise—running and cycling—has taught me more about myself than graduate school in psychology, therapy, or reading," he told me. We're all athletes, says Jerry. "Every one of us is a naturally born athlete. We are all given that gift." Some of us grew up believing in our natural athletic ability, while the rest of us were discouraged or ridiculed. Called "clumsy" by our parents, "fat" or "skinny" by our peers, we developed negative attitudes toward our bodies. Whatever your experience, a regular exercise practice can restore your natural relationship with your body, making you stronger both physically and emotionally.

Strategies for Excellence

When Jerry works with college athletes—over thirty years younger than he is—he rides his mountain bike to the top of the mountain first, then tells them he did it because he is "mentally stronger." "I'm an ordinary person but I'm capable of doing extraordinary things," he says, sharing strategies he calls "mental mechanics." Because the young athletes have seen the results, they listen and learn, developing their own potentials.

Jerry's tools are "to compete with your heart, with courage, perseverance, compassion."

"When athletes fight their inner battles with the weapons of the heart—courage, patience, perseverance, integrity, tenacity—they build inner strength," he says. "Your soul is getting nourished. Your heart is getting stronger. It's soul food." You, too, can use these strategies to overcome challenges in your personal Renaissance.

Facing Challenges

One common challenge is reaching a plateau. By now you've set your goal, followed some pathways, and made some progress, but there are times when your progress can seem so slow it feels like you're standing still. It's easy to start doubting yourself and your dreams. By bringing you greater perspective, a good exercise practice can renew your faith in the process. "There's a real connection between a good two-hour bike ride and persevering, patience in life," says Jerry.

Dealing with plateaus requires a paradigm shift, as Jerry learned from George Leonard. "When we feel like we're not getting anywhere, that's the western way of looking at it," Jerry says. Actually, "plateau is progress. It's nature's way of allowing your mind and heart to adjust to your progress" before you move up to the next level. "It takes time," he says, "to assimilate to changes about to happen." Plateaus are a natural part of the process, a necessary adjustment. If we try to surge forward and skip the plateau, he says, "there are setbacks, injuries, burnout."

So whether you're building strength through exercise or climbing to new levels in your calling, the important thing is to recognize the plateau and relax with it. "When I relax," Jerry says with a smile, "I actually get there faster."

When approaching our goals, many of us hesitate, but "champions go all out," Jerry told me.

"Why don't more people go all out?" I asked.

"Fear," Jerry answered. "Our biggest inner battle is with our fears."

Fear again, that recurrent challenge when we seek a new Renaissance in our lives. When we face the unknown, when we reach out to do something we care about, we struggle with fear and self-doubt. Exercise helps us overcome our fears.

One reason we feel so much fear, Jerry says, is that "people don't like to be uncomfortable." As a coach and sports psychologist, he sees his task as helping people "become comfortable with being uncomfortable." "The pain going up a hill is your body's way of dealing with the unfamiliar," he says. But he sees this discomfort as a "pathway to enlightenment." By dealing with discomfort, we make breakthroughs to the next level.

"We become complacent with comfort," Jerry believes. When we let complacency dictate our behavior, this is limiting, like an illness. "The cure is commitment of the heart. That's your intuition. That's the truth," he says. In his life's work, Jerry helps people find this truth in themselves. Becoming "comfortable with being uncomfortable" leads to "growth, change, forward movement." Jerry estimates that about 98 percent of the population is stuck in the complacent category: "The other 2 percent are the movers, shakers, doers."[11] When you move forward into the unknown, following your heart into a new Renaissance, you become part of this group.

Shadows on the Path: Overcoming Perfectionism

Another form of "being comfortable with being uncomfortable" is facing our imperfections, overcoming the shadow that still haunts many of us today: the passion for perfection. In the Renaissance, whenever someone criticized one of artist Cimabue's paintings or he himself noticed a small imperfection, no matter how beautiful the total picture might be, he would destroy that painting because it wasn't perfect.

Cimabue's reaction struck a common chord in many of my students. "We've all had to face our imperfections," I told them. In grade school, whenever I brought home a spelling test, my parents praised me when I got 100 percent, but with anything less, even a 95, they focused on what I did wrong. Filled with shame when my scores were less than perfect, I hid my mistakes by crumpling up the tests and throwing them under my bed. My students laughed but got the message: hiding our mistakes is ridiculous. I asked them to hold up their pencils and notice the erasers, there because we're all human. We all make mistakes. That's how we learn.

Another Renaissance artist, Raphael, faced his imperfections, continuing to learn from them. As a boy, he had learned to draw by imitating his master, Pietro Perugino. When he grew older, Raphael was amazed by the subtle facial expressions in the paintings of Leonardo da Vinci. Carefully studying these paintings,

Raphael learned how to blend his own colors to achieve this natural grace. Then, when he saw Michelangelo's paintings, he realized that his own knowledge of the human body fell far short. For many long months, Raphael became a student again, studying anatomy, drawing nudes, dissecting bodies to understand the complexities of the human form. Finally, he could accurately portray the human body but found that his drawings still lacked the power that was Michelangelo's alone. Then Raphael focused on his own gifts, developing a distinctive portrayal of landscapes, clothing, light, and shadow. He refined his skill in portraiture, capturing in exquisite detail the uniqueness of each person he painted. After bringing his work up to the desired level, Raphael focused on his strengths, developing his own standard of excellence.[12]

Personal Exercise: Take Positive Steps

If you've fallen short or made a mistake, stop obsessing about perfection. Ask yourself:

- What can I learn from this?
- What *can* I do?
- How can I use my gifts?

Take positive steps to improve your performance. Then develop your own strengths. Embrace the living process of growth that made Raphael a great artist.

The Importance of Little Things

The conclusion of Milton's Renaissance epic, *Paradise Lost,* reminds us to keep faith with our gifts and stay on the path, "by small, accomplishing great things."[13] Jerry Lynch knows the importance of little things. "There's a Japanese expression," he told me, "'from little streams come big rivers.'" Jerry has hiked to the highest point in the Colorado Rockies, watched the trickle of snowmelt turn into tiny streams that become the mighty Colorado River.

Great accomplishments always begin with small steps. My husband, Bob, began running two or three miles around the neighborhood, gradually building up to four miles. Then he ran six miles with his friend Milo, and longer distances with new friends Terry, Dave, Patti, and Sandy, increasing his workouts to eight or ten miles. He read books on marathon training, developing stamina by running six to ten miles four days a week, with a longer twelve- to twenty-mile run on Saturdays. In 1987, he ran his first marathon, twenty-six miles through the morning fog on the Golden Gate Bridge and the hills of San Francisco, followed by many races thereafter.

Little things are essential to your personal Renaissance. But most people don't realize this. According to Jerry Lynch, "Everyone thinks they have to do something gargantuan. Then they get performance anxiety. In national championships or the Olympics, athletes think they need to do something really big." He tells them, "No, you have to do the little things that got you there." In basketball, it's the "dive for the fifty/fifty ball, boxing out under the backboards, sprinting back on defense" that lead to a championship performance.

In relationships, too, it's the little things, Jerry says, "not the expensive dinners, the flashy jewelry, but the small gestures of caring, the time you take to really be with that person." With his family, he makes it a point to "see" his children when they leave the house, to make eye contact with them, showing that he cares.

When Jerry went to New Zealand to give a keynote address, he could have gotten all caught up in thinking he had to do some "big thing." But instead, he told me, he concentrated on the little things: being present, meeting people the day before, making eye contact. Then, he told himself, "When you are speaking, remember who you are, that you're here to serve. Stay in touch with your purpose."

RENAISSANCE QUESTION

What little things can I do to move forward with greater purpose?
You'll be exploring this question more fully in the next chapter.

Moving Forward

Now it's time to review your progress in your exercise practice.
Write your answers and today's date in your Renaissance Notebook:

1. Have you been practicing mindful walking? What difference
   has it made in your life?
2. What is your personal exercise practice? Has it increased
   your CS joy?
3. Have you begun to relax in plateaus? Become more comfortable with being uncomfortable? See imperfections as opportunities to learn?
4. What was your creative victory in this chapter and how are
   you celebrating it?

Taken together, the small steps in this chapter will add greater
activity to your days, greater strength and wisdom to your life.

RENAISSANCE REMINDERS

Small actions over time produce monumental results.
As you pursue your personal Renaissance:

- Make active choices, adding more mindful walking to your days.
- Use the power of exercise to open your heart to greater wisdom
  and strength.
- Remember the importance of little things.

CHAPTER 12

Discipline and Dedication

Bringing Your Dreams to Life

And as imagination bodies forth
The forms of things unknown, the poet's pen
Turns them to shapes, and gives to airy nothing
A local habitation and a name.

—WILLIAM SHAKESPEARE, *A MIDSUMMER NIGHT'S DREAM*[1]

Throughout this book, you have been developing your gifts and discovering your calling, adding one practice at a time to support you on your journey to a new Renaissance life. Now you're ready for the final practice, discipline and dedication, which builds upon all the others, giving you the power to bring your dreams to life.

Many people begin a personal growth program with enthusiasm but give up before reaching their goals. Without discipline and dedication, their visions of a better life fade into the distance. Terri has tried it all, going from one personal growth workshop to another. She's studied with celebrity gurus and consulted psychics, tried sweat lodges in Arizona, hot tubs at Esalen, fire walking, bioenergetics, and dozens of other approaches. With each new workshop she's excited, certain that this time she's found the answer. But in a few days, the workshop "high" wears off, leaving her with the same unresolved issues in her life. Restless, unhappy, yearning for change, she scans the Internet and checks New Age bookstores for the next speaker, the next workshop, the next stairway to heaven.

Terri has missed the secret known by Renaissance artists and those who live Renaissance lives today: that consistent effort in the direction of your dreams will open the gateway to a new life. The key is to persevere, to practice, to keep faith with your dreams. Discipline and dedication have characterized the lives of achievement throughout history, according to a classic Stanford University study. With these strengths, the great Renaissance artists transformed their dreams into realities. Centuries ago, in a Florentine warehouse, a giant block of marble lay on its side, abandoned by a sculptor who had begun carving, hacked a hole through its base, and then given up. The spoiled marble had lain idle for years, with people wondering what to do with it. In 1504, Michelangelo carefully studied the marble, then with discipline and dedication transformed it into his heroic statue of David.[2]

As you've followed the program in this book, you've been chipping away at the blocks within and around you to uncover the life of your dreams. In this final chapter, you will take this process to the next level by developing a sustaining discipline.

Looking Back

John Milton wrote that there is nothing "in the world of more grave and urgent importance throughout the whole life of man, than is discipline." Today we often associate discipline with punishment—parents discipline a child and students are sent to the principal's office for "disciplinary action." But in the Renaissance, discipline meant ongoing education, essential for developing your gifts and keeping faith with your dreams.

Each calling has its own discipline, its own precepts, its own code. In the Renaissance the Reverend John Hooper wrote that doctors must study medical principles, musicians the rules of music, and farmers the principles of agriculture, each learning "the rules that belong unto his profession, or else he shall never profit in his science or art." Cennino Cennini reminded young artists to learn the language and principles of art by continuing to practice drawing. "Do not fail," he said, "to draw something every day . . . no matter how little," for daily discipline develops essential skills.[3]

In our own time, after studying nearly one hundred artists, actors, musicians, architects, scientists, philosophers, writers, and political leaders, psychologist Mihaly Csikszentmihalyi found that to make a creative contribution we must work within a creative system, internalize the language and principles of a domain, reproducing its structure within our minds. Neuroscience research has shown that disciplined practice produces new neural connections, actually preparing your mind for flashes of creative insight.[4]

The statue of David emerged from Michelangelo's disciplined quest for domain knowledge. As a young man, he studied classical sculptures in the gardens of Lorenzo de' Medici. To learn anatomy, he dissected bodies in the church of San Spirito until he could transform cold marble into statues so lifelike they seemed ready to move and breathe. So dedicated was he that he often worked at night, lighting his way with a helmet he made with a candle on top to free both hands for carving.

Other Renaissance men and women developed their own sustaining disciplines. Sculptor Madonna Properzia de Rossi developed her skills by carving peach stones into miniatures of Christ and the saints. St. Francis de Sales began a daily discipline at age twelve, rising early to study, read, and contemplate. Philosopher John Locke spent years reading in politics, religion, history, classics, and ethics, gaining the foundation knowledge for his work on politics and human understanding.[5]

This is the secret of this chapter: you, too, can achieve excellence, becoming an artist in your life through disciplined, consistent effort. Far from being monotonous, productive effort brings purpose and vitality to our lives. Studies have shown that when done mindfully, this practice will help you develop a powerful forward momentum, promoting "flow" and bringing you higher levels of joy and meaning.[6]

Making an Effort to Finish

Neuroscientists have found that you and I each have "designer brains," continuously shaped in response to our daily actions. During adolescence, our activities develop the neural connections we bring into adulthood. Now you are building new neural connections for perseverance, focus, and precision by pursuing your Renaissance practices. Psychologists tell us that engaging in intense, concentrated effort develops these strengths, promoting healthy personal development and future success.

Without these strengths, people cannot reach their goals. Brad's life was a series of impressive beginnings, his resume filled with stops and starts. With his flashing smile, personal charm, and high IQ, he coasted through high school, voted student council president and "Most Likely to Succeed." Impatient and easily bored, he went to the state university where he changed majors repeatedly, finally settling on English, then going on to law school. He impressed his law professors and made important contacts, but couldn't coast through the bar exam. When he didn't pass the first time, he decided he'd rather be a Hollywood screenwriter. But when he took a screen-writing class and saw all the hard work beneath the glamour, he changed his mind again. Going into sales, he's worked for a number of firms, beginning each new job with enthusiasm, then slacking off when novelty becomes routine. Brad hasn't learned that all the talent and charm in the world will not get him far without the inner strength of discipline and dedication. Discipline and dedication are the building blocks of success in any domain. Veterinarian Dr. David Reed can tell in a week which high school students he mentors will be successful. He's found that those with a good work ethic, punctuality, professional demeanor, and commitment not only became good veterinary technicians but go on to become successful veterinarians, attorneys, and business professionals.[7]

Daily Discipline as Spiritual Practice

By becoming deeply involved in what we do, by practicing life's daily rituals with care, commitment, and focused attention, we develop inner strength and find greater meaning in life. Concert pianist Hans Boepple began piano lessons at age four. At ten, he made his concert debut with the Los Angeles Philharmonic. He has played in major orchestras and his students have earned more than one hundred state, national, and international awards. As professor and chair of the music department at Santa Clara University, Hans teaches, oversees his department, instructs private students, performs—and practices seldom less than three hours a day.

After a magical Chopin recital of his in 2006 that received three standing ovations, I told Hans that when people find their callings, their life's work not only brings them joy but enhances the lives around them. His music, I said, is a gift to us all.

Hans makes sure he practices by coming to campus at 6:30 a.m. He exercises at the gym three days a week, then practices an hour or two before handling his duties as department chair. He also works in an hour or two of practice during the day. Maintaining this daily discipline is not easy. In 1995, when Hans became department chair, there was so much to do—so many meetings, protocols, memos, and demands on his time—that for the first time in his life he stopped practicing. From August 1995 to March 1996, he "did virtually no personal work at the piano." Then, he said, "I had a remarkable experience: a feeling of deep, deep sadness, like I had never known." It was as if someone he loved, a close family member, had died. He realized that this profound sadness came from the absence of music from his life. He went back to the piano and has been practicing daily ever since.

For Hans, "There is no 'right amount of time' to practice music, or anything else, for that matter." We must each find that out for ourselves. However, he believes that "There are some who seem born to something, such as music, who love it more than any other activity in their life, who find the deepest meaning and self-expression in it, and who never think of doing anything else as their life's work. I never think of piano practice (no matter how much) as work: I think of work as something I would rather *not* be doing."

When people find their callings, he says, "Their work comes from passion, not obligation, and brings them joy. Any sort of activity that springs from a sense of obligation or duty or parental expectation will not likely lead to happiness, or result in something beautiful or significant. But I believe in every person is a passion that can be found and should be cultivated. If every person's profession could be what fills his life with light, I think this would be a better, certainly a happier, world."[8]

RENAISSANCE QUESTIONS

What is my passion, the activity that fills my life with light?

Do I have a daily practice to sustain it?

Personal Exercise: Pursue Your Daily Practice

Every one of us has a calling and each calling has its own sustaining discipline. Musicians practice, artists sketch, scientists experiment, writers write, and members of the clergy minister to their congregations. Novelist Ron Hansen writes every day. My husband, Bob, does experiments and reads scientific journals. In the Renaissance, Leonardo da Vinci sketched in his notebook, capturing in exquisite drawings people in the public square, the flight of birds, the power and grace of horses, the daily details of his world. Shakespeare wrote, acted, and read history and romances to get ideas for his dramatic plots. As a country parson, George Herbert not only ministered to people on his daily walks, he also rebuilt the church and parsonage of Bemerton, paying attention to the smallest detail, seeing that all was "in good repair," the church "swept, and kept clean without dust or cobwebs," creating an atmosphere of beauty and harmony.[9]

Your calling, too, has a daily practice that develops your strengths, brings you joy, and inspires new insights. In the last chapter, you learned the importance of "little things." Now ask yourself, "What one little thing would make me more of the person I want to be?" Your answer will depend upon where you are in life, your personal passion and priorities.

- This small act can be practicing your instrument, developing one of your strengths, learning a new skill, exploring a new subject, balancing your life by taking better care of yourself, or staying in touch with someone you love.
- Don't get carried away with a list of resolutions. Focus on one important little action.
- Write it in your Renaissance Notebook and on an index card.
- Sign and date the card: "I, [your name], promise myself to practice [your chosen activity] each day."
- Review your card each morning as you plan your day, incorporating this new discipline into your life.

Developing habits takes time, but cultivating excellence through your own daily discipline will bring you increasing joy and power. In a month, review your progress, either renewing your commitment to this action or adding another essential discipline.

The Power of Dedication

Your daily discipline builds dedication, powerful momentum to help you move forward in your calling. Positive psychologists Martin Seligman and Christopher Peterson call this quality "integrity," "persistence," and "perseverance." It is the moral courage to follow your star, to push through resistance to achieve your dreams.[10]

Many Renaissance men and women had such dedication. Elizabeth I overcame arrest and imprisonment, political and religious controversy, to become a great Renaissance leader. Michelangelo worked four long years to paint the ceiling of the Sistine Chapel. St. Teresa of Avila reformed the Carmelite order, founding seventeen new convents, traveling through the rugged mountain terrain from her forties through her sixties, despite chronic arthritis, a weak heart, a broken shoulder, and recurrent malaria.[11]

Persevering despite illness and accusations of heresy, Galileo Galilei transformed the way we see ourselves and our world. Born in 1564, the same year as Shakespeare, Galileo's fascination with the stars as a boy led to a lifelong curiosity about the cosmos. His father sent him to study with the monks at Vallombroso and then to the University of Pisa to study medicine, intending for him to become a doctor, but Galileo's gifts drew him to science and mathematics. At twenty-two, he improved on Archimedes' method for weighing metals, later becoming professor of mathematics at the University of Pisa and the University of Padua. He invented the thermometer and built his own telescope. In 1610, he discovered the craters of the moon and the moons of Jupiter, publishing his findings in *The Starry Messenger* and becoming chief mathematician to the Medicis in Florence. The next year, he journeyed to Rome to show his telescope to the Papal Court. A devout Catholic, Galileo believed that science and faith were compatible, representing different forms of truth. But in 1633, after publishing his *Dialogue on the Two World Systems,* he was summoned to Rome, tried for heresy, and condemned by the Inquisition. Legend has it that as he left the courtroom, Galileo muttered under his breath, "Eppur si muove" ("But yet it moves," referring to the earth's orbit around the sun). He spent his final years sick, blind, and under house arrest, continuing to write and receive visitors. In 1638 he published his greatest work, *Discourses on Two New Sciences.*[12]

As a boy, John Milton dreamed of writing a great epic poem. Since an epic poet must acquire "an all-around foundation in all the arts and sciences," he set himself a personal discipline to learn languages, classical literature, philosophy, theology, and history. Beginning at age twelve, he tells us, "I hardly ever left my studies or went to bed before midnight." Convinced that a poet should live the values he portrays, to be himself "a true poem," Milton developed his courage, strength of character, and skill with the sword. He produced impressive early poetry, earned his bachelor's and master's degrees at Cambridge, then spent five more years in intensive study. In 1638, he traveled to Italy, where leading Renaissance poets and scholars encouraged him in his vocation. There, he says that he "found and visited the famous Galileo, grown old, a prisoner to the Inquisition, for thinking in astronomy otherwise than the Franciscan and Dominican licensers thought."

Milton returned home in the summer of 1639, to a country torn by controversy and demands for government reform. Setting aside his planned epic, for the next twenty years he wrote about political reform and freedom of the press, becoming Latin secretary for the new Puritan government, equivalent to our secretary of state. His eyes grew weak, but he forged on, determined to explain the new English democracy to the world. Losing his sight, he continued working, supported by able assistants. When the Puritan government collapsed in 1660, King Charles II returned from exile, declaring Milton a public enemy. Legend has it that only the intervention of Andrew Marvell prevented his execution. Spending his final years old, blind, and under house arrest, Milton published his greatest work, the epic *Paradise Lost,* in 1667.[13]

Dedication Today

Dedication takes many forms: persevering through challenge and change, political upheaval, personal tragedy, violent storms, and government negligence. From the Renaissance to today, creative men and women have always shown us that when we persevere we have the power to reach our dreams.

On August 29, 2005, Hurricane Katrina ravaged America's Gulf Coast, flooding the city of New Orleans, where my aunt and uncle lost their home and thousands lost their lives. Karel Sloane had just published her first book, won an award for research on art and the immune system, and planned to continue her research with a professor from the Louisiana State University medical school. Now the medical school was under water, her plans swept away by deluge and desolation that stunned the world. Evacuated to Memphis with friends, she volunteered to work at the evacuated River Oaks Hospital, answering phones, running errands, making coffee, because, she says, "I wanted to be of service in any way I could."

"I believe New Orleans will rise again," she told me. "There is so much artistry connected to it, and so much life. Watching the news," she said, "can make people feel powerless, yet each person has power, whether it's volunteering, donations, arts benefits, all of us have some kind of personal power we can use to transform this tragedy." Since *With the Naked Eye,* her book about New Orleans, had just come out, she began scheduling book signings, donating her royalties to Katrina relief.

Karel's mantra is Gandhi's quote: "Be the change you wish to see in the world." Affirming the power of creativity, she spent the year after Katrina commuting between Memphis and New Orleans, networking with other displaced artists, serving as a visiting artist in public schools, working on a multimedia piece about life in exile, and organizing a grants workshop to help other New Orleans artists rebuild their lives. In June 2006, she moved back to New Orleans and began working with the Ashé Cultural Arts Center on the "Katrina Monologues: Swimming Upstream," a partnership with Eve Ensler and fourteen other artists. In November 2006, Karel was honored by Maybelline New York and *People* magazine with an "Inspiring Confidence through Education" award for her work with the Jefferson Performing Art Society's cultural crossroads program.

Karel has many gifts. She writes, acts, paints, works with new media, does outreach work with young people and other artists, and is pursuing her research on art and health as a master's student at Tulane University. "I believe everyone is an expert in their own life," she says. "People just need an opportunity to connect to their own unique and individual inner wisdom."[14]

❧ *Personal Exercise: Strengthen Your Dedication*

Like Karel, you, too, have the power to make a difference by connecting with your gifts, living your values, and following your own guiding star. By living your calling, you inspire others to live more creatively and make a positive difference in the world.

You can strengthen your dedication by practicing your daily discipline and cultivate a powerful forward momentum by discovering what activities enhance your personal energy. To do this, each evening for the next two weeks rate your day in your Renaissance Notebook.

- Using a scale of one to ten, ask yourself how *strong, happy, enthusiastic, on track with your calling, most truly yourself* you felt that day, with ten being the highest (a truly wonderful day), one being the absolute lowest (an abysmal, awful day), and five being neutral.
- Then list the day's activities. This process should take no more than five minutes.
- At the end of two weeks, review your high and low days, looking for patterns.
- You will find your own personal pattern, when you feel most truly and powerfully yourself. For me, good days are when I learn something new—anything from a new research insight to programming my cell phone or fixing something around the house. Psychologist Christopher Peterson, whose research inspired this exercise (I had a good day when I learned about it), says that his good day involves finishing something—a project, a chapter, a piece of work.[15]
- Once you've discovered your personal energy pattern, include more of it in your daily life to become stronger, more confident, more fully yourself.

Seek New Challenges

Throughout this book, you have seen how people find their callings through Discovery, Detachment, Discernment, and Direction, a process that begins in childhood and continues throughout life. Yet Renaissance men and women, past and present, are *always* in discovery. There is a light in their eyes, a joy in their days as they follow their hearts to new possibilities. "One cannot rest in a vocation," psychologist Larry Cochran has said, "rather, one strives unceasingly to realize it."[16]

The further you go, the more you discover. As you develop your strengths, you will seek greater challenges—and they will seek you out. Michelangelo found challenge throughout life, as a sculptor, painter, and architect, creating breathtaking statues, painting the Sistine Chapel, building St. Peter's, and he worked actively until the end of his life, a month before his eighty-ninth birthday. Psychologist Patti Simone, who directs Santa Clara's Osher Lifelong Learning Program, says that seeking out new challenges and remaining active adds more years to our lives, more health and vitality to our years.[17]

Look around you. The most vibrant people are always in discovery. Linus Pauling pursued new ideas at his research institute into his nineties. My friend, veterinarian Dr. David Reed, says, "I cannot fathom retirement," finding new challenges in treating animals, learning new skills, and mentoring young people.[18]

Following your calling may draw you more deeply into your current field or take you in new directions as you respond to curiosity, a blocked pathway, a pressing need, or a sense of restlessness. Over a decade ago, Erna Wenus was a successful anesthesiologist in Germany. Concerned with some patients' negative reactions to anesthetics, she began exploring alternatives, learning about acupuncture from exchange doctors visiting from China. When her husband got a job in California, Erna found that to practice medicine in the United States she would have to do her residency all over again. With a two-year-old daughter, she saw this as a blocked pathway, but another pathway opened up: a chance to study traditional Chinese medicine at Pacific College in San Diego. Discovering a new, holistic approach to health and wellness, Dr. Erna Wenus now combines the wisdom of East and West as a licensed acupuncturist and herbalist in northern California.[19]

You may be called to respond to a pressing need around you. In 1980, when Paula Leen retired from her job as secretary, she went to rural Zimbabwe to work for her church. Finding the children hungry and malnourished, she brought them a car load of food, then contacted friends at home to send used clothing and supplies. She used her Social Security checks to buy food, planting gardens to grow more food. Developing new skills and pathways, recruiting help, learning what she needed along the way, she set up dams and dug wells for irrigation. Her work has become the Zimbabwe Orphan Project, whose gardens and orchards now feed over two thousand people.[20]

Some changes come about gradually. Robert Mason has been a successful attorney since 1980. A few years ago, he watched the Bill Moyers interviews with Joseph Campbell and began examining his life. Looking for greater purpose, he made small adjustments, asking himself what he could do to be a better son to his parents, brother to his siblings, and companion to his partner. He also began rereading the classics he'd enjoyed as an English major in college, along with books on theory and contemporary culture. Now he is entering Stanford's master of liberal arts program to gain a deeper understanding of literature, art, and politics, because, he says, "I don't want to be one of those people who lived his life but never learned."[21]

Whether you are called to pursue art, music, science, political action, or another direction, following your calling is a journey that blesses your life as it brings new possibilities to the world.

Shadows on the Path: Threshold Guardians

Following your dreams more deeply or pursuing a new direction inevitably takes you into unknown territory, where you face what Joseph Campbell called "threshold guardians," sentinels at the edge of the known world and the great unknown.

Braving the great unknown was the lot of Renaissance explorers. Campbell tells of Columbus's crew, setting out for what they believed was the edge of the world through dark seas guarded by monsters of the deep. In your life, threshold guardians can take many forms. Externally, they can be limited finances, social stereotypes, friends accustomed to your old self and threatened by the new, or well-meaning relatives with their own ideas about your future. Internally, they can be fears, self-doubt, feelings of inadequacy, telling you "You're not good enough," "You've never done this before." Yet, from the Renaissance to today, the path of human progress has been charted by people of courage, faith, and perseverance who dared to follow their dreams into the great unknown.[22]

In 1988, in the wake of student demonstrations at Gallaudet University, the world's only college for the deaf, psychology professor I. King Jordan became the first deaf college president in history. At first there were many threshold guardians. People said that Jordan couldn't succeed because no deaf person had been a college president: interacting with the media, meeting with foundations, senators, and congressional representatives. Yet for eighteen years he led the school, building programs, obtaining grants, appearing on radio and television. He lectured internationally, received eleven honorary degrees, a congressional resolution, and the President's Citizen's Medal.

An average student in high school, Jordan had enlisted in the navy after graduation, losing his hearing in an automobile accident when he was twenty-one. He entered Gallaudet with a new dedication to education, learning sign language, excelling in his studies, and majoring in psychology. He then went on to graduate school in psychology at the University of Tennessee. Competing with hearing students, Jordan earned his master's and doctoral degrees, returning to Gallaudet as a psychology professor, later becoming department chair and dean. In 1987, he applied for the presidency, doing research on administration, budgeting, and university relations.

After retiring in 2006, Jordan remains an advocate for people with disabilities. In an interview, he said his greatest accomplishment as president was helping people realize that "deaf people can do anything except hear." King Jordan showed us all that we can succeed, defeating threshold guardians by following our own guiding star.[23]

Whenever you take on a new challenge, seek a new level, and head out for the great unknown, expect threshold guardians. They come with the territory. My friend, minister and spiritual counselor Tina Clare, says that we need to "up level our self-acceptance" whenever we aspire to new heights.[24]

Dealing with inner threshold guardians helps you overcome those around you. I am confident that when your heart calls you to create something new, you are given the power to bring it about. That power, developed with discipline and dedication, will lead you to your dreams. Take a moment now to visualize yourself succeeding in this new territory. What are you doing? What does it look like? Feel like?

Smile as you see yourself achieving your dreams, moving forward with the lessons from this book to live your personal Renaissance.

Moving Forward

Let's review your progress and reflect on your personal Renaissance. Write your answers and today's date in your Renaissance Notebook.

1. What little thing are you doing to become more of the person you want to be?
2. What are you doing to increase your CS joy?
3. How are you using your gifts?
4. How are you exercising ongoing discernment?
5. What was your creative victory in this chapter and how are you celebrating it?
6. Where do you feel your calling taking you now?

You have now completed twelve chapters, twelve steps in your personal Renaissance. As your journey continues, keep moving forward by maintaining your new Renaissance habits, reviewing the lessons in this book, recording your progress, and remembering that within you lives the promise of tomorrow—your own unique gift to the world.

RENAISSANCE REMINDERS

Your calling is your vocation of destiny that brings greater joy and meaning to your life.
As you pursue your personal Renaissance, remember to:

~ Develop forward momentum with discipline and dedication.

~ See threshold guardians as part of the journey, a sure sign you are making progress.

~ Always follow what brings you joy and meaning.

~ Remember that you are a unique individual, here to use your gifts to bring greater joy to your life and make a positive difference in the world.

~ Reflect on how the Renaissance principles have become a vital part of your life.

A Renaissance Valediction

In the Renaissance, St. Teresa of Avila reminded people "to take care that they do not hide their talent; for it may be that God has chosen them to be the edification of many others, especially in these days." Her words are equally true for us today.

Living your new Renaissance, following your calling, means keeping faith with your gifts, recognizing the patterns within and around you. This was said many times in the Renaissance by saints, scholars, writers, and artists who upheld both the treasure of our uniqueness and our relationship with the larger whole. This powerful Renaissance principle remains with us today as we realize that, on this planet, everything is connected. As John Donne wrote, no one "is an island, entire of itself."[25] You are a vital part of the tapestry of life, your own life and gifts an essential part of the whole. Without them, something valuable, something beautiful, would be lost. As you go forward in life:

- Never forget the treasure of your own uniqueness,
- Keep faith with your gifts,
- Steer by your inner compass,
- And follow your path with heart.

Now and forever, I wish you joy on the path.

RENAISSANCE PRINCIPLES

~ Your calling is your vocation of destiny, bringing greater joy and meaning to your life.

~ Your daily choices shape your life and inform the world.

~ There is a part of you that is forever young, playful, curious, and true that leads you to your calling.

~ Detach from the noisy world around you to follow the deepest values of your heart.

~ You are here to discover your gifts and use them to fulfill your destiny.

~ Discernment means following what inspires you and releasing what diminishes you.

~ You excel by focusing on your strengths, not dwelling on your weaknesses.

~ New Renaissance men and women affirm creative growth for themselves and one another.

~ Small actions over time produce monumental results.

~ When you reach out to follow your calling, the universe supports you with a world of possibilities.

Notes and Resources

Your Personal Renaissance is drawn from years of research on Renaissance lives, validated by studies in positive psychology and neuroscience. These notes offer documentation of how the four stages and eight practices in this book have informed Renaissance and contemporary lives, along with resources on personal growth, meaningful work, balance, and spirituality to support you on your path.

Introduction

1. C. Marlowe, *Tamburlaine,* 2.7.18–20, in *Christopher Marlowe's Tamburlaine,* part one and part two, ed. I. Ribner (New York: Odyssey Press, 1974).

2. For a study of spiritual development in the Renaissance, see D. E. Dreher, *The Fourfold Pilgrimage* (Washington, DC: University Press of America, 1982). For the hero's journey in world mythology, see J. Campbell, *The Hero with a Thousand Faces* (Princeton, NJ: Princeton University Press, 1968). (Originally published 1949.) W. Shakespeare, *As You Like It,* 2.7.141. All references to Shakespeare's works are from S. Greenblatt, W. Cohen, J. E. Howard and K. E. Maus, eds., *The Norton Shakespeare* (New York: Norton, 1997). For data on the international study, see D. E. Super and B. Sverko, *Life Roles, Values, and Careers,* with C. M. Super (San Francisco: Jossey-Bass, 1995). For information on calling, health, and happiness, see M. Csikszentmihalyi, "If we are so rich, why aren't we happy?" *American Psychologist* 54 (1999): 821–827; C. Peterson and M. E. P. Seligman, *Character Strengths and Virtues: A Handbook and Classification* (New York: Oxford University Press, 2004); M. E. P. Seligman, *Authentic Happiness* (New York: Free Press, 2002);

and A. Wrzesniewski, C. McCauley, P. Rozin, and B. Schwartz, "Jobs, careers, and callings: People's relations to their work," *Journal of Research in Personality* 31 (1997): 21–33. For a discussion of creativity and "flow," see M. Csikszentmihalyi, *Creativity: Flow and the Psychology of Discovery and Invention* (New York: Harper-Collins, 1996).

3. M. Luther, "Lectures on Galatians: Chapters 1–4," in *Luther's Works,* vol. 26 (St. Louis, MO: Concordia, 1963), 3–461. (Originally published 1535.); J. Calvin, *Institutes of the Christian Religion,* ed. J. T. McNeill (Philadelphia: Westminster Press, 1960). (Originally published 1536.) An earlier form of this discussion and a measure of the sense of vocation appear in D. E. Dreher, K. A. Holloway, and E. Schoenfelder, "The vocation identity questionnaire: Measuring the sense of calling," *Research in the Social Scientific Study of Religion* 18 (2007): 99–120; for a history of work and vocation, see L. Hardy, *The Fabric of This World* (Grand Rapids, MI: Eerdmans, 1990).

4. M. E. P. Seligman, *Learned Optimism* (New York: Knopf, 1991), v, 57–59, 68–70, and (2002), 117–119. See also P. A. Gore, Jr., W. E. Leuwerke, and J. D. Krumboltz, "Technologically enriched and boundaryless lives: Time for a paradigm upgrade," *The Counseling Psychologist* 30 (2000): 847–857; Csikszentmihalyi (1999); and T. Kasser, *The High Price of Materialism* (Cambridge, MA: MIT Press, 2002).

5. See the affirmation of human agency in G. Pico della Mirandola, *On the Dignity of Man,* in *On the Dignity of Man, On Being and the One, Heptaplus,* trans. C. G. Wallis (Indianapolis: Bobbs-Merrill, 1965), 1–34. (Originally published 1496.); and F. Bacon, *The New Organon,* in *The New Organon and Related Writings,* ed. F. H. Anderson (New York: Bobbs-Merrill, 1960). (Originally published 1620.)

6. L. Belkin, "One good career deserves another," *The New York Times Education Life,* November 6, 2005, 4A, p. 32.

7. For example, in *Will in the World: How Shakespeare Became Shakespeare* (New York: Norton, 2004), Stephen Greenblatt says that Shakespeare's plays are informed by the language of vocation (p. 13). Naming a feeling brings it from implicit to declarative memory. My thanks to Robert Numan, professor of psychology, Santa Clara University, for insights about declarative memory. See R. Numan, ed., *The Behavioral Neuroscience of the Septal Region* (New York: Springer-Verlag, 2000).

8. For studies of the self-fulfilling prophecy, see R. K. Merton, "The self-fulfilling prophecy," *The Antioch Review* 8 (1948): 193–210; R. Rosenthal and L. Jacobson, *Pygmalion in the Classroom* (New York: Holt, Rinehart & Winston, 1968) and R. Rosenthal, "Critiquing Pygmalion: A 25 year perspective," *Current Directions in Psychological Science* 4 (1995): 171–172. Greenblatt (2004), 24–25, contrasts Shakespeare's parents' minimal literacy with his remarkable achievements.

9. Information from G. Fox, *The Journal of George Fox,* ed. R. M. Jones (New York: Capricorn, 1963). (Originally published 1644.); F. Manuel, *A Portrait of Isaac Newton* (New York: Da Capo Press, 1990). (Originally published 1968.); and M. F.

Jerrold, *Vittoria Colonna and Some Account of Her Friends and Times* (Freeport, NY: Books for Libraries Press, 1969). (Originally published 1909.)

10. For an extensive study of calling and a new measure for men and women today, see Dreher, Holloway, and Schoenfelder (2007).

11. Psychologist Tom Plante and I presented this approach to therapists and health care professionals in "Finding Your Vocation: A Spiritual Perspective" at the Spirituality, Science, and Health national conference, cosponsored by the Society of Behavioral Medicine and the Spirituality and Health Institute at Santa Clara University on March 22, 2006. I also presented it in "Renaissance Lessons for To-day" Best Practices, at the Osher Lifelong Learning national conference in San Jose, CA, April 20, 2006, and as "Your Vocation Identity: Blessing Your Calling," to the Parent Coaching Institute, Bellevue, Washington, July 7, 2006. I've described it in D. Dreher, "Renaissance lessons for today: A course to promote purpose and personal growth in later life," *The LLI Review* 1 (2006): 105–112, and in D. Dreher and T. G. Plante, "The Calling protocol: Promoting greater health, joy, and purpose in life," in *Spirit, Science, and Health: How the Spiritual Mind Fuels Wellness,* eds. T. G. Plante and C. E. Thoresen (Westport, CT: Greenwood Press, 2007), 129–140. The book was the subject of a panel at the American Psychological Association annual conference in San Francisco in August 2007.

12. Research on intrinsic motivation and health in E. L. Deci and R. M. Ryan, "The general causality orientations scale: Self-determination in personality," *Journal of Research in Personality* 19 (1985): 109–134; Ryan & Deci (2000). Quote is from W. Shakespeare, *Hamlet,* 3.2.60.

13. C. L. Flinders, *Enduring Grace* (San Francisco: HarperSanFrancisco, 1993), 106.

Chapter One

1. Facts about Giotto's life from G. Vasari, *Lives of the Painters, Sculptors, and Architects,* vol. 1 (1550; repr. New York: Knopf, 1996), 96–97. Descriptions and dialog are my additions.

2. Reference to diversities of gifts in I Corinthians 12:1–12. See Renaissance discussions of vocation by Luther (1535/1963), Calvin (1536/1960), and also W. Perkins. "A Treatise of the Vocations or Callings of Men," in *The Work of William Perkins,* ed. I. Breward (Abingdon, Berkshire, England; Sutton Courtenay Press, 1970), 441–476. (Originally published 1603).

3. Information on Galileo from M. Sharrat, *Galileo: Decisive Innovator* (New York: Cambridge, 1996) and P. Ferrucci, *Inevitable Grace* (Los Angeles: Tarcher, 1990).

4. Teresa of Avila, *The Life of St. Teresa of Avila,* trans. D. Lewis (Westminster, MD: Newman Press, 1962).

5. Information on Newton from Manuel (1968/1990) and R. S. Westfall, *Never at Rest: A Biography of Isaac Newton* (New York: Cambridge University Press, 1980).

6. Information from M. Pynsent, *The Life of Helen Lucretia Cornaro Piscopia* (Rome: St. Benedict's, 1896).

7. Sor J. I. de la Cruz, *A Woman of Genius: The Intellectual Autobiography of Sor Juana Inés de la Cruz,* ed. M. S. Peden. (Salisbury, CT: Lime Rock Press, 1987). (Originally written 1691.)

8. R. C. Gorman's Navajo Gallery, P.O. Box 1756, Taos, New Mexico 87571; telephone (505) 758-3250; Web site, www.RCGormanGallery.com.

9. Information on Goodall's early life from J. Goodall, *Reason for Hope* (New York: Warner Books, 1999). Motto used by permission of the author, Dr. Jane Goodall, DBE, Founder, the Jane Goodall Institute, UN Messenger of Peace. Information on the Jane Goodall Institute available from www.JaneGoodall.org.

10. See H. Gardner, *Creating Minds* (New York: HarperCollins, 1993), 32; T. B. Kashdan, P. Rose, and C. D. Fincham, "Curiosity and exploration: Facilitating positive subjective experiences and personal growth opportunities," *Journal of Personality Assessment* 82 (2004): 291–305.

11. For a discussion of how our feelings from the limbic system work with the prefrontal cortices to aid in decision making, see A. Damasio, *Descartes' Error: Emotion, Reason, and the Human Brain* (New York: Putnam, 1994). I am grateful to Dr. Robert Numan for this reference. For the Renaissance perspective, see Pico della Mirandola (1496/1965).

12. Discussion of peak experiences in A. H. Maslow, *The Farther Reaches of Human Nature* (New York: Viking, 1971), 162–172.

13. Ryan & Deci (2000); see also T. B. Kashdan and F. D. Fincham, "Facilitating curiosity: A social and self-regulatory perspective for scientifically based intervention," in *Positive Psychology in Practice,* eds. P. A. Linley and S. Joseph (Hoboken, NJ: Wiley, 2004), 482–503.

14. Quote from John Donne, "The Canonization" (1633), l. 36, in *John Donne's Poetry,* A. L. Clements, ed. (New York: Norton, 1992), 6. For details of Donne's life, see I. Walton, "The Life of Dr. John Donne," in *Isaac Walton: The Lives of John Donne, Sir Henry Wotton, Richard Hooker, George Herbert, and Robert Sanderson,* ed. George Saintsbury (London: Oxford University Press, 1927), 8–89. (Originally published 1640.) Quote from "Meditation 17" in J. Donne, *Devotions upon Emergent Occasions* (Ann Arbor: University of Michigan Press, 1959), 108–109. (Originally published 1623.)

15. J. Donne, "The Autumnal," ll.1–2, in Clements (1992), 48–49. For details of Magdalen Herbert's life see J. Donne, "Sermon No. 2: A Sermon of Commemoration of the Lady Danvers, Preached at Chelsea where She was Lately Buried," in *The Sermons of John Donne,* vol. 8, eds. E. M. Simpson and G. Potter (Berkeley: University of California Press, 1956), 61–93. (Originally published 1627.); I. Walton, *The Life of Mr. George Herbert* in Saintsbury (1927), 251–319. (Originally pub-

lished 1675.); A. M. Charles, *A Life of George Herbert* (Ithaca: Cornell University Press, 1977); J. Powers-Beck, *Writing the Flesh: The Herbert Family Dialogue* (Pittsburgh: Duquesne University Press, 1998); F. E. Hutchinson, ed, "Introduction," in *The Works of George Herbert* (Oxford: Clarendon Press, 1941), xxi–xxxix; and S. Stewart, *George Herbert* (Boston: Twayne, 1986).

16. For joy when using strengths, see Seligman (2002) p. 160. For "flow," M. Csikszentmihalyi, *Flow* (New York: HarperCollins, 1990). For happiness and meaning, see Lykken (1999), p. 63.

17. For "signature strengths," see Peterson and Seligman (2004), Seligman (2002), and Csikszentmihalyi (1990). Seligman's signature strengths questionnaire is available in *Authentic Happiness* and on his Web site, www.authentichappiness.org. The Gallup organization has also done extensive survey research on personal strengths. See M. Buckingham and D. O. Clifton, *Now, Discover Your Strengths* (New York: Free Press, 2001). For contrasts between the fleeting pleasure of consumption and the joy of using our gifts, see Csikszentmihalyi (1990) and (1999); S. S. Luthar and S. J. Latendresse, "Children of the affluent: Challenges to well-being," *Current Directions in Psychological Science* 14 (2005): 49–53; and Seligman (2002).

18. Gallup survey in T. D. Hodges and D. O. Clifton, "Strengths-based Development in Practice," in *Positive Psychology in Practice*, eds. P. A. Linley and S. Joseph (Hoboken, NJ: Wiley, 2004), 256–268.

19. For the beneficial effects of focusing on our strengths, see Hodges and Clifton (2004); Seligman (2002) and (1991); D. Whitney and A. Trosten-Bloom, *The Power of Appreciative Inquiry* (San Francisco: Berrett-Kohler, 2003).

Chapter Two

1. T. Traherne, "Century I, Meditation 29," in *Centuries of Meditation* (Oxford: Mowbray, 1908). (Originally written c. 1670.)

2. Neuropsychologist Robert Numan sees implicit or nondeclarative memory as the source of intuition, revealing itself in "hunches" or feelings. For information on how sleep deprivation weakens memory, see W. C. Dement and C. Vaughan, *The Promise of Sleep* (New York: Dell, 1999). Chronic stress damages the hippocampus, the part of our brains that facilitates formation of long-term memories; for research on this, see R. M. Sapolsky, "Why stress is bad for your brain," *Science* 273 (1996): 749–750, and J. D. Bremner, "Hypotheses and controversies related to effects of stress on the hippocampus: An argument for stress-induced damage to the hippocampus in patients with posttraumatic stress disorder," *Hippocampus* 11 (2001): 75–81. For a discussion of how fear narrows our perspective by sending an alarm message from the sensory thalamus to the amygdala, bypassing the cortex, which allows for detailed reasoning, see J. LeDoux, *The Emotional Brain* (New York: Simon & Schuster, 1996); J. P. Neafsey, "Psychological dimensions of the discernment of vocation," in *Revisiting the*

Idea of Vocation, ed. J. C. Haughey (Washington, DC: Catholic University of America Press, 2004), 166. A treatment protocol explaining how the authors have used detachment in clinical practice and spiritual counseling can be found in Dreher and Plante (2007).

3. For research on the healing effects of positive emotions, see B. Fredrickson, "Positive Emotions," in *Handbook of Positive Psychology,* eds. C. R. Snyder and S. J. Lopez (New York: Oxford, 2002), 120–134; and K. Neff, "Self-compassion and psychological well-being," *Constructivism in the Human Sciences* 9 (2002): 27–37; and "Self-compassion: An alternative conceptualization of a healthy attitude toward oneself," *Self and Identity* 2 (2003): 85–101. For evidence that using our gifts can dramatically increase our happiness, see M. E. P. Seligman, T. A. Steen, N. Park, and C. Peterson, "Positive psychology progress: Empirical validation of interventions," *American Psychologist* 60 (2005): 410–421. For research on how personal values can buffer stress, see J. D. Creswell, W. T. Welch, S. E. Taylor, D. K. Sherman, T. L. Gruenewald, and T. Mann, "Affirmation of personal values buffers neuroendocrine and psychological stress responses," *Psychological Science* 16 (2005): 846–851.

4. Details of Elizabeth's early life from C. Hibbert, *The Virgin Queen: Elizabeth I, Genius of the Golden Age* (New York: Addison-Wesley, 1991), 47–60; J. E. Neale, *Queen Elizabeth I: A Biography* (Garden City, NY: Doubleday, 1957), 13–17, 46–47. Elizabeth's words at the Tower of London from Neale (1957), 39; her couplet and first public speech in 1558 from *Elizabeth I: Collected Works,* eds. L. S. Marcus, J. Mueller, and M. B. Rose (Chicago: University of Chicago Press, 2000), 46, 51–52.

5. For a discussion of resilience and moral growth through crisis, see R. A. Emmons, P. M. Colby, and H. A. Kaiser, "When Losses Lead to Gains: Personal Growth and the Recovery of Meaning," in *The Human Quest for Meaning,* eds. P. T. P. Wong and P. S. Fry (Mahwah, NJ: Erlbaum, 1998), 163–178.

6. See A. Van Gennep, *The Rites of Passage,* trans. M. B. Visedom and G. L. Caffee (Chicago: University of Chicago Press, 1960). (Originally published 1909.); and Campbell (1949/1968).

7. Traherne, "Century III," 7, 13. See Gloria DeGaetano's analysis of the effects of this cultural conditioning in *Parenting Well in a Media Age* (Fawnskin, CA: Personhood Press, 2004).

8. The four needs are adapted from Kasser (2002), 24–26, and Kasser, "The Good Life or the Goods Life? Positive Psychology and Personal Well-being in the Culture of Consumption," in *Positive Psychology in Practice,* eds. P. H. Linley and S. Joseph (Hoboken, NJ: Wiley, 2004), 55–67. For the effects of corporate branding and consumerism, see also T. Beaudoin, *Consuming Faith* (New York: Sheed & Ward, 2003); E. Erikson, "Sense of Industry," in *Childhood and Society,* 2nd ed. rev. (New York: Norton, 1963), 258–261. Research on consumerism and disorders from Kasser (2002), 14–17.

9. See N. Chesley, "Blurring boundaries? Linking technology use, spillover, individual distress, and family satisfaction," *Journal of Marriage and Family* 67 (2005): 1237–1248.

10. Quote from Walton, 264.

11. Greenblatt (2004, p. 70) says Shakespeare was "good company" but did not waste his time in drinking and debauchery like many of his contemporaries. Marlowe's life was a mystery, and some say that he was a spy, the "tavern brawl" no accidental death. See D. Hilton, *Who Was Kit Marlowe?* (New York: Taplinger, 1977); J. Vrooman (1970).

12. See Eknath Easwaran's discussion of the "hurry sickness" in *Meditation* (Tomales, CA: Nilgiri Press, 1991). See T. M. Amabile, C. N. Hadley, and S. J. Kramer, "Creativity Under the Gun," *Harvard Business Review* 80 (2002): 52–61, for research on how hurrying impedes creativity.

13. For statistics on TV viewing, low morale, and materialism, see Kasser (2002, pp. 54–55) and J. Schor, *The Overspent American* (New York: Basic Books, 1998), 74. For insights on raising children with healthy brains, see DeGaetano (2004) and her Web site, http://www.parentcoachinginstitute.com/. Others who have advocated media fasts include Beaudoin (2003), Kasser (2002), M. Pipher, *The Shelter of Each Other* (New York: Putnam, 1996), and M. Berman, *Dark Ages America* (New York: Norton, 2006).

Chapter Three

1. Heraclitus, *On the Universe* (c. 500 BCE), Fragment 121, also commonly translated as "Character is fate." An English translation, *The Riddles of Heraclitus and Democritus,* was published in London by W. Hatfield for J. Norton in 1598. I am grateful to Santa Clara University librarian Leanna Goodwater for this reference. For a recent edition, see B. Haxton, trans., *Fragments: The Collected Wisdom of Heraclitus* (New York: Viking, 2001).

2. For insights into how the values and choices of Shakespeare's characters influence their fates, see the classic A. C. Bradley, *Shakespearean Tragedy* (London: Macmillan, 1929). For a psychological study of values and meaning today, see R. F. Baumeister, *Meanings of Life* (New York: Guilford, 1991).

3. See A. H. Maslow, *Motivation and Personality* (New York: Harper & Row, 1954). For psychological studies of optimal health and altruistic values, see R. F. Baumeister and K. D. Vohs, "The Pursuit of Meaningfulness in Life," in *Handbook of Positive Psychology,* eds. C. R. Snyder and S. J. Lopez (New York: Oxford, 2002), 608–618; and C. D. Ryff and B. Singer, "From Social Structure to Biology: Integrative Science in Pursuit of Human Health and Well-being," in *Handbook of Positive Psychology,* eds. C. R. Snyder and S. J. Lopez (New York: Oxford, 2002), 541–555.

4. For common values in world cultures, see S. Bok, *Common Values* (Columbia: University of Missouri Press, 1995). For research on lack of meaning and human disease, see E. Klinger, "The Search for Meaning in Evolutionary Perspective

and Its Clinical Implications," in *The Human Quest for Meaning*, eds. P. T. P. Wong and P. S. Fry (Mahwah, NJ: Erlbaum, 1998), 27–50.

5. For research on the lack of meaning and failure, see P. T. P. Wong, "Academic Values and Achievement Motivation," in *The Human Quest for Meaning*, eds. P. T. P. Wong and P. S. Fry (Mahwah, NJ: Erlbaum, 1998), 261–292; and R. L. Ochberg, "College dropouts," *Journal of Youth and Adolescence* 15 (1986): 287–302. For origins of logotherapy, see V. E. Frankl, *Man's Search for Meaning* (New York: Simon & Schuster, 1984), 96–169. (Originally published 1946). For the UCLA study, see Cresswell et al. (2005).

6. Theologian James Fowler has explained that vocation is simultaneously personal fulfillment and public service: J. W. Fowler, *You Bet Your life: Finding Meaning and, Perhaps, Vocation* (Santa Clara University: Bannan Center for Jesuit Education, 2004). For a Renaissance perspective on the difference between calling and workaholism, see D. E. Dreher, "Milton's warning to Puritans in *Paradise Lost:* Another look at the separation scene," *Christianity and Literature* 14 (1991): 27–38. For research on time pressure and creativity, see Amabile et al. (2002). For research on calling and optimal health, see Wrzesniewski et al. (1997).

7. Love and duty questions are adapted from M. Silf, *Inner Compass* (Chicago: Loyola Press, 1999), 141.

8. Information on the life of St. Ignatius is from H. Gray, "The experience of Ignatius Loyola: Background to Jesuit education," in *The Jesuit Ratio Studiorum: 400th Anniversary Perspectives*, ed. V. J. Duminuco (New York: Fordham University Press, 2000), 1–21; and J. C. Olin, ed., *The Autobiography of St. Ignatius Loyola,* trans. J. F. O'Callaghan (New York: Harper & Row, 1974), 21–29. (Originally published 1555.) For a discussion of "twice-born" individuals, see W. James, *The Varieties of Religious Experience* (New York: Penguin, 1982), 166–173. (Originally published 1902.) For a contemporary approach to discernment, see Silf (1999). A treatment protocol offering a brief life of St. Ignatius and explaining how the authors have used discernment in clinical practice and spiritual counseling can be found in Dreher and Plante (2007).

9. My thanks to Michelle Chappel for her story, used with permission. For information on Michelle's music and creativity workshops, visit her Web site: http://www.michellechappel.com.

10. See the neoplatonic discussion of desires in Pico della Mirandola (1496/1965), 5, and the discussion of self-actualization in Maslow (1954), 91–92. Quote from *Hamlet* IV, 4.11.23–25. References are to act, scene, and line.

11. See Neafsey (2004) and D. Lonsdale, *Eyes to See, Ears to Hear: An Introduction to Ignatian Spirituality* (Chicago: Loyola Press, 1990).

12. See D. W. Winnicott, *The Maturational Process and the Facilitating Environment* (New York: International Universities Press, 1965) and Neafsey (2004).

13. For insights into consolation and desolation, see L. J. Puhl, ed., *The Spiritual Exercises of St. Ignatius* (Chicago: Loyola Press, 1951). Some helpful guides are

Lonsdale (1990), Silf (1999), and *Prayer for Finding God in All Things: The Daily Examen of St. Ignatius of Loyola* (St. Louis, MO: Institute of Jesuit Studies, 2005).

14. Fox (1694/1963), 84. Information on Locke is from R. I. Aaron, *John Locke* (Oxford: Clarendon Press, 1971).

15. See Seligman (2002), 8–9. For a discussion of values and vocation, see L. Cochran, *The Sense of Vocation* (Albany: SUNY Press, 1990), 193; Neafsey (2004), 195.

16. R. Burton, *The Anatomy of Melancholy* (London: H. Cripps, 1660). For a guide to consolation and desolation, see Silf (1999).

17. See research on altruistic values and happiness in Seligman (2002); J. Fabry, "The Calls of Meaning," in *The Human Quest for Meaning,* eds. P. T. P. Wong and P. S. Fry (Mahwah, NJ: Erlbaum, 1998), 295–305; and D. G. Myers and E. Diener, "Who is happy?" *Psychological Science* 6 (1995): 10–19.

Chapter Four

1. Shakespeare, Sonnet 116, lines 5–8. In the Renaissance, "bark" (or barque) meant a small ship or sailing vessel.

2. Recent studies have connected a sense of direction and meaningful goals with greater happiness, health, and well-being. See C. L. Keyes and C. D. Ryff, "Psychological Well-being in Midlife," *Life in the Middle: Psychological and Social Development in Middle Age,* eds. S. L. Willis and J. D. Reid (San Diego, CA: Academic Press, 1999), 161–180.

3. For Leeuwenhoek's life, see C. Dobell, *Antony van Leeuwenhoek and His "Little Animals"* (New York: Russell & Russell, 1958). See Luther (1535/1964).

4. Maslow (1954), 91.

5. See the dissociation exercise recommended by psychologist C. R. Snyder in *The Psychology of Hope: You Can Get There from Here* (New York: Simon & Schuster, 1994), 214.

6. For a classic study of identity formation, see Erikson (1950/1963). For research on brain development in young adulthood, see E. Goldberg, *The Executive Brain* (New York: Oxford, 2001) and J. M. Fuster, "The prefrontal cortex—an update: Time is of the essence," *Neuron* 30 (2001): 319–333. For studies of meaning, see Ryff and Singer (2002). For brain development throughout life, see P. R. Huttenlocher, *Neural Plasticity* (Cambridge, MA: Harvard University Press, 2002).

7. H. Markus and P. Nurius, "Possible selves," *American Psychologist* 41 (1986): 954–969, and S. Cross and H. Markus, "Possible selves across the life span," *Human Development* 34 (1991): 230–255. For More's life, see N. Harpsfield, *The Life and Death of Sir Thomas Moore, Knight, Sometymes Lord High Chancellor of England,* ed. E. V. Hitchcock (London: Oxford University Press, 1932). (Originally published 1557.); R. Marius, *Thomas More: A Biography* (New York: Knopf, 1985); and L. Martz, *Thomas More* (New Haven: Yale University Press, 1990).

8. For studies of values, health, and well-being, see Baumeister and Vohs (2002). Best possible self writing exercise is adapted from K. M. Sheldon and S. Lyubomirsky, "How to increase and sustain positive emotion: The effects of expressing gratitude and visualizing best possible selves," *The Journal of Positive Psychology* 1 (2006): 73–82, and L. A. King, "The health benefits of writing about life goals," *Personality and Social Psychology Bulletin* 27 (2001): 798–807. Snyder (1994), 244, describes how visualizing best possible selves can strengthen hope.

9. Frankl (1946/1984), 127, discusses this creative tension. Research shows how moving successfully toward meaningful goals builds health while the opposite, "learned helplessness," is equated with chronic depression. See Seligman (1991); R. A. Emmons, "Personal Goals, Life Meaning, and Virtue: Wellsprings of a Positive Life," in *Flourishing,* eds. C. L. M. Keyes and J. Haidt (Washington, DC: American Psychological Association, 2003), 105–128. I am grateful to Dr. David B. Feldman for insights about Rick Snyder and the origins of hope psychology, in a personal communication, October 2006. For an excellent overview of hope psychology, see Snyder (1994).

10. Information on "stretch goals" is from D. B. Feldman, personal communication, October 2006; see Snyder (1994) for research on performance-based goals and Emmons (2003) for positive goals and greater subjective well-being.

11. Jerry Lynch, personal communication, 2006.

12. For further advice about Goals, Pathways, and Agency, see Snyder (1994). A treatment protocol explaining how the authors have used direction and hope skills in clinical practice and spiritual counseling can be found in Dreher and Plante (2007). For the "win-win friendships" (both the concept and the reality), I am grateful to my friend, psychologist and musician Michelle Chappel.

13. Hope Assessment is from C. R. Snyder, C. Harris, J. R. Anderson, S. A. Holleran, L. M. Irving, S. T. Sigmon, L. Yoshinobu, J. Gibb, C. Langelle, and P. Harney, "The will and the ways: Development and validation of an individual-difference measure of hope," *Journal of Personality and Social Psychology* 60 (1991): 570–585 (scale on p. 585: Copyright 1991 by the American Psychological Association, adapted with permission from the APA and Dr. Sandra Sigmon). The test also appears in Snyder (1994), 26.

14. Information on Bacon from P. Zagorin, *Francis Bacon* (Princeton: Princeton University Press, 1998). Bacon quote from his prayer of 1621, in H. G. Dick, ed., *Selected Writings of Francis Bacon* (New York: Modern Library, 1955), 542.

15. Details of Michelangelo's life from Vasari (1568/1996), vol. 2, pp. 642–769.

16. Details of Sor Juana's life from de la Cruz (1987).

17. Aphra Behn's life from V. Sackville-West, *Aphra Behn: The Incomparable Astrea* (New York: Russell, 1970). (Originally published 1927.); and J. Fitzmaurice, J. A. Roberts, C. L. Barash, E. R. Cunnar, N. A. Gutierrez, eds., *Major Women Writers of Seventeenth-century England* (Ann Arbor: University of Michigan Press, 1997).

18. Advice on roadblocks based on Snyder (1994). For information about POST, see www.openspacetrust.org. For more about KIVA, see www.kiva.org. For the hero's struggle with opposition in world literature, see C. Booker, *The Seven Basic Plots: Why We Tell Stories* (New York: Continuum, 2004). For "life theme" development in response to challenge, see M. Csikszentmihalyi and O. V. Beattie, "Life themes: A theoretical and empirical exploration of their origins and effects," *Journal of Humanistic Psychology* 19 (1970): 45–64; and J. Nakamura, M. Csikszentmihalyi, "The construction of meaning through vital engagement," in Keyes and Haidt (2003), 83–194.

19. J. Milton, *Areopagitica,* in *John Milton: Complete Poetry and Major Prose,* ed. M. Y. Hughes (New York: Odyssey, 1957), 733. (Originally published 1644.)

Chapter Five

1. I am grateful for conversations on vocation with Dr. William C. Spohn, Augustin Cardinal Bea, S.J., Professor of Religious Studies at Santa Clara University, in the spring of 2002. See also W. C. Spohn, "Spirituality and its discontents: Practices in Jonathan Edwards' *Charity and Its Fruits,"Journal of Religious Ethics* 31 (2003): 253–276, and A. MacIntyre, *After Virtue* (Notre Dame, IN: University of Notre Dame Press, 1984). For neuroplasticity, see Huttenlocher (2002). Research on developmental assets in P. C. Scales, P. L. Benson, N. Leffert, and D. A. Blyth, "Contribution of developmental assets to the prediction of thriving among adolescents," *Applied Developmental Science* 4 (2000): 27–46, and T. A. Steen, L. V. Kachorek, and C. Peterson, "Character strengths among youth," *Journal of Youth and Adolescence* 32 (2003): 5–16. Supporting research for each Renaissance practice will be cited separately in chapters 5–12 of this book.

2. For research on faith and meaning, see Frankl (1946/1984); Cochran (1990); J. W. Fowler, *Stages of Faith* (San Francisco: Harper & Row, 1981); S. D. Parks, *Big Questions, Worthy Dreams* (San Francisco: Jossey-Bass, 2000); M. E. P. Seligman, "Positive psychology: Fundamental assumptions," *The Psychologist* 16 (2003): 126–127; and Fabry (1998). For research on faith and health throughout life, see T. G. Plante and A. C. Sherman, eds., *Faith and Health: Psychological Perspectives* (New York: Guilford Press, 2001). For a discussion of Hillel, see A. Cohen, *Everyman's Talmud* (New York: Schocken, 1995), 184.

3. Milton, *Paradise Lost* I, 22–26, in Hughes (1957), 212.

4. See "gratitude" in *The Oxford English Dictionary,* compact edition (New York: Oxford University Press, 1971). A number of studies have found daily gratitude diaries an effective practice. See Peterson and Seligman (2004), R. A. Emmons and M. E. McCullough, "Counting blessings versus burdens: An experimental investigation of gratitude and subjective well-being in daily life," *Journal of Personality and Social Psychology* 84 (2003): 377–389; D. P. McAdams and J. J. Bauer, "Gratitude in modern life: Its manifestations and development," in *The Psychology of Gratitude,* eds. R. Emmons and M. E. McCullough (New York: Oxford University

Press, 2004), 81–99; G. Bono, R. A. Emmons, and M. E. McCullough, "Gratitude in practice and the practice of gratitude," in *Positive Psychology in Practice,* eds. P. A. Linley and S. Joseph (Hoboken, NJ: John Wiley, 2004), 464–481.

5. For St. Francis, see H. Burton, *The Life of St. Francis de Sales* (New York: Kennedy, 1925).

6. For St. Jeanne, see E. Bougard, *St. Chantal and the Foundation of the Visitation,* trans. A. Visitandine (New York: Benziger, 1895).

7. T. Browne, *Religio Medici,* in A. Witherspoon and F. J. Warnke, *Seventeenth-century Prose and Poetry* (New York: Harcourt Brace, (1642) 1982), 335. Einstein's quote from *Mein Weltbild* (1933) is widely cited. One English translation is A. Einstein, *The World as I See It,* trans. A. Harris (New York: Covici Friede, 1934), 242.

8. My thanks to Ron Hansen for the grace of this interview, used with permission, personal communication, Santa Clara University, June 14, 2006. See his essays on his faith and fiction in R. Hansen, *A Stay Against Confusion* (New York: HarperCollins, 2001).

9. D. Oman and C. E. Thoresen, "Spiritual modeling: A key to spiritual and religious growth?" *The International Journal for the Psychology of Religion* 13 (2003): 149–165; J. Haidt, "The positive emotion of elevation," *Prevention and Treatment* 3 (2000): Article 3; Dreher, [Initial vocation identity surveys], unpublished raw data, 2003. See also Parks (2000); Steen, Kachorek, and Peterson (2003).

10. C. L. Flinders, talk and signing at Santa Clara University, May 31, 2006. See C. L. Flinders, *Enduring Lives* (New York: Jeremy P. Tarcher, 2006).

11. See, for example, David L. Fleming, S.J., *The Spiritual Exercises of St. Ignatius: A Literal Translation and a Contemporary Reading* (St. Louis: Institute of Jesuit Sources, 1978), 69.

12. For despair, see Burton (1660), part 3, subsection iv. For gentleness, see F. de Sales, *Introduction to the Devout Life,* ed. and trans. A. Ross (Westminster, MD: Newman Press, 1948), 137–138. (Originally published 1608.) For research on compassion and self-compassion, see P. R. Steffan and K. S. Masters, "Does compassion mediate the intrinsic religion-health relationship?" *Annals of Behavioral Medicine* 30 (2005): 217–224. Definition of self-compassion used by permission of Dr. Kristin Neff. For the self-compassion scale, see K. D. Neff, "Development and validation of a scale to measure self-compassion," *Self and Identity* 2 (2003): 223–250, as well as K. D. Neff, "Self-compassion and psychological well-being," *Constructivism in the Human Sciences* 9 (2004): 27–37.

13. My thanks to Shauna Shapiro for the Metta mantram she shared at her class on mindfulness meditation, Santa Clara University, November 5, 2005 (used by permission), as well as for her friendship and her own radiant expression of loving kindness.

Chapter Six

1. Socrates, quoted in Plato, *Dialogues: The Apology of Socrates,* in *The Norton Anthology of World Masterpieces,* eds. S. Lawall and M. Mack, trans. B. Jowett, vol. 1, *The Western Tradition,* 7th ed. (New York: Norton, 1999), 726–746.

2. Phaedria is found in bk. 2, canto 6, of E. Spenser, *The Faerie Queene,* in *Renaissance Literature: An Anthology,* eds. M. Payne and J. Hunter (Malden, MA: Blackwell, 2003), 294–304. (Originally published 1596.)

3. See D. Gilbert, *Stumbling on Happiness* (New York: Knopf, 2006); For studies of metacognition and conscience, see T. D. Albright, T. M. Jessell, E. R. Kandel, and M. I. Posner, "Neural science: A century of progress and the mysteries that remain," *Neuron* 25 (2000): 1–55; A. Bandura, "On the psychosocial impact and mechanisms of spiritual modeling," *International Journal for the Psychology of Religion* 13 (2003): 167–173; R. F. Baumeister, D. M. Tice, and T. F. Heatherton, *Losing Control: How and Why People Fail at Self-regulation* (New York: Academic Press, 1994); and C. M. Shelton, *Achieving Moral Health: An Exercise Plan for Your Conscience* (New York: Crossroad, 2000).

4. Information about Francis de Sales is from Burton (1925).

5. Information about Brother Lawrence's life and method of prayer was collected and published after his death by the Abbé de Beaufort. See Brother Lawrence of the Resurrection, *The Practice of the Presence of God,* ed. H. M. Helms, trans. R. J. Edmonson (Orleans, MA: Paraclete Press, 1985). (Originally published 1692.)

6. "Know thyself" was said to be inscribed in Greek on the temple of the oracle at Delphi, in the sixth century BCE. This saying, attributed to many Greek sages, including Socrates, became a guide for many Renaissance philosophers. The Latin translation is *nosce te ipsum.* J. Davies, *Nosce teipsum,* ll.45–48, in *The Renaissance in England,* eds. H. E. Rollins and H. Baker (Boston: Heath, 1954), 475. (Originally published 1599.) Shakespeare, *Hamlet,* 1.3.78; M. Fox, *The Reinvention of Work* (San Francisco: Harper San Francisco, 1955), 21; P. J. Palmer, *The Courage to Teach* (San Francisco: Jossey-Bass, 1998), 3.

7. Seligman (1991), 70; M. E. P. Seligman, P. Verkuil, and T. H. Kang, "Why lawyers are unhappy," *Cardozo Law Review* 33 (2001): 33–53; see also W. D. McCausland, K. Pouliakas, and I. Theodossiou, "Some are punished and some are rewarded: A study of the impact of performance pay on job satisfaction," *International Journal of Manpower* 26 (2005): 636–659. (My thanks to Cameron Boehmer for pointing out this source to me.) A. Bandura, "Toward a psychology of human agency," *Perspectives on Psychological Science* 1 (2006): 167.

8. For "inner focus," see Csikszentmihalyi (1996), 185.

9. Study information is from I. M. Eigsti, V. Zayas, W. Mischel, Y. Shoda, O. Ayduk, M. B. Dadlani, M. C. Davidson, J. L. Aber, and B. J. Casey, "Predicting cognitive control from preschool to late adolescence and young adulthood," *Psychological Science* 17 (2006): 478–484; See also Scales et al. (2000).

10. I. Csikszentmihalyi, "Flow in a historical context: The case of the Jesuits," in *Optimal Experience: Psychological Studies of Flow in Consciousness,* eds. M. Csikszentmihalyi and I. Csikszentmihalyi (New York: Cambridge, 1988), 232–249. See Ignatius's discussion of the Examen in Puhl (1951) and a guide to the Examen in *Prayer for Finding God in All Things* (2005). I am grateful to Theodore J. Rynes, S.J., for giving me a copy of this guide.

11. B. Franklin, *The Autobiography of Benjamin Franklin,* eds. L. W. Labaree, R. L. Ketcham, H. C. Boatfield, and H. H. Fineman (New Haven, CT: Yale University Press, 1964), 148–160. (Originally published 1791.) See H. Smith, *The 10 Natural Laws of Successful Time and Life Management* (New York: Warner, 1994) and S. Covey, *The Seven Habits of Highly Effective People* (New York: Simon & Schuster, 1989).

12. J. Lynch, *The Way of the Champion,* with C. A. Huang (Rutland, VT: Tuttle, 2006), 77. Used with permission; T. G. Plante, personal communication, August 26, 2006. Tom Plante is professor of psychology and director of the Spirituality and Health Institute at Santa Clara.

13. Seligman et al. (2005).

14. See E. Kross, O. Ayduk, and W. Mischel, "When asking 'Why' does not hurt: Distinguishing rumination from reflective processing of negative emotions," *Psychological Science* 16 (2005): 709–715; A. Miller-Tiedeman, *Learning, Practicing, and Living the New Careering: A 21ˢᵗ Century Approach* (New York: Taylor & Francis, 1999); A. Miller-Tiedeman, "The Lifecareer® Process Theory: A Healthier Choice," in *Connections between Spirit and Work in Career Development,* eds. D. P. Bloch and L. J. Richmond (Palo Alto, CA: Davies-Black, 1997), 87–113; quote is from personal communication with Dr. Miller-Tiedeman, January 25, 2007, used with permission. Lifecareer® is a registered trademark of Anna Miller-Tiedeman. Her Web site is www.life-is-career.com; phone (304) 697–1110.

15. For studies of how using our gifts productively increases health and happiness, see R. A. Emmons, "Personal strivings: An approach to personality and subjective well-being," *Journal of Personality and Social Psychology* 51 (1986):1058–1068; Lykken (1999); P. T. P. Wong, "Spirituality, meaning, and successful aging," in *The Human Quest for Meaning,* eds. P. T. P. Wong and P. S. Fry (Mahwah, NJ: Erlbaum, 1998), 359–394; and Wrzesniewski et al. (1997).

Chapter Seven

1. Donne (1623/1959), "Devotion 17," 108.

2. For information on apprenticeships, see C. D. Cennini, *The Craftsman's Handbook (Il libro dell' arte),* trans. D. V. Thompson, Jr. (New York: Dover, 1960). (Originally published 1437.); J. L. Singman, *Daily Life in Elizabethan England* (Westport, CT: Greenwood, 1995); L. Stone, *The Family, Sex, and Marriage in England, 1500–1800* (New York: Harper & Row, 1977).

3. For the lack of positive role models, see Steen, Kachorek, and Peterson (2003); R. W. Larson, "Toward a psychology of positive youth development,"

American Psychologist 55 (2000): 170–183; and M. Csikszentmihalyi and B. Schneider, *Becoming Adult: How Teenagers Prepare for the World of Work* (New York: Basic Books, 2000), statistics pp. 14–15, 44. Statistics on American families are from D. G. Myers, *The American Paradox* (New Haven: Yale University Press, 2000), 179.

4. For mentoring communities, see Parks (2000).

5. For the early life of Michelangelo, see Vasari (1568/1996) and G. Bull, *Michelangelo* (New York: St. Martin's Griffin, 1998); G. Herbert, in *A Priest to the Temple: The Works of George Herbert,* ed. F. E. Hutchinson (Oxford: Oxford University Press, 1945), 223–290. (Originally published 1652.)

6. B. Deimling, *Sandro Botticelli* (New York: Taschen, 2000); A. R. Turner, *Inventing Leonardo* (New York; Knopf, 1993).

7. For information on mentoring in Renaissance lives, see M. Casper, *Kepler,* trans. and ed. C. D. Hellman (New York: Abelard-Schuman, 1959); G. Keynes, *The Life of William Harvey* (Oxford: Clarendon Press, 1966); Hutchinson (1941); Jerrold (1906/1969).

8. D. Hilton, *Who Was Kit Marlowe?* (New York: Taplinger, 1977).

9. J. Vrooman, *René Descartes* (New York: Putnam, 1977); B. K. Lewalski, *The Life of John Milton* (Walden, MA: Blackwell, 2002).

10. For Locke, see Aaron (1971).

11. For domain knowledge, see Csikszentmihalyi (1996).

12. See Deimling (2000) and Turner (1993).

13. See Rosenthal and Jacobson (1968); R. Rosenthal, "Interpersonal expectancy effects: A 30-year perspective," *Current Directions in Psychological Science* 3 (1994): 176–179; and Rosenthal (1995).

14. See J. Kabat-Zinn, *Wherever You Go, There You Are* (New York: Hyperion, 1994), a classic book on the wisdom of mindfulness.

15. P. Ekman, "Facial expressions of emotions: New findings, new questions," *Psychological Science* 3 (1992): 34–38; P. Ekman and R. J. Davidson, "Voluntary smiling changes regional brain activity," *Psychological Science* 4 (1993): 342–345; see also Damasio (1994).

16. For research on mentoring, meaning, and fulfillment, see Nakamura and Csikszentmihalyi (2003) and J. Haidt, "Elevation and the positive psychology of morality, " in *Flourishing,* eds. C. L. M. Keyes and J. Haidt (Washington, DC: American Psychological Association, 2003), 275–289.

17. My thanks to Dr. David Reed, DVM, for an interview on establishing apprenticeships today: personal communication, June 26, 2006, Lawrence Pet Hospital, Santa Clara, CA. Used by permission.

18. Information on R. C. Gorman is from Associated Press obituary, "Picasso of American Art dies at 74," printed in *The Albuquerque Tribune,* November 4, 2005, http://www.abqtrib.com/albq/nw_state/article/0,2564,ALBQ_19863_4212369,00. html (accessed November 20, 2005).

19. Information on Denise Levertov and William Carlos Williams from D. Gingerich, "Poets as Mentors," *The Writer's Chronicle* 37 (December 2004): 11.

20. Information on Michael Collopy from personal communications at Santa Clara University, 2003–2004, and N. Marchetti, "Promoting peace with a camera," *The Daily Journal,* June 21, 2004, http://www.smdailyjournal.com/article_preview.php?id=31738&reddate=06/21/2004 (electronic version retrieved December 13, 2005).

21. See S. E. Taylor, "Tend and befriend: Biobehavioral bases of affiliation under stress," *Current Directions in Psychological Science* 15 (2006): 273–277.

Chapter Eight

1. J. Milton, *Paradise Lost,* bk. XII, line 587, in M. Y. Hughes, ed., *John Milton: Complete Poems and Major Prose* (New York: Odyssey Press, 1957), 207–469. (Originally published 1674.)

2. For contemporary discussions of action and contemplation, see H. J. M. Nouwen, *Out of Solitude* (Notre Dame, IN: Ave Maria Press, 1974); P. J. Palmer, *To Know as We Are Known* (San Francisco: HarperCollins, 1993); Maslow (1954); D. Goleman, R. Boyatzis, and A. McKee, *Primal Leadership* (Boston: Harvard Business School Press, 2002). For studies by the UCLA Center on the Everyday Lives of Families (CELF), see C. Mithers, "The Fractured Family," *UCLA Magazine,* July 2006, 26–29, 58, and www.celf.ucla.edu. For creativity studies, see T. M. Amabile, *Creativity in Context* (Boulder, CO: Westview, 1996); Gardner (1993); and Csikszentmihalyi (1996).

3. For the health effects of meditation, see B. R. Cahn, and J. Povich, "Meditation states and traits: EEG, ERP, and neuroimaging studies," *Psychological Bulletin* 132 (2006): 180–211; S. L. Shapiro, G. E. R. Schwartz, and C. Santerre, "Meditation and positive psychology," in *Handbook of Positive Psychology,* eds. C. R. Snyder and S. J. Lopez (New York: Oxford University Press, 2002), 632–645. The three types of meditation are from R. Walsh, and S. L. Shapiro, "The meeting of meditative disciplines and western psychology: A mutually enriching dialogue," *American Psychologist* 61 (2006): 227–239.

4. For meditation's effects on the brain, self-compassion, and healthier aging, see Cahn and Povich (2006); R. J. Davidson, J. Kabat-Zinn, J. Shumacher, M. Rosenkranz, D. Muller, S. F. Santorelli, F. Urbanowski, A. Harrington, K. Bonus, and J. F. Sheridan, "Alterations in brain and immune function produced by mindfulness meditation," *Psychosomatic Medicine* 65 (2003): 564–570; B. L. Fredrickson, "Cultivating positive emotions to optimize health and well-being," *Prevention and Treatment* 3 (2000): article 0001a; Shapiro, Schwartz, and Santerre (2002); Walsh and Shapiro (2006); E. S. Epel, E. H. Blackburn, J. Lin, F. S. Dhabhar, N. E. Adler, J. D. Morrow and R. M. Cawthon, "Accelerated telomere shortening in response to life stress," *Publication of the National Academy of Sciences* 101 (2004):

17312–17315. For meditation and wisdom, see Walsh and Shapiro (2006); Shapiro, Schwartz, and Santerre (2002).

5. See A. Dijksterhuis, M. W. Bos, L. F. Nordgren, and R. B. van Baaren, "On making the right choice: The deliberation-without-attention effect," *Science* 311 (2006): 1005–1007; A. Dijksterhuis, and L. F. Nordgren, "A theory of unconscious thought," *Perspectives on Psychological Science* 1 (2006): 95–109. I am grateful to Dr. Robert Numan for pointing this research out to me. See also discussion in M. Gladwell, *Blink: The Power of Thinking without Thinking* (New York: Little, Brown, 2004).

6. See B. Zimmerman, ed., *The Autobiography of St. Teresa of Avila,* trans. D. Lewis (Rockford, IL: Tan Books, 1997) ; Shakespeare, *As You Like It,* 2.1.16–17; J. Hall, *Occasional Meditations,* in *Bishop Joseph Hall and Protestant Meditation,* ed. F. L. Huntley (Binghamton, NY: Center for Medieval and Early Renaissance Studies, 1981), 119–198. (Originally published 1633.)

7. For Herbert, see Stewart (1986); Charles (1977); Walton (1675/1927); J. H. Summers, *George Herbert: His Religion and Art* (Cambridge: Harvard University Press, 1968).

8. For Descartes, see Vrooman (1970).

9. J. Hall, *The Art of Divine Meditation,* in Huntley (pp. 65–118, quote on p. 77). (Originally published 1606.)

10. Adapted from *Meditation* by Eknath Easwaran, founder of the Blue Mountain Center of Meditation, copyright 1991; adapted by permission of Nilgiri Press, P. O. Box 256, Tomales, CA 94971, www.easwaran.org. A selection of passages for meditation in E. Easwaran, *God Makes the Rivers to Flow: Sacred Literature of the World* (Tomales, CA: Nilgiri Press, 2003). For a study of passage meditation and health, see D. Oman, J. Hedberg, D. Downs, and D. Parsons, "A transcultural spiritually-based program to enhance caregiving self-efficacy: A pilot study," *Complementary Health Practice Review* 8 (2003): 201–224. Quote from St. Teresa in Zimmerman (1565/1997), 115.

11. My thanks to David Feldman, PhD, assistant professor of counseling psychology at Santa Clara University, personal communication at a Santa Clara stress-management workshop on October 19, 2006. Used with permission.

12. My thanks to C. L. Flinders and T. Flinders, personal communication, July, 2006. Used with permission.

13. My thanks to W. J. Rewak, S.J., personal communication, July, 2006. Used with permission.

14. My thanks to J. Velasco, personal communication, July, 2006. Used with permission.

15. My thanks to S. L. Shapiro, personal communication, July, 2006. Used with permission.

16. My thanks to J. Ferguson, personal communication, July, 2006. Used with permission.

17. C. L Flinders, T. Flinders, Rewak, Velasco, Shapiro, and Ferguson, (2006).

18. W. Blake, "Auguries of Innocence," in *The Poetical Works of William Blake,* vol. 1 (London: Chatto & Windus, 1906), lines 1–4, p. 138. Blake was an early Romantic poet who wrote these lines around 1793.

19. From *Take Your Time: Finding Balance in a Hurried World* (pp. 46–47) by Eknath Easwaran, founder of the Blue Mountain Center of Meditation, copyright 1994; adapted by permission of Nilgiri Press, P. O. Box 256, Tomales, CA 94971, www.easwaran.org.

20. Advice on the mantra (or mantram) from *Meditation* (pp. 70–75) by Eknath Easwaran, founder of the Blue Mountain Center of Meditation, copyright 1991; adapted by permission of Nilgiri Press, P. O. Box 256, Tomales, CA 94971, www.easwaran.org. An extensive list of mantras can be found in Eknath Easwaran, *The Mantram Handbook* (Tomales, CA: Nilgiri Press, 1998) and on the Blue Mountain Web site, www.easwaran.org. For the San Diego study, see J. E. Bormann, D. Oman, J. K. Kemppainen, S. Becker, M. Gershwin, and A. Kelly, "Mantram repetition for stress management in veterans and employees: a critical incident study," *Journal of Advanced Nursing* 53 (2006): 502–512; quote is from p. 504.; de Sales (1608/1948), 90.

Chapter Nine

1. W. Shakespeare, *A Midsummer Night's Dream,* 5.1.14–17.

2. Singman (1995); Lewalski (2002); and C. M. Cox, *The Early Mental Traits of Three Hundred Geniuses,* vol. 2, *Genetic Studies of Genius,* ed. L. M. Terman (Stanford: Stanford University Press, 1953). (Original edition 1926.)

3. B. Castiglione, *The Courtier,* in *The Renaissance in England,* trans. T. Hoby, eds. H. E. Rollins and H. Baker (Boston: Heath, 1954), 522–530. (Original edition 1528, translation 1561.)

4. Information is from G. Bull, ed. and trans., *The Courtier: Baldesar Castiglione* (New York: Penguin, 1967); J. Cartwright, *The Perfect Courtier: Baldassare Castiglione* (New York: Dutton, 1927); A. Quondam, "On the Genesis of the *Book of the Courtier,*" in *Baldassare Castiglione: The Book of the Courtier,* ed. D. Javitch, trans. C. S. Singleton (New York: Norton, 2002), 283–295.

5. For creativity and health, see Maslow (1971), 55; Peterson & Seligman (2004); Myers, Sweeney, and Witmer (2000); N. Leffert, P. L. Benson, P. C. Scales, A. R. Sharma, D. R. Drake, and D. A. Blyth, "Developmental assets: Measurement and prediction of risk behaviors among adolescents," *Applied Developmental Science* 2 (1998): 209–230; Wong (1998). For studies of the arts and identity in adolescents, see A. S. Waterman, "Identity development from adolescence to adulthood: An extension of theory and a review of research," *Developmental Psychology* 18 (1982): 341–358, and J. Marcia, "Ego identity: Research review," in *The Power of Identity: Politics in a New Key,* eds. K. R. Hoover with J. Marcia and K. Parris (Chatham, NJ: Chatham House, 1997), 85–122. For the effect of music on performance, see E. G. Schellenberg, "Music and cognitive abilities," *Psychological*

Science 14 (2006): 317–320; J. S. Catterall, "Involvement in the arts and success in secondary school," *Americans for the Arts* (Los Angeles: UCLA Imagination Project, 1997); reference to musicians in the Silicon Valley in G. Venerable, *The Paradox of the Silicon Savior* (San Francisco: MVM Productions, 1987). For effects of music on the brain, see F. H. Rauscher, G. L. Shaw, L. J. Levine, E. L. Wright, W. R. Dennis, and R. L. Newcomb, "Music training causes long-term enhancement of preschool children's spacial-temporal reasoning," *Neurological Research* 19 (1997), 2–8; see also Huttenlocher (2002).

6. For music, depression, and stress, see Burton (1660), subsection III; B. Bittman, L. Berk, M. Shannan, M. Sharaf, J. Westengard, K. J. Guegler, D. W. Ruff, "Recreational music-making modulates the human stress response: A preliminary individualized gene expression strategy," *Medical Science Monitor* 11 (2005): 31–40. For "broaden and build," see Fredrickson (2002).

7. J. Milton, "L'Allegro," 11.143–144, in Hughes (1957), 71. (Originally published 1646.); Browne (1642/1982), 347.

8. For the effects of art, harmony, and natural beauty, see Csikszentmihalyi (1990), 235; M. Csikszentmihalyi and R. Larson, *Being Adolescent: Conflict and Growth in the Teenage Years* (New York: Basic Books, 1984); and C. Lewis, "The Evolutionary Importance of People-plant Relationships," *Investigating the Relationship between Health and the Landscape* (University of Minnesota: Landscape Arboretum, 2000), 27.

9. For information on Mary Sidney Herbert's life and works, see M. P. Hannay, *Philip's Phoenix: Mary Sidney, Countess of Pembroke* (New York: Oxford, 1990) and M. P. Hannay, N. J. Kinnamon, and M. G. Brennan, eds., *The Collected Works of Mary Sidney Herbert, Countess of Pembroke* (Oxford: Clarendon, 1998). Other information about Mary Sidney from Janette Lewis, PhD, personal communication at UCLA in the 1970s and September 2006.

10. For insights on the therapeutic effect of writing, see Baumeister and Vohs (2002).

11. B. F. Skinner, "What is wrong with daily life in the western world?" *American Psychologist* 41 (1986): 568–574, quote on p. 572.

12. Definition of flow is from Csikszentmihalyi (1990), 6. Studies of flow are from M. Carli, A. Della Fave, and F. Massimini, "The Quality of Experience in the Flow Channels: Comparision of Italian and United States Students," in *Optimal Experience: Psychological Studies of Flow in Consciousness,* eds. M. Csikszentmihalyi and I. Csikszentmihalyi (New York: Cambridge, 1988), 288–306; Csikszentmihalyi (1999); Csikszentmihalyi and Schneider (2000); F. Massimini, and M. Carli, "The systematic assessment of flow in daily experience," in Csikszentmihalyi and Csikszentmihalyi (1988), 266–287.

13. For flow and play, see Amabile (1996), 131; J. Panksepp, *Affective Neuroscience: The Foundations of Human and Animal Emotions* (New York: Oxford, 2004); and M. Chappel, personal communication, September 11, 2006.

14. Shu-Park Chan, personal communication, 1993; earlier account published in D. E. Dreher, "Shu-Park Chan," *Quality Living* (Winter 1993): 25–27. For further information on Jimmy Carter and the Carter Center, see www.cartercenter.org. M. Numan, personal communication, May, 2006.

15. For the creative spirit in the Renaissance, see Pico Della Mirandola (1496/1965); quote on agency is from Larson (2000), 177. Hilltop information and quote are from L. Welch, personal communication, September 8, 2006. For more information about Hilltop Artists in Residence, visit www.hilltopartists.org or contact them at P. O. Box 6829, Tacoma, WA 98406, telephone (253) 571–7670. I am grateful to my research assistant, Erin Schoenfelder, for making me aware of this program.

16. Information on Lorenzo de' Medici is from Bull (1998).

17. Information on Djerassi is from his autobiography, C. Djerassi, *The Pill, Pygmy Chimps, and Degas' Horse* (New York: Basic Books, 1992). For further information on Djerassi and the foundation, see http://www.djerassi.com and http://www.djerassi.org.

18. Adapted from the Time-Pressure/Creativity Matrix in T. M. Amabile, C. N. Hadley, and S. J. Kramer, "Creativity Under the Gun," *Harvard Business Review* 80 (August 2002): 56. Copyright by the Harvard Business School Publishing Corporation; all rights reserved. Used by permission of *Harvard Business Review.*

19. P. Sidney, "The Defense of Poesy," in *The Renaissance in England,* eds. H. E. Rollins and H. Baker (Boston: Heath, 1954), 605–624, quote on 608. (Originally published 1595.)

20. J. Edman, personal communication, August 22 and September 1, 2006, used with permission. Josepha Edman has an MBA, worked with a Canadian networking company, and is currently studying Shiatsu and Chinese medicine. Her company, Business & Pleasure (www.bizandp.com), trains people in personal leadership through seminars and coaching (telephone: +972–544494607).

Chapter Ten

1. Milton, *Areopagitica* (1644/1957), 720.

2. See W. J. F. Davies, *Teaching Reading in Early England* (New York: Barnes & Noble, 1974); A. E. McGrath, *In the Beginning* (New York: Doubleday, 2001); D. Riggs, *The World of Christopher Marlowe* (New York: Holt, 2004).

3. First quote is from D. N. Rapp, and P. van den Broek, "Dynamic text comprehension: An integrative view of reading," *Current Directions in Psychological Science* 14 (2005): 276–279, quote on p. 276; Quote from Dana Gioia, Director of the National Endowment for the Arts on p. 4 of R. A. Schroth, "Facing the reading crisis," *Conversations in Jesuit Higher Education* 30 (2006): 2–5. Statistics about readers' involvement are from *Reading at Risk: A Survey of Literary Reading in America,* Research Division Report #46 (Washington, DC: National Endowment for the Arts, 2004), vii. See also *To Read or Not to Read: A Question of National Consequence,* Re-

search Division Report # 47 (Washington, DC: National Endowment for the Arts, 2007).

4. For reading and social mobility, see L. S. Gottfredson, "Gottfredson's Theory of Circumscription, Compromise, and Self-Creation," in *Career Choice and Development,* 4th ed., ed. D. Brown et al. (San Francisco: Jossey-Bass, 2002), 85–148.

5. For details about Shakespeare's life, see Greenblatt (2004).

6. Quote and information about Locke is from Aaron (1971), 24, and http://oregonstate/edu/instruct/ph1302/philosophers/locke.html.

7. For the life of Stephen Douglass, see F. Douglass, *Life and Times of Frederick Douglass Written by Himself* (Secaucus, NJ: Citadel Press, 1983), quote on p. 70. (Originally published 1881.)

8. My thanks to William J. Rewak, S.J., for his advice on *lectio divina,* personal communication, July 2006.

9. Quote is from Rapp and van den Brock (2005), 276. For a good introduction to brain function and reading, see R. Restak, *The Secret Life of the Brain* (Washington, DC: Dana Press and Joseph Henry Press, 2001); research on reading comprehension, memory, and the brain is in M. I. Posner and Y. G. Abdullaev, "Neuroanatomy, circuitry and plasticity of word reading," *Neuroreport* 10 (1999): 12–23; M. St. George, M. Kutas, M. I. Martinez, M. I. Sereno, "Semantic integration in reading: engagement of the right hemisphere during discourse processing," *Brain* 122 (1999): 1317–1325; T. A. Keller, P. A., Carpenter, M. A. Just, "The neural basis of sentence comprehension: A fMRI examination of syntactic and lexical processing," *Cerebral Cortex* 11 (2001): 223–237; Numan (2000); I am grateful to Robert Numan, PhD, for his insights on memory and advice on this section.

10. W. Iser, *The Act of Reading* (Baltimore: Johns Hopkins Press, 1978), 107; my thanks to Dr. Marilyn Edelstein for this reference. For reading and self-awareness, see J. McQuillan and G. Conde, "The conditions of flow in reading: Two studies of optimal experience," *Reading Psychology* 17 (1986): 109–135; for international studies of reading and flow, see M. Csikszentmihalyi and I. S. Csikszentmihalyi, eds., *Optimal Experience: Psychological Studies of Flow in Consciousness,* (New York: Cambridge University Press, 1988); for education, see E. D. Hirsch, *The Schools We Need* (New York: Doubleday, 1996); for adolescent development, see Leffert et al. (1998); and for reduced risk of Alzheimer's, see R. S. Wilson, C. F. Mendes De Leon, L. L. Barnes, J. A. Schneider, J. L. Bienias, D. A. Evans, and D. A. Bennett, "Participation in cognitively stimulating activities and risk of incident Alzheimer disease," *JAMA* 287 (2002): 742–748, and D. Snowden, *Aging with Grace* (New York: Bantam, 2001).

11. For the UCLA study, see L. J. Sax, A. W. Astin, J. A. Lindholm, W. S. Korn, V. B. Saenz, K. M. Mahoney, *The American Freshman* (Cooperative Institutional Research Program, Los Angeles: University of California Los Angeles Higher Education Research Institute, 2003). Discussion of diminished ability and SAT renorming is in C. J. Sykes, *Dumbing Down Our Kids* (New York: St. Martin's, 1995). Gioia quotes are from *Reading at Risk* (2004), vii, xi, xiii.

12. See D. Talbot, *Brothers: The Hidden History of the Kennedy Years* (New York: Simon and Schuster, 2007).

13. F. Scogin, C. Jamison, and K. Gochneaut, "The comparative efficacy of cognitive and behavioral bibliotherapy for mildly and moderately depressed older adults," *Journal of Consulting and Clinical Psychology* 57 (1989): 403–407. See discussion in D. D. Burns, *Feeling Good: The New Mood Therapy* (New York: Collins, 1980), xxiii-xxx.

14. Happy's story is in G. G. Jampolsky, *Forgiveness: The Greatest Healer of All* (Hillsboro, OR: Beyond Words Publishing, 1999).

15. My thanks to Anne Quaranta for her story, from an interview on April 25, 2007. For reading on bibliotherapy and its long-term effects, see C. Jamison and F. Scogin, "The outcome of cognitive bibliotherapy with depressed adults," *Journal of Consulting and Clinical Psychology* 63 (1995): 644–650, and N.M. Smith, M. R. Floyd, C. Jamison, and F. Scogin. "Three-year follow-up of bibliotherapy for depression," *Journal of Consulting and Clinical Psychology* 65 (1997): 324–327. Information on reading and personal assets is from Leffert et al. (1998).

16. For story and psychological development, see Csikszentmihalyi (1990) and Csikszentmihalyi and Beattie (1979); quote is from Hansen (2001), 20–21; for spiritual modeling, see D. Oman and C. E. Thoresen, "Spiritual modeling: A key to spiritual and religious growth?" *The International Journal for the Psychology of Religion* 3 (2003): 149–165.

17. C. F. E. Spurgeon, *Shakespeare's Imagery and What It Tells Us* (London: Cambridge University Press, 1965). (Originally published 1935.)

18. My thanks to Santa Clara University career counselor Elizabeth Thompson, for her story and insights on life themes shared in my vocation class, October 10, 2006.

19. A. Wittman, "Sacred Story: Yours and Mine," July 23, 2006, SCSC Jubilee, http://www.holycrosssisters.org/Our_Spirituality/SACREDSTORY. htm. Used with permission.

20. Insights into narrative psychology are from Baumeister and Vohs (2002); D. P. McAdams, "Personality, modernity, and the storied self: A contemporary framework for studying persons," *Psychological Inquiry* 7 (1996): 295–321; D. P. McAdams, R. Josselson, and A. Lieblich, *Turns in the Road* (Washington, DC: American Psychological Association, 2001).

21. For the hero's journey, see Campbell (1949/1968); for insights into Dorothy's journey in *The Wizard of Oz,* I am grateful to my friend, Michelle Millis-Chappel, PhD. For a contemporary explanation of the hero's journey and the plots of Hollywood films, see C. Vogler, *The Writer's Journey* (Studio City, CA: Michael Wiese Productions, 1998).

Chapter Eleven

1. J. Milton (1674/1957), *Paradise Lost,* bk. XII, lines 566–567.

2. N. Mutrie and G. Faulkner, "Physical activity: Positive psychology in motion," in *Positive Psychology in Practice,* eds. P. A. Linley and S. Joseph (Hoboken, NJ: Wiley, 2004), 146–164.

3. J. Parkes, *Travel in England in the Seventeenth Century* (London: Oxford Clarendon Press, 1968); K. L. Emerson, *Everyday Life in Renaissance England* (Cincinnati, OH: Writer's Digest Books, 1996).

4. Walton (1675/1927), quotes and information are from pp. 303–305, italics are mine. See also Charles (1977).

5. E. M. Hallowell, "The human moment at work," *Harvard Business Review* (January-February 1999): 58–66; Chesley (2005).

6. Case history is recorded in D. E. Dreher, and T. G. Plante, "The Calling Protocol: Promoting Greater Health, Joy, and Purpose in Life," in *Spirit, Science and Health: How the Spiritual Mind Fuels Wellness,* eds. T. G. Plante and C. E. Thoresen (Westport, CT: Greenwood, 2007), 129–140.

7. For exercise, education, and treatment of ADHD, see Myers, Sweeney, and Witmer (2000); Mutrie and Faulkner (2004); and California Department of Education, "State study proves physically fit kids perform better academically," CDE release no. 02–37 (Sacramento, CA: Office of Delaine Eastin, State Superintendent of Public Instruction, 2002); J. Panksepp, "Attention deficit hyperactivity disorder, psychostimulents, and intolerance of childhood playfulness: A tragedy in the making?" *Current Directions in Psychological Science* 7 (1998): 91–98; S. C. Putnam, *Nature's Ritalin for the Marathon Mind* (Hinesburg, VT: Upper Access, 2001). For the effects of exercise on the immune system, see J. Chubak, A. McTiernan, B. Sorensen, M. H. Wener, Y. Yasui, M. Velasquez, B. Wood, K. B. Rajan, C. M. Wetmore, J. D. Potter, and C. M. Ulrich, "Moderate-intensity exercise reduces the incidence of colds among postmenopausal women," *American Journal of Medicine* 119 (2006): 937–942. For exercise and brain health, see Snowdon (2001); J. D. Churchill, R. Galvez, S. Comcombe, R. A. Swain, A. F. Kramer, and W. T. Greenough, "Exercises, experience, and the aging brain," *Neurobiology of Aging* 23 (2002): 941–955; R. P. Friedland, T. Fritsch, K. A. Smyth, E. Koss, A. J. Lerner, C. H. Chen, G. J. Petot, and S. M. Debanne, "Patients with Alzheimer's Disease have reduced activities in midlife compared with health control-group members," *Publication of National Academy of Sciences* 98 (March 13, 2001): 3440–3445. For exercise and mental health, see Csikszentmihalyi and Larson (1984); T. G. Plante "Getting physical: Does exercise help in the treatment of psychiatric disorders?" *Journal of Psychosocial Nursing* 34 (1996): 38–43; T. G. Plante and J. Rodin, "Physical fitness and enhanced psychological health," *Current Psychology: Research and Reviews* 9 (1990): 3–24.

8. Burton (1660), part 2, section 2; Plante (1996). See also Panksepp (1998) and Putnam (2001).

9. Mutrie and Faulkner (2004).

10. Snyder (1994).

11. J. Lynch, personal communication, July 27, 2006. All quotes are from this interview, used with permission. Jerry Lynch's Web site is www.wayofchampions.com. He can be contacted at Way of Champions in Santa Cruz, California 95060, telephone (831) 466–3031, e-mail docj@wayofchampions.com.

12. Vasari (1568/1996), I, 51–57, 710–748.

13. Milton (1674/1957), *Paradise Lost,* bk. XII, lines 566–567.

Chapter Twelve

1. W. Shakespeare, *A Midsummer Night's Dream,* 5.1.14–17.

2. Cox (1926/1953). According to this study, in their youth, men and women of achievement demonstrate not only high intelligence but also motivation, self-discipline, persistence, confidence, and strength of character. For Michelangelo, see Vasari (1568/1996), II, 653–655.

3. J. Milton, *The Reason of Church Government* (orig. pub. 1642), in Hughes (1957), 640–689, quote on p. 642; see "discipline" in the *Oxford English Dictionary* (1971); J. Hooper, *A Declaration of the Ten Holy Commandementes of Almyghtye God,* in *Early Writings of John Hooper* (New York: Cambridge University Press, 1843), 249–430, quote on p. 274. (Original edition 1549); Cennini (1437/1960), 15.

4. For the importance of domain knowledge, see Gardner (1993) and Csikszentmihalyi (1996), quote on p. 47; for disciplined practice, neuroplasticity, and inspiration see Huttenlocher (2002), and J. Kounios, J. L. Frymiare, E. M. Bowden, J. I. Fleck, K. Subramanian, T. B. Parrish, and M. Jung-Beeman, "The prepared mind: Neural activity prior to problem presentation predicts subsequent solution by sudden insight," *Psychological Science* 17 (2006): 882–890.

5. For Michelangelo, see Vasari (1568/1996), II, 642–769; for Madonna Properzia de' Rossi, see Vasari (1568/1996), I, 856–860; for St. Francis, see Burton (1925); for Locke, see Aaron (1971).

6. See Bandura (2006), Lykken (1999), and Csikszentmihalyi (1996).

7. For discipline as essential to healthy development, see Csikszentmihalyi and Schneider (2000) and Restak (2001). For discipline and development, see Baumeister, Tice, and Heatherton (1994) and Csikszentmihalyi and Schneider (2000); for disciplined habits and academic success, see S. A. Wagerman and D. C. Funder "Acquaintance reports of personality and academic achievement: A case for conscientiousness," *Journal of Research in Personality* 41 (2007): 221–229. Dr. David Reed, personal communication, June 26, 2006, used with permission.

8. For disciplined practice and the brain, see J. Nakamura and M. Csikszentmihalyi, "The Motivational Sources of Creativity as Viewed from the Paradigm of Positive Psychology," in *A Psychology of Human Strengths,* eds. L. G. Aspinwall and U. M. Staudinger (Washington, DC: American Psychological Association, 2003), 257–269; Huttenlocher (2002). My thanks to Hans Boepple for his inspiration

and personal communication, Santa Clara University, October 2006 and January 2007, used with permission.

9. Herbert (1652/1945), 246 (spelling regularized).

10. See Peterson and Seligman (2004); Scales et al. (2000). Sports psychologist Jerry Lynch uses a similar approach with his champion athletes, described in Lynch (2006), 140–142.

11. For St. Teresa's illnesses, see Flinders (1993). I am also grateful to Sofia Aboitiz for insights in her research paper, "Teresa de Avila," for my class, English 189, Santa Clara University, December 4, 2006.

12. Information on Galileo's life is from G. de Santillana, *The Crime of Galileo* (Chicago: University of Chicago Press, 1955), quote on p. 357; S. Drake, *Galileo at Work* (Chicago: University of Chicago Press, 1978); J. Reston, Jr., *Galileo: A Life* (New York: HarperCollins, 1994); and Robert Numan, personal communication, December 2006. On October 31, 1992, the Catholic Church admitted that Galileo was right.

13. For information on Milton's life, see Lewalski (2002) and J. Thorpe, *John Milton: The Inner Life* (San Marino, CA: Huntington Library, 1983). Milton quotes about early study habits are from J. Milton, *Second Defense of the People of England,* in Hughes (1957), 817–838, quote p. 828 (orig. pub. 1654); importance of foundation knowledge, J. Milton, "Prolusion VII," in Hughes, 621–629, quote p. 622; and virtues necessary in a poet, J. Milton, *Apology for Smectymnuus* (1642), in Hughes, 690–695, quote p. 694; on Galileo, *Areopagitica* (1644), in Hughes, 737–738.

14. My thanks to Karel Sloane for her inspiration: personal communications, September 2005 through December 2006, used with permission. Karel's paintings are on display at the Barrie Holt Gallery, 509 Royal Street, New Orleans, LA. She can be reached at ksloane@tulane.edu.

15. C. Peterson, *A Primer in Positive Psychology* (New York: Oxford University Press, 2006), exercise on pp. 43–44.

16. Cochran (1990), 160.

17. P. Simone and M. Scuilli, "Cognitive benefits of participation in lifelong learning institutes," *The LLI Review* 1 (2006): 44–51; see also D. E. Dreher, "Renaissance lessons for today: A course to promote purpose and personal growth in later life," *The LLI Review* 1 (2006): 105–111.

18. Dr. David Reed, personal communication, June 26, 2006, used with permission.

19. Dr. Erna Wenus, personal communication, January 19, 2007.

20. For information on Paula Appley Leen, see http://www.aaw.cc/Get Inspired/2006WOYAwardees.aspx. I am grateful to my friend Sunny Lockwood for telling me Paula's story.

21. Robert Mason, personal communication, December 13, 2006, used with permission.

22. See Campbell (1949/1968), 78. For a discussion of vocation and threshold guardians in Eastern philosophy, see D. Dreher, *The Tao of Personal Leadership* (New York: HarperCollins, 1996), 252–259.

23. Information on I. King Jordan is from the Gallaudet Web site, http://www.gallaudet.edu, and my husband, Robert Numan, who went to graduate school with him at the University of Tennessee.

24. My thanks to my friend Rev. Bertina Clare for this quote, used with permission, as well as insights and inspiration over the years.

25. Teresa in Zimmerman (1565/1997), 118. Donne, "Devotion 17" (1623/1959), 108.

Permissions

Index